DESIRING WOMEN:
THE PARTNERSHIP OF VIRGINIA WOOLF
AND VITA SACKVILLE-WEST

16 how she discovered the similarities of V.S with wr y LACAN

On 23 September 1925, Virginia Woolf wrote to Vita Sackville-West: 'if you'll make me up, I'll make you.' In *Desiring Women*, Karyn Sproles argues that the two writers in fact 'made' each other. Woolf and Sackville-West produced some of the most vibrant and acclaimed work of their respective careers during their passionate affair, and Sproles demonstrates how this body of work was a collaborative project – a partnership – in which they promised to reinvent one another.

Sproles argues that in all they wrote during their affair – essays, criticism, novels, poems, biographies, and letters – Woolf and Sackville-West struggled to represent their desire for one another and to resist the social pressures that would deny their passion. At the centre of this literary conversation is *Orlando*, Woolf's biography of Sackville-West. Sproles restores *Orlando* to the context of Woolf and Sackville-West's discussion of gender and sexuality and demonstrates its importance in Woolf's oeuvre. Sexy and provocative, *Desiring Women* re-imagines Woolf and Sackville-West as daring, funny, beautiful, and bent on resisting the repression of women's desires.

KARYN Z. SPROLES is a professor in the Department of English and an associate dean of the General Education Program at James Madison University.

July 2006

Art —

I am so grateful
for your mentoring &
friendship. I hope you
see your influence in
this attempt to give
Wooly a body.

Love, Karen

KARYN Z. SPROLES

Desiring Women

The Partnership of Virginia Woolf and Vita Sackville-West

UNIVERSITY OF TORONTO PRESS
Toronto Buffalo London

© University of Toronto Press Incorporated 2006
Toronto Buffalo London
Printed in Canada

ISBN-13: 978-0-8020-3883-8 (cloth)
ISBN-13: 978-0-8020-9402-5 (paper)

ISBN-10: 0-8020-3883-2 (cloth)
ISBN-10: 0-8020-9402-3 (paper)

Printed on acid-free paper

Library and Archives Canada Cataloguing in Publication

Sproles, Karyn Z.
 Desiring women : the partnership of Virginia Woolf and Vita
Sackville-West / Karyn Z. Sproles.

 Includes bibliographical references and index.
 ISBN 0-8020-3883-2 (bound)
 ISBN 0-8020-9402-3 (pbk.)

 1. Woolf, Virginia, 1882–1941 – Relations with women. 2. Sackville West,
V. (Victoria), 1892–1962 – Relations with women. 3. Lesbians' writings,
English – History and criticism. 4. English literature – Women authors –
History and criticism. 5. English literature – 20th century – History and
criticism. 6. Homosexuality and literature. I. Title

 PR6045.O72Z8773 2006   820.9'3526643'0904   C2005-906735-7

Excerpts from THE LETTERS OF VIRGINIA WOOLF, Volume III: 1923–1927,
copyright © 1977 by Quentin Bell and Angelica Garnett, reprinted by permission of
Harcourt, Inc. Excerpts from THE LETTERS OF VIRGINIA WOOLF, Volume IV:
1929–1931, copyright © 1978 by Quentin Bell and Angelica Garnett, reprinted by
permission of Harcourt, Inc. Excerpts from THE DIARY OF VIRGINIA WOOLF,
Volume II: 1920–1924, copyright © 1978 by Quentin Bell and Angelica Garnett,
reprinted by permission of Harcourt, Inc. Excerpts from THE DIARY OF VIRGINIA
WOOLF, Volume III: 1925–1930, copyright © 1980 by Quentin Bell and Angelica
Garnett, reprinted by permission of Harcourt, Inc. Excerpts from A ROOM OF
ONE'S OWN by Virginia Woolf, copyright 1929 by Harcourt, Inc. and renewed 1957
by Leonard Woolf, reprinted by permission of the publisher. Excerpts from OR-
LANDO, copyright 1928 by Virginia Woolf and renewed 1956 by Leonard Woolf,
reprinted by permission of Harcourt, Inc.

University of Toronto Press acknowledges the financial assistance to
its publishing program of the Canada Council for the Arts and the
Ontario Arts Council.

To Pip and Sadie

Women's erotic
power
is the
deeper issue
17

Contents

Illustrations

Acknowledgments

I would like to thank the foundations and institutions whose financial support made this project possible: the Canada Council for the Arts, the Ontario Arts Council, the Bush Foundation, Hamline University, the Institute for Ecumenical and Cultural Research, James Madison University, and the Joyce Foundation. I am especially grateful to the National Endowment for the Humanities for supporting my participation in a summer seminar on biography led by the late James E.B. Breslin at the University of California at Berkeley. All of the members of that seminar were invaluable in the initial formation of this project.

I would also like to thank the many deans and administrators who encouraged this project and made scarce resources available: Carole Brown, Jeanie Watson, Jerry Greiner, Garvin Davenport, Richard Whitman, Teresa Gonzalez, David Jeffrey, and Linda Halpern. I owe a hundred thank-yous to Adam Nicolson and his patient family for the final research adventure of this project. I am grateful to the many teachers who led me to Woolf and to psychoanalysis and to the many colleagues and friends who have read drafts, suggested references, and helped me to grapple with the various challenges this material presented. My thanks are boundless to Rees Allison, Suzanne Bost, Michelle Brown, Peter Canning and the University of Minnesota Lacan Study Group, Josephine Carubia, Kathy Clarke, Diane Clayton, Art Efron, Mark Facknitz, Marina Favila, Rebecca Feind, Nicole Hagood, Narin Hassan, Nancy Holland and the Hamline University Feminist Seminar, Keith Horton, Bruce Johnson, Stephen Kellert, Leonardo Lansansky, Jack Marmorstein, James E. Morrison, Tim Polk, Don Rice, Tamara Root, Diana Royer, Maureen Shanahan, Sara Lee Silberman, Susie Steinbach, and Valerie Traub. I especially want to thank Ruth Hariu, who could determine the organizational structure of a pile of gravel, and Kristi Shackelford, for her patience, technical abilities, and celebratory surprises. I owe a debt beyond words to Susan Facknitz, whose encouragement and confidence never faltered.

Everyone at the University of Toronto Press has been wonderful to work with throughout. Each of the readers contributed comments that made this a better book. Barbara Porter cheerfully saw the manuscript through publication. Catherine Frost's careful copyediting saved me from many embarrassments. I am particularly grateful to Jill McConkey, whose supportive optimism was nearly always greater than my own.

The International Virginia Woolf Society has been an enormous support throughout the writing of this book, and many of the ideas developed here were first tried out at their annual conferences. Earlier versions of several sections of this book have previously been published: 'Queering Virginia: How'd We Do It?' in chapter 1 in *Virginia Woolf across Generations: Selected Papers from the 12th Annual Virginia Woolf Conference* edited by Eileen Barrett and Merry Pawlowski (online by subscription 2003) and in chapter 6, 'Virginia Woolf Writes to Vita Sackville-West (and Receives a Reply): *Aphra Behn, Orlando, Saint Joan of Arc*, and Revolutionary Biography' in *Virginia Woolf: Texts and Contexts* edited by Eileen Barrett and Beth Rigel Daugherty (New York: Pace University Press, 1996. 179–91).

I would like to thank Adam Nicolson for permission to quote from Nigel Nicolson's *Portrait of a Marriage* and Juliet Nicolson for permission to quote from Vita Sackville-West's *Aphra Behn* and *The Letters of Vita Sackville-West to Virginia Woolf*. All of the photographs in this book are used with the generous permission of the estate of Nigel Nicolson.

DESIRING WOMEN:
THE PARTNERSHIP OF VIRGINIA WOOLF
AND VITA SACKVILLE-WEST

1 Desiring Women

Doing It in Bloomsbury

... if you'll make me up, I'll make you.

Virginia Woolf to Vita Sackville-West (23 Sept. 1925, 3:214)

A young lady rushed up to me in Pasadena and said she was writing a book about you and me. Isn't that nice for us?

Vita Sackville-West to Virginia Woolf (28 March 1933, 367)

In April 1929, soon after their affair had ended, Virginia Woolf wrote to Vita Sackville-West: 'I told Nessa [Woolf's sister, Vanessa Bell] the story of our passion in a chemists shop the other day. But do you really like going to bed with women she said – taking her change. "And how d'you do it?" and so she bought her pills to take abroad, talking as loud as a parrot' (5 April 1929, 4:36). Thus was Virginia Woolf outed, albeit to a very small group of eavesdropping villagers. Woolf turns the incident into copy for the amusement of Sackville-West, who appreciated the thrill of courting exposure mixed with the nostalgia of remembering their secret past.

Woolf's mock chagrin at her sister's tactless questions distracts from the curious nature of Bell's enquiry.[1] There is a widely repeated but probably apocryphal story that, when confronted with the possibility that two women could engage in erotic activity, Queen Victoria found it unimaginable: what could they do to one another?[2] But that was in 1885. Bell and the other members of the Bloomsbury Group openly defied all that Queen Victoria stood for in politics and personal relationships.[3] There is no evidence that Vanessa Bell, who was fifty at the time, was naïve. On the contrary, she invited her husband's mistress to stay for weekends. She lived, at various times, with her male lover's male lovers, one of whom married their daughter. She spent her adult life at the centre of gay Bloomsbury. It was to the stain on her dress that Lytton Strachey pointed in 1908 or 1909 – depending on whose memory one trusts – and enquired with all civility, 'Sperm?' With this question, Woolf wrote in an essay she read to the Memoir Club in 1922, the year she met Sackville-West, 'all barriers of reticence and reserve went down. A flood of the sacred fluid seemed to overwhelm us. Sex permeated our conversation. The word bugger was never far from our lips' ('Old Bloomsbury' 367). In bawdy Old Bloomsbury men enjoyed each other, and women seem to have enjoyed talking about what the men were doing. However, if their discussions included anything more about women and sex than a stained dress, Woolf does not say so.

When 'Sapphism'[4] was discussed in Bloomsbury, it was without much pleasure. Woolf describes a conversation with E.M. Forster in her diary: 'He said he thought Sapphism disgusting: partly from convention, partly because he disliked that women should be independent of men' (31 Aug. 1928, 3:193). If she challenged Forster's position, Woolf does not record it. No wonder Vanessa Bell joined Queen Victoria in wondering how two women could do it, even though she was not surprised that her sister had done it.

The other question that is avoided by the anecdotal form in which Woolf describes the scene in the chemist's shop is how Woolf answered Bell's question. To Sackville-West, Woolf need not repeat the answer. Sackville-West knew exactly how they did it. In her letters she was more forthcoming than Woolf was about the details of the affair: 'she does love me, and I did sleep with her at Rodmell [the Woolfs' house in Sussex],' she wrote to her husband, Harold Nicolson, on 28 June 1926 (150). The Nicolsons habitually shared the news of their affairs with each other, his exclusively with other men and hers primarily with other women. But when Woolf and Sackville-West wrote to each other, they evoked the moments of their physical intimacy through pet names and symbolic references. 'And to think,' Sackville-West wrote twelve years after their affair had ended, 'how the ceilings of Long Barn [Sackville-West's home] once swayed above us' (19 Dec. 1938, 417).[5] Their letters describe their love and longing for each other but not their erotic practice.

How, then, did Woolf answer her sister? Did she say that when she was with Sackville-West the ceiling swayed above their heads? Or did she use the excuse of the crowded chemist's shop to defer responding? Bell's question suggests an open curiosity it would be a shame to leave unsatisfied, but Bloomsbury's women seem to have been chronically unsatisfied. Frances Spalding, Vanessa Bell's biographer, writes that Bell 'had been able over the years to submerge her sexual appetite' (213).[6] Dora Carrington, who was devoted to the insistently gay Lytton Strachey, 'apparently did not even understand the meaning of the word "homosexual" when they met' (Gerzina, *Carrington* 70).[7] In her complex and even-handed biography of Woolf, Hermione Lee argues that Bloomsbury constructed Woolf as 'Virginia the Virgin' (240), who did not benefit from the sexual openness enjoyed by the men: 'what sexual space did this "liberation" provide for Virginia Stephen in her late twenties? ... Perhaps their new freedom of speech ... was not after all so enfranchising for her, but rapidly became a game in which she had to compete ... but in which her own desires had to be discounted' (239). Sackville-West wrote that Leonard and Virginia Woolf's sex life 'was a terrible failure, and was abandoned quite soon' (letter to Harold Nicolson, 17 Aug. 1926, 159).[8] For Woolf, heterosexuality was not particularly satisfying, but, unlike 'buggery,' erotic practice between women was not celebrated in Bloomsbury.

Sackville-West, who never became a part of Bloomsbury, introduced the pleasures of sapphism into Woolf's life and into her writing.[9] Critics typically credit Woolf with influencing Sackville-West,[10] but I will argue throughout this book that their influence on one another was reciprocal and profound. Their literary dialogue – public and private – was bent on resisting the repression of women's desires (see appendix B for a chronology of their publications during this period). Woolf brought to their exchange formal experiments in representing subjectivity; Sackville-West brought an insistence on the presence of desire, particularly women's erotic desire for one another. In all that they wrote during their affair – essays, literary criticism, novels, poems, and most especially biographies and letters to each other – Woolf and Sackville-West struggle to articulate their desire for one another and to resist the social pressures that work to repress women's desire altogether. Woolf and Sackville-West were engaged in a collaborative project – a partnership – in which they promised that, as Woolf wrote to Sackville-West: 'if you'll make me up, I'll make you' (23 Sept. 1925, 3:214). In this book, I have tried to recover the shared fantasy they created as a result of this promise. It is a fantasy they developed, I believe, most overtly in the letters they wrote to one another and in the biographies they wrote of other women writers. Their letters are promises to imagine each other. The biographies they wrote imagine other women. Through this public and private literary partnership they created desiring women. They knew exactly how to do it.

Queering Virginia: How D'We Do It?

Queen Victoria: 'We have arrived.'

Woolf, *Freshwater* (53)

Woolf's conversation with her sister about her 'passion' for Sackville-West illustrates the way readers of Woolf of my generation – those of us who started reading Woolf in the 1970s and 1980s – imagined Woolf's sexuality. Guided by Quentin Bell's biography, I learned to 'know' without knowing, while continuing to wait patiently in line, hoping for an insight into Woolf's work that she herself had not already had.[11] Woolf wrote both *Mrs. Dalloway* and *To the Lighthouse* during her growing intimacy with Sackville-West between 1924 and 1927 (see appendix A for a more detailed chronology of their relationship), and both novels drop fairly obvious hints. How could I have missed Sally Seton's kiss and Lily's head on Mrs Ramsay's knees? Toni McNaron asks herself the same question in the first essay of Eileen Barrett and Patricia Cramer's important anthology, *Virginia Woolf: Lesbian Readings*: 'I cannot remember what I told myself from my closet about the significance of Sally Seton's kissing Clarissa ... perhaps I read that moment ... through tightly fitted heterosexist blinders, which prevented me from attaching sexual or intimate excitement to anything other than a male-female liaison' (11). Clarissa Dalloway describes this kiss to herself as 'the most exquisite moment of my whole life' (52), yet there is something about the narrative that works to repress knowledge of Sally and Clarissa. Even though Sally's kiss is *marked* by Clarissa as essential to her sense of self, she acts as if she does not know this. Her behaviour and even her associations elide its significance. This encourages a reading experience in which desire is repressed. It is raised, felt, and made vivid, but it is inconsistent with the rest of the narrative. It is interrupted, just as the kiss itself is interrupted by Peter Walsh. A reading that seeks to produce a unified narrative would need to repress the exquisite memory of Sally's kiss and focus, as Clarissa does, on Peter. But Woolf's narrative

personal
exp of Karyn

equally resists the urge towards a stable, unified reading. Something nags, something tugs. The kiss returns from the repressed as a trace, a thread of disruption that weaves throughout the novel. Woolf gives plenty of clues. When I go back to the novels, it is right there on the page. Typically, in my experience of reading Woolf, when I think I have figured something out and go back to look for evidence, I find she has said it outright: the kiss was the most important thing, the not quite forgotten centre of Clarissa's life. This is how you do it. Then I realize that I have known all along.

The clues are especially thick in *Orlando*, where Woolf writes openly: 'Orlando enjoyed the love of both sexes equally' (221). But in the reading experience, it seems that what is given with one hand is covered over with the other. In *Orlando* I am distracted by the changes of clothing that allow Orlando to be scholar, gardener, lady, and nobleman throughout the course of the day. Borrowing a phrase from Jane Gallop, Pamela Caughie calls it 'Virginia Woolf's Double Discourse' in her analysis of *Orlando*'s rhetoric as unstable, ambiguous, and contradictory.[12] Even in novels that oscillate less rapidly, something is there to distract the reader's attention. When Peter Walsh interrupts Sally and Clarissa (53), the reader's attention, like Clarissa's, is diverted.

Esther Newton and Terry Castle have suggested that self-censorship was a deliberate strategy used by Woolf to protect her work from being banned as Radclyffe Hall's writing was. Jane Marcus argues that the in-jokes of *A Room of One's Own* seduce readers into a conspiracy 'of women in league together against authority' (*Language* 166). Feminist anger is a useful distraction from even more dangerous ground, and *Orlando*, like *A Room of One's Own*, gives its readers plenty of material with which to distract themselves. Elizabeth Meese suggests that androgyny itself is a distraction from sexuality. Similarly, Bell's biography taught me that whatever might have been going on between Woolf and Sackville-West, it was the emotional intensity of the relationship that was important.

As a student in nascent women's studies classes, I was drawn to Woolf by her politics and for something that I was also finding in psychoanalysis (about which more later): the intensity of her expression of the interior lives of women characters. Bell's biography dominated my understanding of Woolf as damaged, frigid, and witty, but depressed. Now I see that version of Woolf as naïve and pathologizing. So, I wonder, how did I and other readers of my generation come to *know* about Woolf's sexual attraction to women? For many readers, Woolf

personal

was transformed by the publication of her diaries and letters and by the remarkable feminist critics whose imagination was stirred by her. For me it was reading Victoria Glendinning's biography of Vita Sackville-West followed by DeSalvo and Leaska's edition of Sackville-West's letters to Woolf.[13] My subsequent rereading of *Orlando* then became the revolutionary experience Woolf had promised it would be. I discovered desire in Woolf herself and in Woolf's writing through Sackville-West, so it was to their relationship that I turned to try to better understand desire and the construction of female subjectivity.[14]

Jane Lilienfeld argues persuasively that Woolf's relationship with Violet Dickinson was 'a consummated lesbian love' (Barrett and Cramer 41), but the nature of Sackville-West's relationships with women requires no persuasion. Even Woolf says of Sackville-West: 'these Sapphists *love* women; friendship is never untinged with amorosity' (*Diary*, 21 Dec. 1925, 3:51). Unlike Woolf, Sackville-West resists repression, an ability, I think, Sackville-West inspired, briefly, in Woolf. During their affair, Woolf's work becomes more openly sensual, more overtly sexual in topic. This is the time in which Lily (mirroring a favourite pose of Woolf and Sackville-West) leans against Mrs Ramsay's knees, as 'close as she could get' (*To the Lighthouse* 78). This is the time in which Orlando 'was seen to dance naked on a balcony' (*Orlando* 222) and in which 'Chloe liked Olivia' (*A Room of One's Own* 87). These moments are, I believe, the result of Sackville-West's influence.

Woolf helps us to repress this knowledge by prevaricating about her sexuality. As Patricia Cramer says: 'Woolf's aim was to write as clearly as she could about love between women while avoiding detection. To do so, Woolf crafted works that could "pass" within the dominant culture and at the same time communicate subversive in-group messages to savvy readers' (Barrett and Cramer 123). Breaking Woolf's code requires reading her letters, which provide a key to her erotic imagery. The letters are full of puns on having and coming, exploring budding flowers, and romping with licking dogs. Many critics have written about these encoded messages.[15] They become quite obvious after one receives the wink or a poke in the ribs that gives permission to read Woolf as one as wished to do all along. Feminist criticism has served as the nudge many readers needed in order to get the joke.

Woolf is not popularly known for her sense of humour or her ribaldry; again, it is the letters that most overtly show this side of her, after which it is impossible to miss. As the codes are broken, Woolf is recreated in individual executions of the cultural process Brenda Silver describes as 'the "versioning" of Virginia Woolf' (xvi). Silver celebrates the fluidity of the 'Virginia Woolf Icon' because it is 'situated on the borders [and thus] continually threatens to undo them and the categories or norms they name and contain' (11). This wonderful fluidity also allows evasiveness. Woolf's persona – created by her and after her – has assisted in repressing knowledge of her sexuality. It is all well and good to see her rejection of categorization as an anticipation of Foucault's more elaborately theorized position against positions, but in practical terms it has made things more difficult. It allows even the most balanced of biographies, by Hermione Lee, to conclude that, despite participating in affectionate physical contact with women, Woolf did not define herself as lesbian (484). This is true enough, but neither did Sackville-West call herself a lesbian. Nevertheless, for Lee, Sackville-West is the lesbian and Woolf is a woman who, beginning with her mother and sisters, has close relationships with women. We must be careful when prevarication threatens to throw us back into the sticky arms of Havelock Ellis, where Woolf can once again become the 'sexless Sappho' of Bell's biography, temporarily corrupted by Sackville-West in the role of the congenital sexual invert. Lee writes: 'If Virginia Woolf was lesbian and Sackville-West confirmed that identity, she accepted it only evasively and ambivalently' (487). Many people are evasive and ambivalent about their sexuality – one might say that Sackville-West was – but thanks to unflinching biographies by Nigel Nicholson and Victoria Glendinning, critics cannot avoid Sackville-West's complex sexual history, and many see her as unequivocally lesbian. In her influential *Vita and Virginia*, Suzanne Raitt describes Sackville-West as 'already a self-identified and experienced lesbian by the time she met Woolf' (2).[16] If we are more comfortable labelling Sackville-West as lesbian, and we admit that she had some sort of intimate relationship with Woolf, then the door opens onto Woolf's sexuality as well. This, for me as a reader of Woolf, was the key. It was Sackville-West who led me to a vision of Woolf as someone who had a sexual identity to be ambivalent about, and from there there was no return.

It was Sackville-West's transformation of my readings of Woolf's work coupled with my realization that both women were writing biographies of women writers during the time of their relationship that motivated this book. I was particularly curious about the biographies they wrote, since this was a relatively unusual genre for each of them and because this work has received comparably scant critical attention.[17] Out of the approximately fifty books Sackville-West published,

the germ of the book

seven could be called biographies. The first two bookend her affair with Woolf. When they met, she had just published *Knole and the Sackvilles*, a biography of her family and estate. A copy of this book was the first of many presents Sackville-West would send to Woolf. In the summer of 1927, as the intensity of their affair was cooling, Sackville-West wrote a biography of Restoration playwright Aphra Behn. Woolf also wrote her first biography at the end of their affair, taking Sackville-West herself as the subject for *Orlando: A Biography*. This work was immediately followed by *A Room of One's Own*, which, I will argue, makes use of biography to revise history as well as the literary canon.[18] Biography seems to me to be especially relevant to the shared project they engaged in to imagine one another, and by extension other women, since in biography that is precisely what the biographer is called upon to do. In the chapters that follow I will consider these biographies, along with their letters and the fiction (Sackville-West's *The Heir* and *Seducers in Ecuador* and Woolf's *Mrs. Dalloway* and *To the Lighthouse*) that I believe make up their conversation about how to imagine women, especially desiring women.

My project builds on previous publications on the work and lives of Woolf and Sackville-West: for example, Joanne Trautmann's early *The Jessamy Brides*, Suzanne Raitt's *Vita and Virginia*, and, more recently, Eileen Barrett and Patricia Cramer's *Virginia Woolf*. However, there is a long history of criticism on Woolf and sexuality (see appendix C for a more detailed chronology of this important work). I am surprised at the early dates of the first essays: Blanche Wiesen Cook's '"Women Alone Stir My Imagination"' was published in 1979, Catharine Stimpson's 'Zero Degree Deviancy' in 1981, Louise DeSalvo's 'Lighting the Cave' in 1982, and Bonnie Zimmerman's 'Is "Chloe Liked Olivia" a Lesbian Plot?' in 1983. While these essays and others only gradually trickled down to the common reader, they were being published in a rich context of feminist historical and cultural analysis. Jeffrey Weeks (1977), Lillian Faderman (1978), Carroll Smith-Rosenburg (1985), and Martha Vicinus (1989) showed us that there was more to the lesbian subculture than the mannish lesbian. Happily, this important work still continues.

Some readers of Woolf are now comfortable imagining her as lesbian. Others see her as queer. Many readers are still unsure. Uncertainty seems to me to be consistent with the changing nature of Woolf's own attitudes towards her body and desires, and while it may be uncomfortable, it seems to me the most appropriate position to take. Not only is uncertainty consistent with Woolf's own position (and, as I will later argue, central to the notion of subjectivity and desire she and Sackville-West worked together to develop), but it also allows us to hold open the question of sexuality rather than risk dismissing it by way of stable conclusions.

Desire, of course, needs contextualization. It might be that at various moments in Woolf's life she could be described as homo-, hetero-, bi-, or asexual, although she never used any of these words to describe herself.[19] Even if her sexuality were stable, it is the fantasies of her generated by readers of her work, including students, critics, and biographers, that concern me here. And while I want to be careful not to elide the important distinctions between lesbian and queer sexualities, it seems to me that Woolf can be imagined either way, depending on who is imagining her. Woolf is a powerful figure of identification. Readers frequently (and inadvertently) imagine her, so as to repress the ways in which she is different from them, thus stabilizing both their and her identities. This fantasy can be immensely pleasurable, but it is illusory. I believe that, the more one reads Woolf's work, the more difficult it is to maintain this imaginary identification in which she is a mirror for the reader and the more powerfully complex she begins to appear in her own right. How readers imagine her is telling, and it can also be liberating.

Very few readers are still afraid of a sapphic Woolf. There is a growing trend, at least among critics, towards queering Virginia, or at least recognizing that she felt sexual desire for several of the women in her life.[20] When the early volumes of Woolf's diaries and letters had been published, Blanche Wiesen Cook advised: 'Because of the disparity between Virginia Woolf's own words, the fact of her changing sensibilities over time, and the prevailing interpretation of the meaning of her words, feminists may want to read every newly available letter and journal entry to decide for themselves such questions as whether or not Woolf was an elitist aristocrat or a socialist, asexual or woman-loving' (726). This is exactly what many readers have done.

I believe that it is important not to create two tracks in Woolf studies, in which some critics produce work focused primarily on issues of sexuality and some critics produce work that does not consider sexuality at all. I am afraid that Woolf's complex sexuality is not commonly integrated into readings of her work in the way that, say, Gertrude Stein's or Proust's or Sackville-West's sexuality is simply a part of the exquisite baggage readers carry as they read. I suspect that the initial repression of Woolf's sexuality, combined with subsequent resistance to imposing a single label on her, is largely responsible for this lack of integration. It is a dilemma that will be difficult to resolve. Even as I advocate maintaining Woolf's own fluid notion of sexuality and subjectivity, when I read Patricia Cramer's description in the introduction to Part II of *Virginia Woolf: Lesbian Readings*, which gives us an unambivalently lesbian Woolf, I feel an enormous sense of relief. As much as I recognize and wish to preserve the instability of Woolf's sexuality, I also enjoy being released from the tension of uncertainty. In those moments of stability, I look forward to a time when a Queer Virginia will be less surprising than the tailless cat glimpsed by the narrator of *A Room of One's Own* (13).[21] It can be difficult not to make her up as I would like her to have been.

Despite the chic of Queer Theory, there is still plenty of anxiety about sexuality, especially lesbian sexuality, in American universities and society. The publication of Woolf's diaries and letters and Vita Sackville-West's letters to Woolf have given readers a new perspective on Woolf. Prominent critics from Louise DeSalvo and Jane Marcus to Sherron Knopp and Elizabeth Meese have asked critics to integrate Woolf's sexual history into readings of her work and understandings of her life. In the last thirty years, readers of Woolf have been transformed painfully, resistantly, unconsciously, or joyfully. We cannot go back to waiting patiently in line for change, ignoring Woolf's hints and revelations.

But what happens when we take this knowledge to our students? Woolf is now unquestionably a part of the canon, but when I introduce her in my sophomore survey of British literature, there is squirming at the first mention of feminism. By the time I get through her childhood sexual abuse to her relationship with Vita Sackville-West, all I can see of the students in the back row are the tops of their baseball caps. I fear that the relative tolerance of the academy allows me to live in a great big closet – a walk-in closet, somewhat like a room – that I must leave from time to time to go into another sort of room – a classroom – where the work of queering Virginia continues. My students have all sorts of assumptions about sexuality, many of them created or supported by films and other forms of popular culture. It is difficult to disrupt these assumptions. Sometimes the media can be useful. One of my most successful experiments in disrupting assumptions about gender has been taping to my office door a picture of Russell Crowe knitting (*ChicKnits*). Visitors do a double take. But Crowe does not always call into question assumptions about masculinity and sexuality. To justify the omission of John Nash's alleged bisexuality in Ron Howard's film *A*

Beautiful Mind, the *Washington Post* quoted Crowe as saying, 'we didn't want to imply that there was any possibility that schizophrenia and homosexuality are related' (3 Jan. 2002, C3). While attempts to avoid pathologizing homosexuality are to be commended, it is worrying when they come at the expense of not representing homosexuality at all.

Crowe's comment points to the difficulties inherent in fashioning a biography of a person recognized as complex and in whose reputation many feel a vested interest. I think this is a problem in all biographies. It is certainly a problem with Virginia Woolf's. As Woolf criticism struggles to integrate the repressed knowledge of the sexual abuse Woolf suffered, it is important to avoid pathologizing lesbian desire. It is equally important not to avoid doing so by censoring sexuality. My confrontation with this issue occurs primarily in the classroom. I do not want to put students off Woolf before they have had a chance to fall in love with her prose, but I have no ambivalence about insisting that they recognize that her biography is just as complex as those of Wordsworth or Byron. Still, I recognize that it is more difficult for some of them to do so. The students I worry about most are those who identify with a single aspect of Woolf. Anxious about uncertainty, my students tend to pin Woolf down as a suicide or an incest victim and to read her work only in those contexts. As teachers and critics, we must struggle against this reductive impulse.

I hope that scholars and teachers of Woolf's work will fully integrate sexuality into readings of Woolf and her work and that this will not be interrupted by our culture's tendency, reflected and supported in most biographies, to affirm the existence of a unified identity. Even after Woolf herself, in 'The New Biography,' called for biography to take on the challenges of modernist fiction, British and American biographies still tend to imagine lives that are unified, explicable, and progress linearly towards a climax (Nagourney). Can we imagine Woolf, as she herself challenged us to imagine her, like the unstable Orlando, whose biographer could capture only a few of her thousands of selves (*Orlando* 309)? Can some of those selves be 'Sapphic' without eliminating all the others? When we queer Virginia, what do we change and what do we gain? If we gain discomfort because we can no longer avoid the difficult topic of sexuality, then we make this change in order to gain a more fully human Woolf, with all the pain and pleasure and loss and joy that goes along with lovely, messy life. As scholars and teachers, we are passing on Woolf to a new generation. We imagine a Woolf different from the one that was first presented to us. How do we do it? By continuing to follow Woolf's charge to us at the end of *A Room of One's Own* to prepare for the arrival of Shakespeare's sister, so that she can 'put on the body which she has so often laid down' (118). By 'versioning' a sexual Woolf, we imagine her as the woman she herself desired.

Resisting Feminine Sexuality

For Lacan ... language itself is structured as desire.

Butler, 'Desire' (383)

Lacan lived for eighty tumultuous years and made a very successful career out of saying things that just about no one could understand.

Schneiderman, *Jacques Lacan* (vi)

Before their first meeting on 14 December 1922 Sackville-West was, according to Woolf, 'one of those scribbling Sapphists.' Within two years she was 'My dear Vita' (8 Jan. 1924, 3:83) and after that 'My Dear Honey' (31 Jan. 1927, 3:319). As their intimacy increased, Woolf did not hesitate to express her own love and longing. She happily behaved like one of the scribbling sapphists she had once mocked. Woolf never defined herself as a sapphist, and it is not a term I intend to use for her. While sapphist might be taken as an early equivalent of 'lesbian,' I want to hold open the definition of this term, which for us suggests neither a culture nor an identity but might evoke an identity and certainly indicates a woman who desires women. Neither lesbian nor queer, as we understand the terms, was available to Woolf. Had they been, it is unlikely that she would have used either to describe herself, although we can graph either onto her. For myself, I am not interested in retrofitting Woolf's sexuality. Rather, I want to advance the work she and Sackville-West did in understanding desire and, through desire, the construction of the subject.

In seeking direction from Woolf and Sackville-West, I have been influenced by my background in feminist, psychoanalytic, and poststructural theory. While I hope this perspective arouses insight into the literary texts, I also believe that these texts enlighten contemporary critical theory. My goal, therefore, is a sort of praxis, in which textual analysis illuminates social conflicts that have resulted from the ways in which we imagine ourselves and one another. Woolf and Sackville-West have helped me to make sense of Lacan, and Lacan has helped me to see what I believe to be radical implications in the work of Woolf and Sackville-West. In the interest of readability, I have relegated the theoretical derivations of my critical perspective to the chapter notes whenever possible, but there are several terms privileged by psychoanalysis that should be understood within a Lacanian context. 'Identity' and 'subject' are carefully distinguished: identity is external, culturally constructed, and (relatively) stable, while the subject, because it includes the unconscious, is by definition unstable.[22] I am primarily concerned throughout with the subject. References to 'Law' or 'the Law of the Father' indicate restrictions enforced by cultural expectations as well as those governed by legal restraints. Following Lacan, I will capitalize Law when it is used in this way in order to distinguish this broader concept from legislation.[23] As I use it throughout, 'feminine' suggests not only the constructed nature of gender but also the way in which it points to the feminine position as repressed by the symbolic (or patriarchal) order.[24] Similarly, 'desire' for Lacan and, I suggest, for Woolf and Sackville-West is not exclusively sexual. While sexuality is central to desire, desire is greater than sexual desire alone. Desire is fundamental to the construction of the very subject that experiences desire. It is also bound up with language. As Judith Butler explains: 'Desire will be that which guarantees a certain opacity in language, an opacity that language can enact and display, but without which it cannot operate' ('Desire' 369). Desire, then, compels speech (or writing), even as it prevents language from being transparent. My quest for desiring women, which I believe I have found in Woolf and Sackville-West, is a search for women who persist in using language to express desire even in the knowledge that the direct communication of desire will be frustrated. In this way, Woolf and Sackville-West anticipate, recognize, and resist feminine sexuality as it has been described by Lacan. The parallels in Woolf and Sackville-West and Lacan make it productive to read them together.

I am acutely aware that this reciprocal reading pulls Lacan, Woolf, and Sackville-West into unusual and perhaps uncomfortable positions. The readings that follow may seem at best idiosyncratic and at worst misinformed. In this, I follow in the tradition of Lacan himself, since, as Stuart Schneiderman writes, 'Lacan's true reading [of Freud] is closer to being a misreading' (31). It is also the path of feminists who have found in Lacan an escape from the battle within the dominant structures to an understanding of those structures that suggests alternatives. Knowing full well that this strategy for resistance would not necessarily be sup- ·

ported by Lacan, feminists such as Hélène Cixous, Catherine Clément, Luce Irigaray, Julia Kristeva, Juliet Mitchell, Toril Moi, and Jacqueline Rose have worked to forge a feminist Lacanian critical practice. In response to criticism that such work runs afoul of orthodox Lacanian theory, Mitchell has said that feminists in England during the 1960s 'made Lacan our own' (Kapnist and Roudinesco). It is within this tradition that I am working, and it is in keeping, I believe, with the spirit of Woolf's *Three Guineas*, in that the theoretical reformulations I propose have political implications that are public and private, social and psychical, for external and internal regulatory structures. While it is crucial to address public, social, and legal conflicts, I think it is equally imperative (and much more difficult) to confront the private, psychical, and internal restrictions that govern desire. Taken together, Lacan, Woolf, and Sackville-West suggest a way to do so.

Modernism and psychoanalysis share a preoccupation with representing internal experience. Like Woolf, Lacan (who was her junior by nineteen years) was influenced by his reading of Freud in the 1930s. While Woolf and Sackville-West were well-established writers at this time, Lacan did not begin his influential Paris seminars until the 1950s, and *Écrits* was not published until 1966. There is no question, then, of Lacan's having any direct influence on Woolf (who died in 1941) or Sackville-West (who died in 1962). The usefulness of Lacan in reading Woolf's and Sackville-West's work arises in the similarity of their formulations of psychic structures.[25] I first saw the divided and unstable subject demonstrated in Woolf's fiction (especially *The Waves*); when I later read Lacan, I recognized Woolf's work in his theorization of the instability of the subject. When I turned for help in understanding Woolf's sexuality to Sackville-West, I found her grappling with the same unstable subject in her fiction, journal, and biographies.

Woolf and Sackville-West anticipated Lacan's theorization of the instability of the subject. In 'The Subversion of the Subject' Lacan posits that desire is constant, whereas the ego is intermittent (*Écrits* 312–13). One is, in this sense, one's desire.[26] These concepts are elaborated most explicitly, albeit briefly, in Sackville-West's journal,[27] in *Orlando*, and in what is, I believe, their shared understanding of androgyny (discussed further in ch. 3). My aim in the readings that follow is to tease out the nuances of these ideas as they are enacted in the textual conversation shared by these two desiring women.

Vita Sackville-West brought passion into Virginia Woolf's life. Woolf requested, and received from her, intimate letters and a story, *Seducers in Ecuador.* This was not the limit of their influence on one another: their intimate correspondence crept beyond the borders of their private lives into their published work. As they wrote during the course of their affair, they wrote to and for one another. This correspondence is most overt in the biographical writing that they did during that time period. Woolf influenced Sackville-West to bring higher standards to her prose, standards evident in the formal quality of later novels such as *All Passion Spent*, which, DeSalvo argues, articulates a more pronounced feminism than Sackville-West had previously demonstrated ('Every Woman' 97–8). More fundamentally, Woolf encouraged Sackville-West's inclination to recognize the instability of the subject position and the centrality of indeterminacy. For her part, Sackville-West increased Woolf's confidence and focused her attention on sensuality and sexuality. She brought out her senses of humour and play. *Orlando* is a tribute to both Woolf and Sackville-West as it demonstrates the integration of these qualities in the subject and her author. The climax of their partnership, *Orlando* is an explicit call for the recognition of the instability of sexuality and subjectivity. Woolf's influence on Sackville-West is well accepted. In this book I want to consider the reciprocal nature of their relationship, to place their work in that context, and to see it as an extended conversation that sought to understand and express their own desires. They pushed one another in form and content to imagine desiring women.

In 1979 Blanche Wiesen Cook wrote: 'But lesbianism is not, in the final analysis, the real issue. What our dominant society so fundamentally opposes is women's independent access to our erotic power' (739). Writing now, in the next century, I believe Cook's conclusions are correct. I was recently chastised by a feminist colleague for continuing to talk about 'patriarchy,' which sounded out of date to her. Would that it were so. My daily experience offers painful proof that, at least where I live, the patriarchy is alive and well, as is the unified subject with which it is inextricably entwined.

In their letters Woolf and Sackville-West imagined each other. As they took photographs of each other – but almost never appeared in one together – so, too, did they pose and frame each other. How they imagined each other affected how they saw themselves. Sackville-West wanted Woolf to respect her as a writer. Woolf struggled to see herself as a sexual being. Both asked the impossible. Imagining their lives spilled over onto their thinking about the construction and representation of gender, sexuality, and subjectivity.

the un stable

or Woolf did not 'respect'
V S-W's WRITING [?]

2 Forbidden Knowledge:
Vita Sackville-West's Secret Fruit

this ch. is mostly about Vita

And the serpent said unto Eve ... on the day ye eat of the fruit of the tree of knowledge of good and evil, then your eyes shall be opened.

Genesis 3. 4–5

Vita Sackville-West invited Virginia Woolf to enjoy, perhaps for the first and last time, the forbidden fruits of desire.[1] How was that possible? What was it about Sackville-West that allowed Woolf to resist the discouragement of acting on her erotic desire for women? Sackville-West's economically privileged background, national identity, sexual education, and development of an alternative theory of sexuality and gender suggest answers to these questions. Sackville-West was in a position, because of class and of her own making, that made it possible for her to profoundly influence Woolf's life and work.

Sackville-West represents all that the bohemian literati of her day despised. When Edith Sitwell called Sackville-West's poem *The Land* 'the worst poem in the English language' (Glendinning 177), Woolf explained away the critique of Sackville-West's lack of formal experimentation as the result of jealousy: 'you sell, and she dont – all good reasons why being a Sitwell she should vomit in public' (letter to Sackville-West, 24 June 1927, 3:394). But it was not only Sackville-West's popularity that nauseated her many critics; a formally traditional and popular writer with an aristocratic heritage is an unlikely literary or sexual revolutionary. Sackville-West was both, and, at least for a time, she shook Woolf's world down to the ground.

The form of Sackville-West's writing is conventional, but, as Suzanne Raitt points out, the content is not (*Vita and Virginia* 13–16). The same can be said of her life. Raitt argues that Sackville-West's marriage was a screen for her erotic practice. The social facade of hyper-conventionality that protected Sackville-West was one commonly used by nineteenth-century aristocrats, including her parents. It is also a structure that organizes her narratives of fact and of fiction. Her journals, letters, biographies, and novels represent the tension between repressing desire in order to maintain the privileges of social position and openly challenging hypocritical conventionality. Regardless of the outcome of the challenge, for Sackville-West the repression of desire was seemingly unendurable. To ignore expectations without suffering the consequences is a fantasy she inherited from her grandfather, Lionel Sackville-West, the 2nd Lord Sackville. This inheritance allowed her to develop a relationship to legal and cultural regulations outside the economy of guilt and obedience. It is from her grandfather, silent patriarch of the family, that she received the secret knowledge of her own hidden strengths, a knowledge she investigated in her life and her writing. It is a gift she shared, briefly, with Virginia Woolf.

Sapphic Desire

Sackville-West and Woolf met at a dinner party given by Vanessa Bell's husband, Clive, on 14 December 1922. Sackville-West was thirty; Woolf was forty. Both were well-known authors. Sackville-West had already published three novels and two books of poems, and she would begin *The Land*, winner of the prestigious Hawthornden Prize, the following year. Woolf had published *The Voyage Out*, *Night and Day*, and *Jacob's Room*, as well as two books of short stories. With her husband, Leonard Woolf, she ran the Hogarth Press, which was publishing T.S. Eliot, Katherine Mansfield, and E.M. Forster, among others. The Press, like Woolf herself, had a reputation for being highbrow, arty, and esoteric. Sackville-West was a much more popular writer, who had received a great deal of critical attention. Married to Harold Nicolson, a successful diplomat and biographer, Sackville-West was distinguished from Woolf in having two sons and a wealthy aristocratic family and having experienced a string of affairs with other women.

Sackville-West never referred to herself as a lesbian. In the early twentieth century, 'lesbian' had no fixed definition(s), either outside or inside scare quotes. Woolf called Sackville-West a sapphist and used that term freely, though never to refer to herself.[2] Unlike 'bugger,' Bloomsbury's favourite slang for a gay man, sapphist does not suggest

any particular erotic practice.[3] 'These Sapphists *love* women' Woolf
wrote of Sackville-West in her diary (21 Dec. 1925, 3:51; emphasis
original), but when posing to herself the question of whether she loved
Sackville-West, Woolf immediately back-pedals: 'But what is love? Her
being "in love" (it must be comma'd thus) with me, excites & flatters; &
interests. What is this "love"?' (20 May 1926, 3:87). Woolf wrote this
passage after she and Sackville-West had begun to 'sleep' together, to
use Sackville-West's euphemism, but Woolf's quote-contained 'in love'
suggests emotional rather than erotic contact.

The displacement of erotic desire by an emotional commitment is
consistent with Victorian doctrine on the sexual education of girls.
Predominant in nineteenth-century England was the notion that the
development of the moral character in men required self-control and
deferred gratification. The Christian gentleman was expected to resist
temptation through proper exercise of his strong will in the business
world and in his private life. Medical texts and educational manuals of
the nineteenth century characterize the model Victorian woman as
inherently lacking sexual awareness and thus lacking sexual desires.
With little or no will of her own, she must be prevented from acquiring
sexual knowledge, since once such awareness was aroused, she would
be powerless to resist the carnal urges that followed.[4] Although this
logic is difficult to take seriously today, it was pervasive in nineteenth-
century England. It was asserted that women were descended from the
fallen Eve and thus retained some kernel of innocence from before the
forbidden fruit was first enjoyed. With no knowledge of good and evil,
all of a woman's energies were to be directed into fulfilling her comple-
mentary duties as devoted wife and loving mother. For a woman, the
tension between duty and unrestrained desire was not a conscious
battle to be manfully fought and won but a matter of remaining ignorant, because she was thought to be insufficiently capable of controlling
her desires once aroused. As long as her innocence was undefiled by
forbidden knowledge, her purity was ensured. Once tainted, she was
fallen. Whether it had been sought, discovered accidentally, or forced
upon her, erotic knowledge created a 'scar' or 'wound' that would
never go away. The metaphor exposes the true object of unseemly
discovery: it is not erotic knowledge in the abstract but consciousness of
the vaginal slit that is frightening. The theory of a woman's natural
innocence represses knowledge of the female body.[5]

Once discovered, the 'scar' cannot be ignored: like the New World, it
must be entered and explored. Knowledge might lead to that which

Victorian medical texts forbade: masturbation. But this concern, too, can be seen as a screen for the greater anxiety over women's knowledge of their bodies' reproductive power. As microscopes enabled the study of reproduction during the nineteenth century, the egg's contribution to propagation was recognized. No longer understood as merely the receptacle for the homunculus deposited by the male, the interaction between egg and sperm was discovered.[6] The myth of male reproduction was destroyed. The doctrine of feminine innocence, however, protected male mastery over female reproductive and sexual power. Women were essentially forbidden to have knowledge of their bodies.

Girls who found themselves scarred by an awareness of their bodies must endeavour to forget the temptation. Miss E.M. Sewell's *Principles of Education, Drawn from Nature and Revelation, and Applied to Female Education in the Upper Classes* (1865) includes a confession to be used by girls who had stumbled upon unwanted knowledge: 'Oh that I had been warned! that I had not been left to the workings of my own mind! that I had learned in infancy to be ashamed of those things which I felt to be evil, though I knew not why! But I was left without a word of caution, and now I can but struggle to forget, what with that caution I might never have learnt' (quoted in Cominos 159). The problem, of course, is that any warning would have functioned to introduce the very knowledge girls must avoid. The warning 'Don't look in the closet!' poses problems for a strategy based on the assumption that women do not realize there is a closet in the first place. Indeed, this was the rationale for not banning female-female erotic acts in a proposed amendment to the Criminal Law Amendment Act debated as late as 1921. The amendment was defeated on the grounds that the prohibition would give women ideas they had not previously had. Women unprotected by ignorance were prey to the unspeakable cravings of their animal nature; unlike men, who could develop strong wills with which to combat temptation, they had no means to resist sinful indulgences of the flesh. The only hope was to ensure they never discovered the possibility, which required total repression of bodily awareness and sexual desire.[7] As the turn of the century approached and sexual knowledge became increasingly public, that requirement became harder to enforce.

Sackville-West was born in 1892, in the last decade of Queen Victoria's reign. This was a transitional period for attitudes towards knowledge – particularly sexual knowledge. The emergence of a scientific epistemology that valued investigation and report over repression and silence was transforming, or at least challenging, popular beliefs. Freud's publication of *Studies in Hysteria* (with Josef Breuer) in 1895 and *The Psycho-pathology of Everyday Life* in 1901, the year of Queen Victoria's death, applied scientific methodology to sexuality. Building on the work of Ernst Brücke and Jean-Martin Charcot, Freud's 1895 book traced the debilitating symptoms of hysteria to their roots in the unconscious conflict produced by nineteenth-century repressions of female sexual-ity. It coincided with a deluge of research into sexuality produced by 'sexologists' such as Havelock Ellis, Richard Krafft-Ebing, Cesare Lombroso, Albert Moll, and Magnus Hirschfeld. But the effects of this change on the public were yet to come. In the 1890s such work, still controversial and energetically opposed, was confined to the medical community. The first English review of Freud in a non-medical journal, written, interestingly enough, by Leonard Woolf, did not appear until 1914,[8] and Edward Carpenter's influential *The Intermediate Sex: Study of Transitional Types of Men and Women* appeared only two years earlier in 1912.[9] In the 1890s typical middle- and upper-class English families were still committed to raising their daughters to become respectable ladies.

Vita Sackville-West's family was far from typical and not altogether English. Nevertheless, it was the conscious and expressed intention of her convent-educated mother to raise her daughter in accordance with the doctrine of feminine innocence. She even went so far as to prohibit Sackville-West from reading suggestive novels such as *The Woman in White* and *The Count of Monte Cristo* (Glendinning 22). But contributions to Sackville-West's sexual education formed a mixture of innocence and knowledge that the educational manuals did not anticipate.

Despite her mother's best intentions, Sackville-West's family history made complete innocence an impossibility.[10] Rather than a genteel family presided over by a controlled father and chaste mother, her family shook with romance, scandal, and glamour; it was not genteel but aristocratic. Her mother, Victoria West, was the illegitimate daugh-ter of Lionel Sackville-West and his mistress, Pepita de Oliva, whose biography Vita Sackville-West would later write. Pepita de Oliva (who was married to the dancer Juan de Oliva) was a Spanish dancer, who raised their children in France under the name of West while Lionel Sackville-West served in the British diplomatic service. Victoria West married her cousin, who was also her father's heir. In a family where lineage was crucial and the stakes (the family estate, Knole) were high, the details of courtships, marriages, and births – or simply courtships and births – would be widely known and carefully taught. An education in the Sackville-West family history was not likely to produce a model of innocence or a stable notion of national identity. Sackville-West was equally proud of her aristocratic lineage and her Spanish heritage, which she conflates with Gypsy traditions. Bilingual, she travelled frequently to France, which was not nearly as draconian as England in its laws or attitudes towards sexuality.[11]

Another contribution to Sackville-West's sexual education was made by her parents' continual affairs. Lady Sackville might have been anxious to raise an innocent daughter, but she herself did not exemplify that model, as her journal attests. By the time Sackville-West was eight, both of her parents were pursuing other romantic interests (Glendinning 17). Lord Sackville's alliances would ultimately become so egregious that his wife left him permanently in 1919. For her part, Lady Sackville had affairs with notables such as William Waldorf Astor, Pierpont Morgan, and the renowned architect Edwin Lutyens. This behaviour was by no means unusual for men and women of their class during the Edwardian era.[12] The title of Miss Sewell's book marks it for the education of the upper class, but the aristocracy existed outside the dominant ideology it enforced. Middle- and upper-class models of male self-restraint and female innocence did not apply to the hyper-privileged.

Sackville-West was certainly privileged. She may have been innocent of the biological details of reproduction, or at least as innocent as a child who grew up in the country surrounded by dogs, horses, and other pets could be, but she understood the consequences of both privilege and reproduction. She knew that her cousin Eddy, because he was male, would inherit Knole in her place.

Despite conditions and events that spoiled the pure and unknowing state her mother took pains to construct, it is evident that the system of enforced innocence had a profound effect on Sackville-West. Indeed, even late in life, the rhetoric that dominated the conception of ideal, chaste womanhood is apparent in her contemplation of her early erotic experiences. At sixty-eight she wrote to Harold Nicolson, in language that closely parallels Miss Sewell's soliloquy of self-reproach: 'I was very young, and very innocent. I knew nothing about homosexuality. I didn't even know that such a thing existed – either between men or between women. You should have told me. You should have warned me. You should have told me about yourself, and have warned me that the same sort of thing was likely to happen to myself ... I simply didn't know' (23 Nov. 1960, 432). She had learned well the discourse of innocence and regret. As Miss Sewell advises, Sackville-West blames her lack of knowledge for the acquisition of knowledge. Sackville-West's letter reprises the lament of the young girl ruined by unwanted knowledge: 'Oh that I had been warned! That I had not been left to the workings of my own mind ... I was left without a word of caution' (Cominos 159). Like her Victorian predecessor, Sackville-West makes the joint assertion of her own innocence and another's failure to absolve her of responsibility for her transgressions.[13] Repeating her own version of Miss Sewell's soliloquy of self-reproach, Sackville-West presents herself as tainted by unwanted experience and despairing of ever ridding herself of the scar. This suggests that, despite a life lived in seeming defiance of sexual conventions, some kernel of the code of innocence remained as a central component of her complex and conflicted sexual identity.

Sackville-West was also in possession of another kind of forbidden knowledge. This knowledge was sought willingly and enjoyed thoroughly. Its acquisition was not something she had protected herself from, even though she would later claim that this was only because she did not know what she was learning. Beginning before her marriage and continuing throughout her life, Sackville-West, to use her own phraseology, slept with women. In certain circles it was no secret.

Even before they met, Woolf and the rest of her set would have heard of Sackville-West's propensity for eloping with other men's wives. 'She is a pronounced Sapphist,' Woolf wrote in her diary, '& may, thinks Ethel Sands, have an eye on me, old though I am' (19 Feb. 1923, 2:235). Two years before meeting Woolf, Sackville-West had run off with Violet Keppel Trefusis, whose mother had been the mistress of Edward VII. The event created a great scandal. Harold Nicolson and Denys Trefusis rented an airplane to fly after their wives and coaxed them home with some difficulty. This was only one incident in the two-year-long affair during which the women gambled heavily at Monte Carlo, dined and danced together in Paris and London, with Sackville-West cross-dressed as 'Julian,' and together went on prolonged – once by as much as three extra months – holidays.

This was not Sackville-West's first experiment in same-sex erotic and romantic behaviour. Like her successor Violet Trefusis, Rosamund Grosvenor was a childhood friend. Their friendship developed into something more: 'my liaison with Rosamund was, in a sense, superficial. I mean that it was almost exclusively physical, as, to be frank, she always bored me as a companion. I was very fond of her, however; she had a sweet nature. But she was quite stupid' (Nicolson 30).[14] Even while they were still in school, Grosvenor's notes to Sackville-West were passionate and filled with erotic innuendo: 'Promise *not* to sit next to me tomorrow. It is not that I don't love you being near me, but that I cannot give my attention to the questions, I am – otherwise engrossed' (Glendinning 31; emphasis original). In retrospect, Sackville-West describes the beginning of their affair: 'by the middle of that summer [1911] we were inseparable, and moreover were living on terms of the greatest possible intimacy. But I want to say again that the thing did start in comparative innocence. Oh, I dare say I realized vaguely that I had no business to sleep with Rosamund' (Nicolson 29). Sackville-West does not romanticize or diminish her relationship with Grosvenor, but neither does she completely integrate it into her life. During their affair Sackville-West became engaged to and married Harold Nicolson; nevertheless, she wrote: 'I really was innocent over the Rosamund affair. It never struck me as wrong that I should be more or less engaged to Harold, and at the same time very much in love with Rosamund' (33). Her relationship with Grosvenor seems to have had no affect on her assumption that her future would be spent in a conventionally defined (i.e., heterosexual) marriage.

As her 1960 protest of innocence to Harold Nicolson suggests, during her early affairs Sackville-West knew how to do it, even if she did not know what to call what she was doing. Clearly female-female erotic practices were enjoyed and acknowledged in England before the term 'lesbian' became part of everyday parlance in the 1930s. Lisa Moore points out that when, in a 1789 diary entry, Hester Thrale described Marie Antoinette as 'the Head of a Set of Monsters called by each other Sapphists,' Thrale understood what she was writing (quoted in Moore 1). Valerie Traub's genealogy of lesbianism in *The Renaissance of Lesbianism in Early Modern England* uncovers a plethora of examples of representations of female homoeroticism in the seventeenth century. As Traub shows, 'The evidence of the early modern period suggests that discrete features of *lesbian* representation acquired more importance as others declined. By the end of the eighteenth century, for instance, the figure [of the tribade] that arguably had the most potential to signify transgressively had almost disappeared from the discourse that first gave her prominence' (358; emphasis original). In the seventeenth and eighteenth centuries, Emma Donoghue concludes, 'Lesbian culture seems to have been understood as a matter of relationships and habitual practices rather than self-identifications' (8). Traub posits that 'cycles of salience [of certain historically specific figures of eroticism] may be

Lesbian Erasure

linked temporally and conceptually to moments of social crisis which have their source in anxieties peripheral to eroticism (such as fears about changing gender roles, nationalist or racist fears of contamination, and broad concerns about morality or social discipline)' (359). While more work must be done before larger conclusions may be drawn, all of these anxieties would seem to have been at play in nineteenth-century England, and while it is not possible to generalize broadly, there is substantial evidence that women frequently lacked access to language for erotic practices between women.

Martha Vicinus points to examples of imprecision and inarticulateness comparable to Sackville-West's in the writing of Dorothy Strachey Bussy and Constance Maynard. Bussy, Lytton Strachey's older sister and long-time friend of Virginia Woolf, wrote of the omnipresence of passionate relationships between women at school in her autobiographical novel, *Olivia* (1949). Written in 1933 and published by the Hogarth Press after Woolf's death, the novel is dedicated: 'To the beloved memory of V.W.' The educator Constance Maynard, a generation older than Woolf and Sackville-West, describes intense feelings for women comparable to those discussed by Sackville-West and Bussy. Vicinus comments: 'Maynard appears never to have linked her passionate love of women with sex, which she defined narrowly as heterosexuality' (524 n32).[15] Laura Doan's analysis of the vocabulary used by the early reviewers of *The Well of Loneliness* concludes: 'The prevalence of euphemistic phrases in these reviews ... suggests that there was as yet no comfortable consensus about or understanding of the appropriate language [to describe lesbianism], even among the most sophisticated reviewers' (26). Carroll Smith-Rosenberg notes that homoerotic practice between women was not codified in the nineteenth century, even in health manuals: 'Until then, it is true, British and American physicians had described behaviour we would now define as lesbian: young women, often schoolgirls or college women, in bed together enjoying genital stimulation, avowing passionate emotional attachment. Although physicians carefully labelled comparable behaviour when engaged in by boys and college men as homosexual and perverted, they categorized the women as masturbators and female homosexuality as a rare and exotic phenomenon'[16] (*Hidden* 268). The only element that appears to be consistent in these registers is the lack of specificity in, even avoidance of, describing homoerotic practices between women.

Indeed, even as late as 1918, knowledge of the female anatomy was suspect, as Lucy Bland demonstrates in her revealing discussion of the libel action taken by Maud Allan. Allan, one of the most gifted and popular modern dancers of her day, brought suit over a review of her performance in Oscar Wilde's *Salome*. The review was entitled 'The Cult of the Clitoris' and implied that Allan was a lesbian. Allan lost the case, largely because she knew what the word 'clitoris' meant. According to Bland, 'to know about the clitoris implied knowledge of women's sexuality autonomous from men. Non-experts such as Allan would only have such knowledge, the defence adamantly claimed, if they were compelled by their perverse proclivities to seek it out' (189). Allan lost the case, like Wilde before her, because, since the implication that she was a lesbian was found to be accurate, it was not libellous to suggest it. The verdict brought an abrupt end to her career. If having a precise vocabulary was damning, it is perhaps no wonder that there are few illustrations of such knowledge.

Sackville-West does not avoid describing her sexual relationships with women in her journal and letters, but, unlike Allan, she does not appear to have had a precise vocabulary with which to detail her affairs. Glendinning concludes that '[Sackville-West] and Rosamund shared a diffuse and sentimental sensuality, but never, then or later, did they technically "make love." They did not think of it' (42). Sackville-West confirms this abstruse conclusion. While she did 'sleep with' Grosvenor, she comments on her characterization of herself as 'passionately in love' with Grosvenor, saying: 'I use the word "passionately" on purpose. It was passion that used to make my head swim sometimes, even in the daytime, but we never made love' (Nicolson 33). However, when describing the first years of her marriage, she writes: 'I never knew [with Harold Nicolson] the physical passion I had felt for Rosamund' (39). We can only guess at what specifically created the distinction between 'sleep with' and 'make love.' Sackville-West is never explicit about her erotic practice. Aside from kissing, which may or may not be code, she is entirely euphemistic. She clearly understands there to be a continuum of erotic behaviour, but she is not explicit as to what practices correspond to which euphemisms. Regardless of the details and distinctions, the emotional intensity and erotic nature of her relationships with women is uncontested.

While a paucity of vocabulary coupled with a lack of precise definitions for the language that *was* available may have kept many women from acting on or even experiencing homoerotic impulses, they may also have screened female-female erotic practice from censorship.[17] For Sackville-West, the flip side of her lack of sexual knowledge was her ability to engage in erotic activities with another woman guilt free. Her early relationship with Grosvenor fostered a mutual exploration of bodies and desires outside cultural restrictions. She acknowledges only mild concern that she was engaging in unsanctioned activities with Grosvenor. 'I should certainly never have allowed anyone to find out, but my sense of guilt went no further than that,' she wrote in her account of their affair (Nicolson 29). Sackville-West presents her early erotic explorations as private, perhaps naughty, but not deviant. Her ignorance facilitated the development of sexual desires and erotic practices with remarkably little interference from cultural or subcultural expectations and prohibitions. She expressed homoerotic desires that she and her partners acted upon. Her relationships were not merely schoolgirl crushes, nor did they simply replicate heterosexual models. As she explored her desire and the bodies of other women, she enjoyed the secret knowledge unscarred.

Sackville-West's Challenge to Sexology

The time of Sackville-West's early homoerotic experimentation was also a period when scientific investigation, sexual exploration, and scandal began to reach the public. The theories of forbidden knowledge produced by late Victorian sexologists Edward Carpenter, Havelock Ellis, et al. contested current notions of gender and sexuality without challenging the central tenant of passivity in feminine sexuality. Sackville-West read the sexologists avidly and experimented with their notions. Ultimately, however, she rejected their conclusions and developed her own experientially derived thesis, an integration of sexology and psychology, which she explicated briefly and elaborated performatively.

In 1895, the year Oscar Wilde was imprisoned after his conviction under the Labouchère Amendment,[18] Edward Carpenter argued, in his popular 'The Intermediate Sex,'[19] that erotic pleasure should be enjoyed as an end in itself rather than regulated as a vehicle for reproduction. This position supported the decriminalization of homosexual, or Uranian, erotic practice. Uranians, according to Carpenter, were the 'Intermediate Sex,' halfway between male and female, who linked the sexes together into one continuous category. Influenced, like Ellis and Symonds, by Walt Whitman and supported by emotional rather than biological evidence, Carpenter celebrated the contributions of 'intermediates' to society (Weeks, *Coming Out* 72–6).

The year Oscar Wilde was released from Reading Gaol, Havelock

Ellis and John Addington Symonds published *Sexual Inversion* (1897).[20] Ellis would become renowned in England for his characterization of the 'sexual invert.' His interest in inversion was shared by continental sexologists Lombroso, Schrenck-Notzing, Moll, Tarnowsky, Tardieu, and especially Krafft-Ebing and Magnus Hirschfeld. Departing from Freud, who argued that everyone is fundamentally bisexual ('Three Essays on the Theory of Sexuality'), they developed a scientific study of deviancy. Ellis, driven by personal motives – his wife Edith was an 'invert' – insisted that homosexuality was the result of heredity, and therefore 'inverts' deserved to be treated compassionately. They were not, he argued, given to such reproachable behaviour as criminality or masturbation. The appeal of Ellis's argument for the congenital nature of inversion may have been strategic. In England, where punishment for male homosexual acts was the most severe in Europe, Ellis's argument for tolerance was politically useful.[21] His theory, however, particularly as regards women, is problematic in both the research methodology and the conclusions.[22]

Sexual Inversion is a collection of thirty-three case histories drawn from questionnaires completed by men and women Ellis termed 'inverts.' Ellis's goal, like that of his greatest influence, Krafft-Ebing, was to categorize the phenomenon he was studying. This both men did. Krafft-Ebing proposes four categories of inversion in women ranging by degrees of increasing masculinity from the female invert who could pass as a 'normal' woman to the female invert who could pass as a man in all respects except her genitals. Although Ellis's questionnaires were obtained randomly, edited, and contained only six samples from women, he nevertheless used these small samples to support his theory of sexual inversion in women and men. He reduces Kraft-Ebing's categories to two: the congenital or 'true' invert and the woman susceptible to 'acquired' homosexuality (33). His 'true' female invert is easily recognized by her masculine appearance and behaviour: she is deep-voiced, likes to smoke, is muscular and athletic, incapable of needlework, shy around women, and unattractive to men (96–8). Sexually aggressive, she preys on innocent, unsuspecting women who are susceptible to her seductive powers. The 'mannish lesbian' is a man trapped in a woman's body.

The stratification proposed by sexology paralleled, with unsubstantiated biological justification, the same tripartite structure created by the Victorian doctrine of innocence, in which women were chaste, being innocent of all sexual knowledge; in danger of falling into sin as a result of gaining sexual knowledge, or fallen, because they had been exposed to and were unable to repress sexual knowledge. Women as constructed by sexology were feminine and sexually passive and therefore categorized as normal; in danger of falling into deviancy as a result of contact with the sexual desires of masculine women; or masculine and sexually aggressive as a result of heredity. Victorian culture denied the existence of feminine sexuality altogether; the sexologists reconstituted it as passive. While sexology's version of women was not the same as the Victorian denial of feminine sexuality, it differed only in ejecting erotic desire from the feminine woman. In order to contain women with sexual knowledge, sexology constructed the masculine female invert, while the tainted Victorian woman was concealed behind the symptoms of hysteria. Both doctrines equated erotic desire with masculinity and considered feminine women to be susceptible to more powerful masculine influences.

The sexologists conflated gender and object choice to excuse the mannish lesbian, whose choice of a female object of erotic desire demonstrated her masculine nature, which in turn explained her active sexuality.[23] Similarly, for a man to prefer a male demonstrated his hyper-masculinity. While Ellis regarded such a choice as perverse – as opposed to the congenital male invert who had no choice – it was tacitly understood that for a man to be aroused by another man was simply a result of men's unquenchable virility. For a feminine woman to prefer a woman to a man, however, was a sign of deviancy, if not insanity.[24]

Empowered by incomes and vocabularies, Gertrude Stein, Natalie Barney, Edna St Vincent Millay, and many, many other women met in, among other places, Paris, Berlin, and Greenwich Village. Their experiments with gender roles and sexual identity coincided with the popularity of the sexologists' characterization of the congenital female invert as masculine. The constructed identity of the 'mannish lesbian' informed both the dominant cultural imagination and the developing lesbian subculture.

The most famous literary example of this style, Radclyffe Hall's *The Well of Loneliness*, with its supportive introduction by Havelock Ellis, neatly dramatizes the theory of inversion. Stephen Gordon is the mannish lesbian, the true congenital invert who recognizes herself in the volume of Krafft-Ebing she finds hidden in her father's study (204). Stephen's lover, Mary, is a feminine woman susceptible to homosexuality. In order to save Mary from deviancy, Stephen, now a famous writer, pretends to reject Mary in order to drive her into the waiting arms of a real man. By this selfless gesture, Stephen proves that inverts are both more talented and more selfless than ordinary mortals. The moral of the story, like the theory of inversion it illustrates, is politically expedient. Also like the theory of inversion, *The Well of Loneliness* has been enormously influential in establishing the image of the mannish lesbian and what has been called the butch/femme couple as one model for female-female relationships in the early twentieth century.[25]

Like Havelock Ellis's *Sexual Inversion*, *The Well of Loneliness* was banned soon after publication. Bloomsbury rallied to its support.[26] Leonard Woolf and E.M. Forster circulated a petition to protest the ban. Virginia Woolf wrote to Sackville-West to explain why the addition of Sackville-West's signature would harm more than help the cause: 'not yours, for *your* proclivities are too well known' (30 Aug. 1928, 3:520; emphasis original). Sackville-West shared more with Radclyffe Hall's heroine than 'proclivities.' Indeed, a case could be made for Sackville-West as the original Stephen Gordon, beginning with their shared aristocratic heritage, physique, and success as writers. Despite similarities, Sackville-West did not ultimately style herself in the role of the mannish lesbian adopted by Stephen and her creator. But she gave it a try.

Like Bussy and Maynard, Sackville-West wrote about her relationships with women and the development of her sexuality. After her death, her son Nigel Nicolson discovered a locked Gladstone bag for which there was no key. He cut the bag open to discover a journal begun on 23 July 1920, five months after Sackville-West's elopement with Violet Trefusis and just days after she wrote to her husband that she had refused to go abroad once again with Trefusis (21 July 1920, 110–11). The affair was not yet over, and Sackville-West wrote in a state of emotional turmoil. The situation had reached a crisis, and while she would have preferred to keep both her marriage and her lover, neither Nicolson nor Trefusis was willing to continue this arrangement. Sackville-West had to decide whether to stop seeing Trefusis or to leave Nicolson. She writes the journal in the hope that it will lead her to a decision. In the journal she attempts to create a narrative that makes sense of her erotic attraction to women and integrates her complex sexuality into her public and personal life. In so doing, she posits a theory of sexuality that recognizes women's active, erotic desires.

The copy of *Sexual Inversion* that Sackville-West kept by her writing table in the tower room used as her study at Sissinghurst was inscribed with the initials of her married name and a quotation from Verlaine in Harold Nicolson's handwriting: '*On est fier quelquefois quand on se com-*

pare.'[27] Next to it were Edward Carpenter's *The Intermediate Sex* and Otto Weininger's *Sex and Character*. Sackville-West read the sexologists with Trefusis and later with Harold Nicolson (Glendinning 405). She possessed the 'mannish' characteristics Ellis uses to define the congenital invert: she was deep-voiced, very tall, physically strong and active, and erotically attracted to women, but she was also attractive and attracted to men. Sackville-West recognized the oversimplifications of sexology; nevertheless, in her journal there is evidence of the sexologists' influence.[28] In the journal, she used the psychoanalytic method of looking back to childhood for clues to her sexual development; specifically, she was looking for evidence of congenital inversion. The trait she found that would seem to prove the case for inversion is her masculinity.

Evidence of masculine characteristics abounds in the journal. As a child, Sackville-West records, 'I wasn't so much of a coward, and I kept my nerves under control, and made a great ideal of being hardy, and as like a boy as possible' (Nicolson 5). She also recalls a preference for her father: 'Dada used to take me for terribly long walks and talk to me about science, principally Darwin, and I liked him a great deal better than Mother, of whose quick temper I was frightened' (5). She describes herself as a man during her first realization of her feelings for Trefusis: 'I might have been a boy of eighteen, and she a woman of thirty-five' (104); and, of course, there is also the cross-dressing and the pet name, Julian.[29]

Writing about cross-dressing to pass as a man is the only moment in her journal when Sackville-West baulks even momentarily: 'the evenings [in Paris with Trefusis in late 1918] were ours. I have never told a word of what I did. I hesitate to write it here, but I must; shirking the truth here would be like cheating oneself playing patience. I dressed as a boy. It was easy' (Nicolson 109). She goes on to explain in some detail how she successfully passed by using make-up and wrapping her head in a bandage (the war was just over). Her height and build were natural advantages. Warming to her subject, she admits that she had cross-dressed previously on one occasion in England. After a stroll down Piccadilly, she went with Trefusis by train to Orpington, where they stayed in a lodging house as husband and wife. The next day they went to Knole, where Sackville-West changed clothes in the stables. 'The extraordinary thing was,' she writes parenthetically, 'how natural it all was for me' (110). Here she echoes Havelock Ellis, who writes: 'There is ... a very pronounced tendency among sexually inverted women to adopt male attire ... because the wearer feels more at home in [it]' (95).

As a young man, she walked through London smoking a cigarette, was called 'sir' by a paper boy, and 'accosted now and then by women' (110). She felt right at home. From a lark, cross-dressing turned into a way of life, at least for a while: 'Well, this discovery was too good to be wasted, and in Paris I practically lived in that role. Violet used to call me Julian. We dined together every evening in cafés and restaurants, and went to all the theatres. I shall never forget the evenings when we walked back slowly to our flat through the streets of Paris. I, personally, had never felt so free in my life' (110–11). Sackville-West continued as Julian when they left Paris for Monte Carlo. There, she developed another venue for Julian as the hero of *Challenge*, a novel that continues her experiments with sexuality and gender identity.[30]

Challenge tells the story of Julian Devenant, the son of an English family made prosperous by grape and olive production on a group of fictional islands attached to the former Greek state of Herakleion. During a vacation from Oxford, Julian becomes a key player in the islands' bid for independence. The plans for rebellion are quickly discovered, and Julian is sent back to school. When he returns two years later, he assumes the presidency of the islands and leads the new state in two successful defences against Herakleion. The islands are recaptured only because of a traitor, Julian's cousin and lover, Eve.[31] Like her Edenic predecessor, Eve is unable to control her passionate desires and thus destroys the innocent paradise Julian longed to create. When she realizes that Julian is devastated by the failure of the rebellion and the murder of his closest comrades, she drowns herself in the ocean.

Eve was modelled on Trefusis and the novel was 'Dedicated with gratitude for much excellent copy to the original of Eve.'[32] Dedications, as evidenced in later works, meant a lot to Sackville-West. As a portrait of Trefusis, Eve must be uncannily accurate. Nigel Nicolson, who was four when the affair ended, confirms that this is so: 'Eve is a portrait of Violet as exact as Vita could make it, having her model always at her side. Physically Eve resembles Violet precisely ... Eve is the portrait of a clever, infuriating, infinitely charming witch' ('Introduction,' *Challenge* 10). Eve seduces Julian into tasting the forbidden knowledge of erotic pleasure in their vaguely incestuous, arousingly transgressive affair. Trefusis was the bearer of a different kind of forbidden fruit; the exact variety was knowledge her family wished to keep secret. Readers who recognized Eve as the apple of Sackville-West's fictional eye would lick their lips over the juicy scandal. Sackville-West's and Trefusis's mothers joined forces to dissuade Sackville-West from publishing the novel in

England. It was brought out in the United States in 1924 and only posthumously in England in 1974.[33]

Violet Trefusis also recognized the similarity, and loved it. Sackville-West read the novel to Trefusis as it was written, and Trefusis offered suggestions for emphasizing the likeness of the characters. She even offered a broad hint to readers by drawing a picture of herself with Sackville-West cross-dressed as Julian to be used on the cover of the novel; this cover was never used (Glendinning 109). Trefusis was particularly delighted by the characterization of Sackville-West as Julian, a comparison the two mothers seem to have missed: 'The description of Julian I thought most adequate,' Trefusis wrote to Sackville-West. 'You say it's not like you! It is you, word for word, trait for trait' (93). In the novel's final scenes, Julian, wounded in battle, even wears a bandage around his head just as Sackville-West did to hide her hair when cross-dressing.

Harold Nicolson recognized Julian. He strongly disapproved of his wife's cross-dressing (Glendinning 107), and he initially supported Lady Sackville's demand that the novel be withdrawn. In his letters to Sackville-West he refers to *Challenge* as 'little smuts' (100). This may suggest more about his attitude towards his wife's affair with Trefusis than about his opinion of the novel.[34] Sackville-West's ultimate agreement to withdraw the novel from her furious publisher shows that she too recognized the story to be about something more than just a fantastic rebellion.

If *Challenge* describes a revolution, the declaration of independence is precipitated not by the trade laws of a fictional state but by early twentieth-century gender conventions. Sackville-West dressed for battle on the streets of Paris and in *Challenge* in the costume of Julian, the wounded soldier. With the psychic wound of her sex in a classic displacement upward, Sackville-West's fantasy of masculinity enabled her to challenge patriarchal Law and act like a man.

The fictional Julian is a perfect stereotype of masculinity. Heroic in battle and passionate in love, he is the embodiment of active desire. The characters articulate as well as perform traditional gender roles. Julian grows up by asserting himself against his father and the law of the land, thus discovering his emotional and erotic passion for Eve. In both situations, political and sexual, he does not hesitate to act on his impulses. He is criticized by his father both for rebelling and for running off with Eve, but the chastisement does not ignore or repress Julian's desires. The consequences of Julian's behaviour will be independence:

at best he will be president of a new and independent state, and at worst he will be disinherited. He will not, like Eve, be dishonoured. Just as Julian represents masculinity, Eve represents femininity. Instead of open, she is secretive. Instead of bold, she is wilful. Instead of visionary, she is selfish. Sackville-West defended Eve against Harold Nicolson's charge that she was a 'little swine,' writing to him: 'she is just all the weaknesses and faults of femininity carried to the nth power' (26 Nov. 1919, 101).

Julian's response to Eve comes directly from the Victorian doctrine of feminine innocence. Before he is seduced by her, Julian is horrified by her erotic advances: 'flinging one arm round his neck, she pulled herself up and kissed him on the mouth. He struggled away, displeased, brotherly, and feeling the indecency of that kiss in that darkened room, given by one whose thinly-clad, supple body he had been holding as he might a child's' (122). The adored and ignorant child is contrasted with the 'indecency' of a woman who acts on her desires. It is only when limp that Eve is desirable, and Julian repeatedly remembers this scene with discomfort over his own arousal by the childlike Eve: 'she had relaxed suddenly, limp and white in his arms; with a long sigh she let her head fall back, her eyes closed. The warmth of her limbs reached him through the diaphanous garment she wore. He thought he had never before seen such abandonment of expression and attitude' (122). Eve uses feminine passivity to seduce Julian, but she is severely punished for acting on her desires when he ultimately rejects her. She internalizes his judgment and kills herself. Active masculinity is extolled; passive femininity is reinforced.

The novel exaggerates, as Sackville-West and Trefusis exaggerated, gender roles. Indeed, in her journal Sackville-West describes Trefusis's seductive behaviour as closely resembling Eve's: 'She pulled me down until I kissed her – I had not done so for many years ... I kissed her again in the dark ... She let herself go entirely limp and passive in my arms' (Nicolson 105). As she narrates it, Trefusis's efforts to seduce her made her conscious of the masculine element in her nature: 'Violet had struck at the secret of my duality; she attacked me about it, and I made no attempt to conceal it from her or from myself' (104). Sackville-West characterizes her duality in terms of gender: 'I had told her how all the gentleness and all the femininity in me was called out by Harold alone, but how towards everyone else my attitude was completely otherwise' (104). Fully aware of her masculinity, Sackville-West acted out, quite consciously, the male role in their affair, which her journal presents in terms of the heterosexual model into which she transforms it in *Challenge*.

This role adoption was particularly apparent when Sackville-West's jealousy of Trefusis's husband, Denys, was triggered. She was tormented by Trefusis's marriage and enraged by Harold Nicolson's insistence that Denys Trefusis claimed to have had erotic contact with his wife. The most detailed description of Sackville-West and Trefusis's erotic practice occurs as a result of such jealousy: 'I treated her [Trefusis] savagely, *I made love to her*, I had her, I didn't care, I only wanted to hurt Denys, even though he didn't know of it' (Nicolson 114; emphasis added). When she meets Denys the next day, Sackville-West writes, 'I wanted to say, "Don't you know, you stupid fool, that she is mine in every sense of the word?"' (114). Sackville-West presents herself as Denys Trefusis's rival – in every sense of the word: in the fight for the woman they love she sees herself as the better man.

Sackville-West's journal account of her affair with Trefusis owes much to the discourse of sexology. The story is a romance with gender trouble. Sackville-West is the congenital invert seduced by the deviant Trefusis. Once she has been overcome, Sackville-West becomes the boyish 'Julian' protecting her feminine, childlike lover and fighting for her against the tyrannical Denys Trefusis. Although, or perhaps because, she is the better man, she knows that it would be wrong to keep the now helpless Violet Trefusis in a passionate but abnormal life. The courageous act would be to give the woman up to the man who will rescue her from deviancy. This Sackville-West does, motivated not by a fear of deviancy but by a commitment to duality. Eight years before the publication of *The Well of Loneliness*, Sackville-West plays out essentially the same plot but with theory of sexuality very different from the one Radclyffe Hall represents in Stephen Gordon.

In her relationship with Trefusis, in her journal, and in *Challenge*, Sackville-West tried on the masculine role of the mannish lesbian. The last name she gave Julian, Devenant, French for 'becoming,'[35] suggests the question the novel and journal propose: should she become Julian? The clothes fit, but the role required a bandage that marked it as flawed. As she imagined it, Julian represented a stable masculinity that left no room for Sackville-West's 'duality.' The novel ends with Eve's suicide, thus destroying any possibility of a union between the masculine and feminine. The Julian fantasized in the novel was only part of who Sackville-West knew herself to be. Trefusis called up the repressed masculine side of her nature that her marriage could not accommodate, but, liberating as that experience was, it was a revolution that would end in the death of her feminine side. For Julian to live, Eve must die. Easily recognizable as the impetuous and seductive Trefusis, Eve is also the embodiment of femininity that Sackville-West pits against the fantasy of the masculine Julian. The conclusion of the novel shows what will be lost if Julian is allowed to declare his freedom: Julian loses the revolution and Eve dies. As the journal and novel show, Sackville-West's final refusal to leave Harold Nicolson for Violet Trefusis was motivated not by a commitment to conventional marriage or a rejection of deviancy, but by a refusal to become either masculine or feminine: she was both.

The development of Sackville-West's sexuality parallels the history of female sexuality in the late nineteenth and early twentieth centuries. Initially immersed in the doctrine of feminine innocence, Sackville-West had little consciousness of her own sexuality as such. She recognized only heterosexuality and did not think of her passion for Rosamund Grosvenor as erotic. Under the influence of the sexologists, she discovered her own sexuality, and, since that discovery uncovered active erotic desires for women, she constructed a masculine persona consistent with her object choice and erotic practice. In attempting to create a unified narrative of herself as 'invert,' however, she fashioned a sexual identity more complex than the stereotype she created in Julian.

Her journal is searchingly honest. Looking for clues that will transform her current confusion into a coherent narrative, Sackville-West does not elide insights that disrupt the easy explanation offered by the sexologists. She records her admiration, as it was in childhood, for lack of cowardice and control of nerves. If these are masculine qualities, then she wishes to have masculine qualities, but she does not conclude from this evidence that she felt like a boy trapped in a girl's body. She recognizes that her standards for behaviour are based on cultural expectations for boys rather than girls and that this is an issue of gender, not sex or sexuality. In her confession to Trefusis she reveals the *duality* of her nature: she is both masculine and feminine, not, as the sexologists would have it, dominated by a masculine nature.

As a stereotype of masculinity, the character of Julian is exactly that. Sackville-West enjoyed the freedom she was allowed as Julian, but she also relished the joke she was playing. She took pleasure in pretending to be a boy and getting away with it. In Monte Carlo she made friends with a French family, flirting with their daughter and exchanging war stories with their son (Nicolson 111). She was exploring masculinity, but she was also making fun of it: 'I never appreciated anything so much as living like that with my tongue perpetually in my cheek, and in defiance of every policeman I passed' (116). Sackville-West tried on the role of the mannish lesbian and explored the masculine aspects of her character, but she did not continue this position after her affair with Trefusis. Indeed, her next affair was with a man, the biographer Geoffrey Scott. Writing to Virginia Woolf many years later, Sackville-West asks, 'Have you read my book? *Challenge*, I mean? Perhaps I sowed all my wild oats then' (11 June 1927, 209).

Even after the wild oats of *Challenge*, two practices characterize Sackville-West's descriptions of her relationships: she made clear distinctions between gender and object choice, and she did not make distinctions between men and women as objects of her erotic desire. Nor did she feel constrained by the available categories of sexual or gender identity. Motivated by the need to decide whether to stay with Trefusis, in her journal Sackville-West reaches a conclusion by articulating her own theory of sexuality:

> I hold the conviction that as centuries go on, and the sexes become more nearly merged on account of their increasing resemblances ... such connections [as that between Trefusis and herself] will to a very large extent cease to be regarded as merely unnatural ... I believe it will be recognized that many more people of my type do exist than under the present-day system of hypocrisy is commonly admitted ... The first step in the direction of such candour must be taken by the general admission of normal but illicit relations. ... I advance, therefore, the perfectly accepted theory that cases of *dual personality* do exist, in which the feminine and the masculine elements alternately preponderate. (Nicolson 105–6; emphasis added)

In writing this bold statement, Sackville-West is clearly much influenced by her reading of sexologists Edward Carpenter and Havelock Ellis. She echoes Carpenter's utopian vision of an evolution or, in Carpenter's terms, 'exfoliation' towards a bisexual, androgynous society and also suggests Ellis's position that her 'type' is inherent and therefore must be tolerated. The notion of 'dual personality,' however, comes not from sexology but from psychology. According to sexologists, the degree to which an invert may be transgendered and homosexual (e.g., the mannish lesbian) falls in a wide spectrum, but for a given individual that position is relatively stable. Individuals may be influenced to exhibit their inversion more or less openly, but the inherent nature of the condition argues for a single, not dual, sexual identity. In her journal, Sackville-West is describing something rather different.

'Dual personality' was an available psychological term in England in the late nineteenth and early twentieth centuries.[36] Used as early as the well-known case of Mary Reynolds in 1816, the more common clinical term was 'double consciousness' (Hacking 150). Described by Freud as a standard feature of hysteria (2:12), dual personality indicates a debilitating state that would seem to have little in common with the condition Sackville-West describes. In his history of the emergence of multiple personality, Ian Hacking summarizes the characteristics of double consciousness, based on the early work of Eugène Azam: 'The characteristic features of the prototype established by Azam are clear. A woman. Early onset. Bad times in childhood. One-way amnesia. Subsidiary quasi-states additional to the *condition seconde* [secondary personality state]. Highly suggestible. Hypnotism reproduces second states. Second state is like (or is) total somnambulism. Above all: the prototypical case of *dédoublement* suffers from florid hysteria, and she is overwhelmed by bodily crises' (169). In its most severe forms, double consciousness, which has evolved into the state described as multiple-personality disorder, refers to a condition that interferes with the individual's ability to function. It is not a condition to be evoked lightly, but there are some important parallels between double consciousness and the state Sackville-West describes. According to Hacking: 'the literature is full of young women who switch from the docile to the daring, from the melancholy to the merry ... Michael Kenny suggests that in general the young women implicitly switched in order to act out a rebellious life that they could not get away with in the normal course of events' (152). Sackville-West's description of herself defying family, class, and policemen when she cross-dressed as Julian fits this aspect of the profile. Her fictional Julian takes this fantasy a step further by transforming her alter ego into a man who actually stages a rebellion. But there are two important differences between Sackville-West's 'dual personality' and double consciousness.

First, there is no evidence that Sackville-West was a 'dual personality' in the clinical sense of the term. As the journal makes clear, she remembered both 'states' equally and consciously put on the role of Julian instead of being overcome by an alternative consciousness. She is describing not so much dual personality as dual gender identity 'in which the feminine and masculine elements alternately preponderate.' Using

the language of double consciousness, Sackville-West makes a powerful case for the recognition of an overwhelming and out-of-control
battle within herself over gender identity.

This points to the second distinction between Sackville-West's and
psychology's descriptions. Clinical descriptions of dual personality do
not consider issues of gender identity. Although in cases of multiple
personality alternative personalities of different sexes are now recognized, multiple-personality disorder has been diagnosed only relatively
recently.[37] Even now the issue of gender, despite the overwhelming
majority of female multiples, is not central to the literature, which
focuses on the presumed origin in childhood sexual abuse. While the
'masculine' aspects of the rebellious and daring alter-ego might seem
obvious, they were recognized only in roundabout ways, such as Freud's
recognition of the female hysteric's identification with her father.

For Sackville-West gender was the main issue. Her own gender instability left her unsure of her ability – indeed her desire – to perform the
roles she was expected to play as wife and mother. Whether she should
leave her husband and children and assist her lover to do likewise was
the question raised by her dual masculine and feminine identity. The
happiness of all the people she loved was rocked by her unstable sense
of herself. Through her journal, Sackville-West makes this instability,
this duality, the central tenet of her identity. Asserting that the difficulties she faces are not in herself but in a lack of social recognition of the
instability of gender identity, she forges a sense of self that accepts her
oscillating sense of her own gender identity.

Sackville-West practised balancing conflicts of identity throughout
her life. She weighed the knowledge of sex against the necessity of
innocence, her parents' behaviour against the social codes of propriety,
her mother's family against her father's. In each of these conflicts the
first term represented passion and rebellion. The second offered conventional respectability that had its advantages, most notably Knole. In
her first novel, *Heritage* (1919), Sackville-West explores the conflict inherent in reconciling the passionate southern and the placid British
temperaments. She tells much the same story when writing of her own
family in *Pepita*, a joint biography of her grandmother and mother. In
Sackville-West's family, the passion is associated with Pepita de Oliva,
her Spanish grandmother, who made her fortune as a dancer before
becoming the mistress of Lionel Sackville-West. It is women, then,
Sackville-West's grandmother and mother, who are associated with
rebellion and daring, even as their femininity is also asserted. Pepita de

Pepita de Oliva,
a woman rebel,
Vito's grandmother
Did she ever marry?

It did not have to be tragic

Oliva was legendary: adventurous, audacious, unpredictable, convention defying. Sackville-West's mother was the same, while her grandfather and father were, by her account, mild-mannered, conservative, quiet, stable, and nurturing as well as masculine. In her family, gender roles were unstable. In her description of her grandmother they are actually in conflict. De Oliva, the beautiful Spanish dancer, is the perfect, desirable, feminine woman, but she also challenges convention, since the perfect woman would never make herself publicly available as a performer, agree to be kept as a mistress, or run her own household, raising her illegitimate children essentially on her own in a foreign country. Whereas in Sackville-West's early novel the conflict leads to tragedy, after writing her journal, with its assertion of the inherent instability of gender, Sackville-West was able to write her dual family history in *Knole and the Sackvilles* and *Pepita*, acknowledging both the conflict in and the heritage of both sides of her past and her identity.

The theory Sackville-West propounds in her journal merges the emotional emphasis and gender focus of the sexologists with the psychological structure of clinical observations to make an original contribution to the study of sexuality and identity.[38] Her theory and supporting documentation were not suppressed when she locked her journal in a portmanteau and lost the key. She internalized her findings and published them through her presence and behaviour. She passed them on to Virginia Woolf, who transformed Sackville-West's knowledge into the theory of androgyny presented in *A Room of One's Own*.

An exploration of gender and sexuality does not lead Sackville-West to a sexual identity. Sackville-West's proto-Darwinian vision of the future adaptation of the species into 'sexes more ... nearly merged' (Nicolson 105) is a nascent theory of androgyny in which gender is flexible and resistant to stable categories. Despite the recognition of her masculine nature, Sackville-West maintains that she has an equally powerful feminine half and that these two aspects of her character can co-exist in a more or less harmonious balance. While *Challenge* exposes the tragic results of exaggerated masculine and feminine characters, Sackville-West's theory of gender-merger subverts the binary equations of female-feminine-passive and male-masculine-active to construct an active feminine sexuality based on a vision of androgyny. This vision, developed by Woolf in *A Room of One's Own*, is one of Sackville-West's most important contributions to their collaboration.

Sackville-West connects her masculinity to her attraction to Trefusis and their homoerotic practices, but this does not lead her to see herself as an 'invert' or to assume the stable identity of the mannish lesbian. The re-evaluation performed in the journal is an integration of her past, previously unconnected experiences with Rosamund Grosvenor and her current relationships with Harold Nicolson and Violet Trefusis. The result is a more complex understanding of her gender identity and sexuality as constituted by her erotic attractions and practices.

For Sackville-West, gender, like object choice, was not singular. She was equally masculine and feminine, and her erotic practice involved women and men. Furthermore, Sackville-West did not identify herself through her erotic practice. She did not refer to herself as lesbian or even bisexual. Her sexuality was conceived in terms of her desire.[39] In his overview of the history of sexuality, Foucault comments: 'between the objectification of sex in rational discourses, and the movement by which each individual was set to the task of recounting his own sex, there has occurred, since the eighteenth century, a whole series of tensions, conflicts, efforts at adjustment, and attempts at retranscription' (33–4). As one element in this series, Sackville-West's journal is a rare performance. She does 'recount her sex' in the journal, but the tension between this task and the redefinition of 'sex' that forces her to reconceive her relations with Grosvenor in erotic terms and to search for the masculine source of her attraction to Trefusis is quickly abandoned to a narrative much more concerned with untangling the emotional netting of the affair. Most of the narrative describes who went where and when, how upset Sackville-West felt at various points, and who said what to whom. The journal represents sexuality not in terms of what Sackville-West was (words such as *invert* and *lesbian* are not used) but in terms of what she did and how she felt. Indeed, what she is going to do – stay with her husband or go away with Trefusis – is the central question the journal aches to resolve. Even so, the decision to stay in her marriage has no impact on her sexuality, gender, or sexual object choice. All remain separate, albeit related, for Sackville-West.

According to Foucault, modern society 'did not exclude sexuality, but included it in the body as a mode of specification of individuals' (47). The sexologists replaced homoerotic acts with homosexuals, constructing an individual identity defined by erotic practice. Sackville-West was immune to the need to define her newly constructed sexuality. She was thus able to escape the regulation that accompanies definition. She saw herself as a woman with some characteristics traditionally defined as masculine. In a culture in which women's sexuality could be either passive or masculine, Sackville-West modelled a third term: active, feminine sexuality.

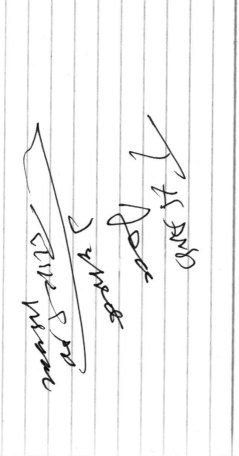

Sackville-West did not assume one available gender or sexual identity, but she did not reject such categories so much as ignore them. She operated outside the constraints of the Law and refused to be labelled. She was not androgynous in conscious rebellion against binary gender positions but oblivious to the availability of only two options. This seeming lack of knowledge of the Law, this inability to speak in the language of her culture, put her into a position from which she could create a language that speaks the active, feminine, erotic desire that is repressed. She spoke the silence that is feminine sexuality and occupied a space that is otherwise non-existent.[40]

The Heir: All and Nothing

In not feeling compelled to find her sexual identity in extant models, Sackville-West participated in the tradition of the hyper-privileged's exemption from the ideological constraints that control the people.[41] Her own parents were excellent examples of the different standards of conduct within the aristocracy, but even within her class Sackville-West went too far, as Lady Sackville's reaction to *Challenge* attested. The novel flaunted her affair with Trefusis, romanticized rebellion against family and country, and introduced Julian to the world. However, Sackville-West had more than privilege – or, more accurately, she had less, considerably less. She had nothing to lose. She had no property. Born into extreme privilege, she could not assume its benefits because, as a woman, she could not inherit Knole.

Knole, covering six acres of ground near Sevenoaks in Kent, is the largest house in England.[42] It may be that the realization that her sex prevented her from inheriting Knole was the founding trauma of Sackville-West's life.[43] It would be difficult to exaggerate her attachment to Knole. In 1947, nineteen years after her father's death and Knole had passed out of her immediate family, she describes it as 'MY Knole which I love more than anything else in the world except [her husband]' (Glendinning 249). Even as late as 1951, at the age of fifty-nine, Sackville-West wrote to her husband, 'If only I had been Dada's son, instead of his daughter' (quoted in Glendinning 368). Again, also to Harold Nicolson, she wrote, 'Knole should have been mine, mine, mine. We were meant for each other' (10 April 1958, 425). This refrain persisted throughout her life.

Raised surrounded by extreme wealth, as an adult she lived on Harold Nicolson's salary, gifts of money from her mother, and the profits of her own writing. She was born into a lifestyle and expecta-

gasp!

tions she could not maintain. She was also unable to preserve the expectations she was taught to have of her marriage. Immediately prior to her affair with Trefusis, Sackville-West learned that Harold Nicolson had had, was having, and planned to continue having erotic relationships with men. She had had no idea of his proclivities. He told her only because he had contracted a venereal disease, and she needed to be tested to see if he had passed it to her.

For the first four and a half years of their marriage, Sackville-West had been a faithful wife. Nicolson contracted the infection at a house party he had attended with her on 20 October 1917. Following his treatment, penetration (apparently the only erotic practice in which they engaged) was not allowed until 20 April 1918. Sackville-West's affair with Trefusis began on 18 April 1918, two days before marital relations were scheduled to resume. Whether Sackville-West was angry at her husband or fearful of future exposure to disease, becoming emotionally and erotically involved with Trefusis perpetuated the interdiction on sexual intimacy with Nicolson. It seems quite possible that Trefusis served as an excuse to avoid future erotic contact long after it was medically allowed. Sackville-West travelled to Italy with Trefusis, writing to Nicolson in response to his wish that they resume intimacy: 'But that is *impossible*, darling; there can't be anything of *that* now' (5 Dec. 1919, 103; emphasis original).

Nicolson's response to her rejection was not sympathetic. When she was critical of a friend's engagement he wrote: '*Damn* those Amazonian theories of yours! Surely it is less ridiculous to marry and have babies, heaps of babies, than to live on through a truculent virginity' (Glendinning 109; emphasis original). If Nicolson makes his wife's position into a caricature of radical feminists to come, it ignores the role he himself played in shaping her views and the personal uses she might be making of such a political position. We have seen from her journal that she did not, in fact, see herself as an 'Amazon' or a mannish lesbian. She used whatever roles came to hand as a *bricaleuse* of sexual and gender identity, but all the while she was devising an alternative identity that was available to her because she had everything and nothing.

The identity Sackville-West fashioned when that of heiress and wife failed her was developed in her writing, first in her journal and then in *The Heir*. In the guise of a story of succession, *The Heir* tells of an alternative inheritance: an identity forged outside recognized options and an erotics outside heterosexuality. A long short story (120 pages in the original edition), *The Heir* is subtitled *A Love Story* and dedicated to Sackville-West's mother.[44] Published in 1922 as the first story in a collection of five, it tells of the transformation of Peregrine Chase, a bland, middle-aged branch manager of a small insurance company, who comes to life as the result of his contact with the estate he inherits from a distant aunt. A stunning Elizabethan mansion complete with gardens, moat, and tenant farmers, the estate is mortgaged to the hilt and in need of costly repairs.[45] His aunt's firm of estate agents and solicitors move ahead with the long-anticipated plans to auction off all the property to pay the mortgage and realize a comfortable income for Chase – not to mention their commission. As the plans move forward, Chase begins to feel an ever greater attachment to the mansion, servants, grounds, and tenants. During a tense auction scene, Chase sacrifices all his future economic comfort to successfully bid on the estate. The story ends with the loyal and aptly named butler, Fortune, asking Chase: '"Will you be having dinner, sir ... in the dining-room or in the garden this evening?"' (120).

While Chase has none of the physical glamour of Sackville-West, he does represent her abiding passion for the family estate. Unlike Sackville-West, Chase has not been disappointed by a lack of inheritance but is unaccountably surprised to become an heir. It takes him some time to grow accustomed to it, spurred by his growing passion for the estate. Novelist and poet Lisa St Aubin de Teran describes the story as 'a medieval romance and a chivalric adventure,' which allegorically represents 'the seduction of the knight by the bewitching temptress' (viii). The temptress is 'the house itself ... eroticized into a sensuous woman' (vii). Indeed, the house is described as feminine. There is an element of the damsel in distress about it, too, especially during the climactic bidding, during which Chase is 'fighting to shield from rape the thing he loved' (116). But Sackville-West does not consistently encode the relationship between Chase and the manor house in conventional heterosexual tropes. If Chase is protecting the house, it is not so that he can possess it. He does not imagine that it is his in every way. The images of contact are not of penetration but of caressing embrace: 'He suddenly stretched out his hands and passionately laid them, palms flattened, against the bricks; bricks warm as their own rosiness with the sun they had drunk since morning' (119). It transmits the sun's warmth through a body that is protected and protecting.

If the house is a seductress or a virgin – images of women defined by their sexual relationships to men – it is also maternal: 'at the centre of all was always the house, that mothered the farms and accepted the homage of the garden ... like a woman gracious, humorous, and dominant, the house remained quiet at the centre' (58).[46] It is fecund, mature, and, though connected to its surroundings, independent. It has multiple points of entry and egress – visitors depart across the park as well as down the avenue (21). It enfolds Chase entirely in nestling protected spaces: the house itself 'seemed to lie at the heart of peace' (24) in a sheltered hollow (26). Chase moves inward, led by Fortune from room to room until they reach the bedroom, which contains yet another, smaller enclosure: 'to realize that he was to sleep inside that brocaded four-poster with the ostrich plumes nodding on the top ... this was a shock that made him draw in his breath' (28–9). But this is not simply a regression to the womb. The house offers complete fluidity of movement. Fortune's final question emphasizes the options in continual readiness: will Chase dine in the garden or the dining room that evening? Inside and outside are equally available. The option will be repeated the next night. That the story ends without an answer emphasizes the openness of the question. In such a house, the sites of pleasure are multiple and repeating. They are enjoyed not only by entering but also through union with the body of the house. As the house is to the hollow where it nestles, so is Chase to the house.

The narrative structure of the developing relationship between Chase and the house is not driven by tension. There is no build-up to a climax, as there is during the auction with its rape metaphor; rather, Chase experiences constant and multiple pleasures from interacting with his new environment. When he buys the house, he rejects the excitement of the marketplace. The private is protected, reclaimed, and experienced as eroticized space in which he lives sensually. Instead of a burst of release, what Chase experiences through the house is a constant circulation of pleasure. Perhaps coincidentally, Chip Chase was the name of the country estate Radclyffe Hall and Una Troubridge owned between 1918 and 1921, around the time Sackville-West was writing *The Heir*. Her hero's name may be a nod in that direction and a clue to those in the know that more is at stake than an exchange of property. When Chase wins the house, he protects his access to the multiple pleasures he has discovered there.

The rhythms and images that organize Chase's experience of the house anticipate *écriture féminine*'s development of metonymics derived from the experience of the female body.[47] As the female body, the house is open for exploration: the slit that scars woman's innocence can be entered, fondled, caressed, encircled, tasted, discussed, and admired. The house is pleasured and pleasure-giving; its spaces always have multiple and fluid entries and meanings.

Secret Fruit

With nothing to lose and everything to gain, Sackville-West left more than her husband when she ran away to Paris with Violet Trefusis. Female to male cross-dressing marks the failure of patriarchal control over women's sexuality, but it does so by allowing women the fantasy of phallic power.[48] As Julian, Sackville-West says she made Trefusis hers 'in every sense of the word' (Nicolson 114) and rivalled even a real man. While Sackville-West's persistent euphemisms make it impossible to know, the erotic practice she suggests she and Trefusis engage in appears to be based on a heterosexual model of penetrative pleasure. As a cross-dresser, Sackville-West may have parodied gender roles, but she does not offer an alternative erotic practice.

In her journal Sackville-West is unflinchingly honest about her experience, conflicts, and beliefs about her sexuality, but even in this private and honest text, she is not able to go beyond convention and euphemism in describing her sexual feelings and practices. This suggests the extent to which feminine desires and erotic practices were absent from public fantasies in the early twentieth century. The virgin/whore dichotomy allows for women who are unavailable/available to men without suggesting anything about the woman's own desires. Feminine sexuality was still forbidden knowledge, which is manifest in the distinction Sackville-West makes in her journal between passively 'sleeping with' and actively 'making love to' another woman. While she 'sleeps with' Grosvenor, which did not count at the time, when Trefusis awakens her masculine side, Sackville-West can 'make love.' In this way, she seems to equate masculinity with activity and femininity with passivity, which is symptomatic of the foreclosure of feminine sexuality mandated by patriarchy. After writing the journal and rejecting the hyper-masculine role of Julian, she wrote two books about houses in which an alternative erotics emerges. What is at stake in performing feminine desire and erotic practice is not only the creation of an alternative to the mannish lesbian but the assertion of the possibility of desire that, because it is not defined in masculine terms, imagines desires and erotic practices that are multiple and active. In her journal, Sackville-West articulates her own gender fluidity and imagines an erotics of active feminine desire that she demonstrates through the metaphor of nurturing domestic space.

In addition to the self-knowledge Sackville-West discovered through writing her journal, her autobiographical writing led her to another memory. When she was a child growing up at Knole, her grandfather, diplomat and lover of the Spanish dancer Pepita, drew 'Vita's Drawer' with coloured chalks on a drawer of his writing table. Every evening after dinner he filled a plate with fresh fruit for his sleeping granddaughter and left it in her special drawer. Sackville-West concludes the history she wrote of her family and their house, *Knole and the Sackvilles*, with a description of her grandfather's daily bequest: 'and this he never once failed to do, even though there might have been thirty people to dinner in the Great Hall, who watched, no doubt with great surprise, the old man who had been so rude to his neighbours at dinner going unconcernedly round with a plate, picking out the reddest cherries, the bluest grapes, and the ripest peach' (219–20). In the morning, she ran through the halls of Knole to her grandfather's sitting room, where she pulled open the heavy drawer to discover the ripe fruit hidden inside. Whether she breakfasted in the dining room or the garden, Sackville-West fed on a mixture of seeds and flesh, innocence and knowledge, lineage and transgression, loss and privilege. With each sweet bite of juicy pulp she tasted her inheritance. She could not have Knole, but she savoured the knowledge of secret fruit.

Usufruit is a French legal term that literally means 'to have use of the fruit.' With the right of *usufruit*, an heir is allowed to spend the interest generated by her inheritance while forbidden to touch the principal. In this way she enjoys the fruit but does not own the tree: in French, to have *la jouissance* of the property. Jacques Lacan refers to the notion of *usufruit* to demonstrate the workings of his concept of *jouissance*, which, like an entailed inheritance, can be enjoyed but never used up. Pleasure, *jouissance*, is the interest, the excess.[49] Sackville-West could not inherit Knole, but she enjoyed the interest it produced. The fruit from her grandfather's writing table bore fruit at her own writing table. She capitalized on that interest literally with the enormously popular *Knole and the Sackvilles*, but more profoundly, she received the *usufruit* of privilege symbolized by her grandfather's daily gift of love. Inheriting fruit instead of property, she learned how to enjoy the excess.

Sackville-West had access to desire because she did not internalize guilt over the father's, or in her case her grandfather's, weakness. For Lacan, internalized guilt of this kind results in the *jouissance* of the superego, which punishes the subject by demanding ever-increasing obedience to the Law. Sackville-West represents a different relationship to the Law. She recognized the Law as external and powerful. Knole was denied to her; that was a fact of her birth. As much as this fact enraged her, it did not lead to the aggression and guilt that comes from the repressed fantasy of the weak father. By accepting the reality of primogeniture, she could enjoy the inheritance she did receive.

In her journal, Sackville-West analyses the structure of desire as she writes of her fixation on Violet Trefusis. Instead of getting over Trefusis by replacing her with another lover, thereby maintaining the structure of that fantasy and the conflicts over gender identity that it perpetuated, Sackville-West traversed the fantasy (Fink, *Reading Seminar* x), putting herself in the place of the object of desire. She thus used the journal to conduct a self-analysis, working through the trauma of being gendered to perform what Fink describes as 'a praxis of jouissance' (ix).[50] After writing the journal, she discarded the symptomatic bipolar roles of Julian and the loving wife/mother and retrieved the fantasy of Knole's fruit salad of identity. Spanish Gypsy oranges rolled around in Vita's Drawer with aristocratic cherries, making a sticky inheritance compote of delicious instability.

Sackville-West discovered young the secrets of her family's past and her body's pleasure. Never one to keep a secret, she told the tales. She wrote of her family openly in *Knole and the Sackvilles* and *Pepita*, of herself in disguise in *Challenge*, and of erotic pleasure in code in *The Heir*. All of these stories are the story of desire. Sackville-West's style of writing may appear conventional, but the passion, the *jouissance*, she describes challenges heterosexual models. Peregrine Chase's relationship with his house is not unlike Sackville-West's homoerotic relationships. Because she did not inherit the dominant culture's sexual assumptions, she forged an erotic practice derived from the experience of her own body. Sackville-West undermined the active/passive, masculine/feminine binary pairs to create active-feminine desire that she reproduced metaphorically in *The Heir* and in practice in her same-sex relationships.

Like Chase, Sackville-West slept in a four-poster bed, but her delight was not confined to architectural interiors. She wrote flirtatiously to Woolf: 'I lie making lovely plans, all firelit and radiant – My bed's at least nine foot wide, and I feel like the Princess and the Pea, – only there is no Pea. It is a four-poster, all of which I like. Come and see for yourself' (25 Dec. 1926, 157). Sackville-West's desire was active and irrepressible. At Clive Bell's dinner party, as at innumerable childhood breakfasts, she sucked the pulp of hot-house grapes, Spanish oranges, and the reddest cherries, then spooned the hard seeds back onto her overflowing plate. 'Feminine' sexuality resists definition. It is fluid, multiple, evasive. It is not passive. It is active in Sackville-West's invitation to Woolf: come, and see for yourself.

Karyn's pronouncement

52 "Feminine'
          Sexuality

why this about spitting out
      the hard seeds

3 Making Use of the Fruit: Vita Sackville-West's Influence on Virginia Woolf

I *have* gone to bed with her (twice), but that's all. Now you know all about it, and I hope I haven't shocked you.

> Vita Sackville-West writing about Virginia Woolf in a
> letter to her husband, Harold Nicolson (17 Aug. 1926, 159)

Virginia Woolf formed attachments to women, usually older women, throughout her life. She clung to them, as she does to Violet Dickinson in the 1902 photograph reprinted in Bell's biography. She acted the child in these relationships. Something was different in her relationship with Vita Sackville-West that allowed that relationship to include sexual desire and erotic practice. One difference may have been that Sackville-West, because she had lost and found Knole, had a rare access to desire that allowed Woolf's positive mother transference to become, briefly, *jouissance*. Another difference was that, for all her aristocratic savoir faire Sackville-West, was ten years younger than Woolf and completely out of her element in Bloomsbury. Woolf felt protective of Sackville-West, even as she felt protected by her. 'I assure you,' Woolf wrote to her, 'I have need of all your illusions' (23 Sept. 1925, 3:214). It was a reciprocal relationship. They traded illusions and letters, Knole and nurture, fruit and books. Sackville-West invited Woolf to share the fruit from the writing table and opened her eyes to desire. She offered *herself* as a safe house, a protective body from which to acknowledge loss and enjoy lack.

When she met Sackville-West, Woolf was ripe for new experiences. She mingled these new desires with a growing interest in the past. Hard at work on *Mrs. Dalloway*, she invented a technique she describes as 'dig[ging] out beautiful caves behind my characters ... The idea is that the caves shall connect, & each comes to daylight at the present moment' (*Diary*, 30 Aug. 1923, 2:263). In the cave of Clarissa Dalloway's memories Woolf discovered Sally Seton, whose kiss is 'the most exquisite moment of [Clarissa's] life' (52). While travelling alone together in France in the fall of 1928, Woolf told Sackville-West the story of her own first crush (Bell 60–1; Lee 511). It was on Madge Symonds Vaughan, a childhood friend who had spent the winter of 1889 with the Stephen family. According to Woolf, Madge, with whom she was still friends, was the original of Sally Seton. In the same journal entry in which she describes her discovery of the tunnelling process she would use in *Mrs. Dalloway*, Woolf also records that she received a visit from Madge Vaughan.

Vaughan's father was John Addington Symonds, who collaborated with Havelock Ellis to produce *Sexual Inversion* (1897), an early contribution to the work of sexology that was so influential for Sackville-West. Woolf's past, like that of her characters, did indeed connect like a series of tunnels and come out at the present moment, when she told Sackville-West of a childhood crush on the daughter of the man who helped to decriminalize homosexuality. The overt awareness of sapphism that Sackville-West brought into Woolf's life, along with Madge Vaughan's sexologist father and Woolf's past feelings for Vaughan, combine to make it hardly surprising that, when Woolf dug a past for Clarissa Dalloway, she would discover homoerotic desire. As she imagined the beautiful caves of Mrs Dalloway's past, Woolf blew Sally Seton's kiss back in time and across the drawing room to Madge Vaughan and forward to Sackville-West.

Woolf and Sackville-West were just becoming friends while Woolf was writing *Mrs. Dalloway*. While Sackville-West was likely influential in stimulating the homoeroticism of *Mrs. Dalloway*, her influence is more directly discernable in *To the Lighthouse*. Writing *To the Lighthouse* allowed Woolf to finally mourn her mother. I believe that Sackville-West provided the additional emotional support necessary to allow Woolf to work through this traumatic loss. *To the Lighthouse* shares with *The Heir* and *Knole and the Sackvilles* the same strong sense of place and maternal presence that suggests that both women are much engaged with thoughts of their mothers and both are able to consciously recognize the power of that childhood relationship. Lily's painting, like Woolf's and Sackville-West's writing, demonstrates the process of simultaneously recreating the lost mother as both internalization and work of art.[1]

Woolf and Sackville-West mother and are mothered by each other. Because they can imagine the mother from the double perspectives of the child and the adult, they can recreate her as a whole being who integrates the maternal and erotic sensuality illustrated by the manor house in *The Heir*. Hermione Lee comments that 'Lily's erotic desire for physical closeness to Mrs. Ramsay is charged up by Virginia's growing feelings for Vita' (474). Mingling, as Lily does, maternal and erotic associations, her intense memory of sitting at Mrs Ramsay's feet originates in a scene shared and remembered by Woolf and Sackville-West: 'Sitting on the floor with her arms round Mrs. Ramsay's knees, close as she could get, smiling to think that Mrs. Ramsay would never know the reason of that pressure ... Could loving, as people called it, make her and Mrs. Ramsay one? for it was not knowledge but unity that she desired ... nothing that could be written in any language known to men, but intimacy itself, which is knowledge, she had thought, leaning her head on Mrs. Ramsay's knee' (78–9). Writing from Moscow on her way to Teheran, Sackville-West refers to a similar scene: 'It's seven o'clock here, but only five in London – so you're having Sibyl [Colefax] to tea at this moment, instead of me, and *she* won't sit on the floor or say my lovely Virginia, and you won't rumple *her* hair' (31 Jan. 1927, 167; emphasis original.[2] Woolf responded with an assurance of the mutuality of their feelings for each other, offering her own head to Sackville-West: 'You shall ruffle my hair in May, Honey' (16 Feb. 1927, 3:331).

Not only did Woolf draw from her relationship with Sackville-West to find material for scenes in *To the Lighthouse*, but she also frequently associated her with that beacon of safety the characters are trying to reach. Describing a party she hopes to give, she writes to Sackville-West: 'Everybody will be discharged into the room, unmixed, undressed, unpowdered. You will emerge like a lighthouse, fitful, sudden, remote. (Now that is rather like you)' (23 Sept. 1925, 1:215). Woolf subsequently used the image of the lighthouse in her novels, drawing on the wealth of her relationship with Sackville-West to produce new work resting on a new relationship to the past. The optimistic conclusions of both novels are united in this improbable connection of lighthouse and party, both of which come to represent the urge for connection. As enigmatic in this letter as it is in Woolf's fiction, the metaphor suggests just how closely Woolf associated her writing with Sackville-West. Receiving maternal comfort from Sackville-West allowed Woolf to reach for the ripe fruit she could now see in their relationship and in her own work. While writing *To the Lighthouse*, she noted in her diary the ease of writing: 'I think this is the proof that I was on the right path; & that what *fruit* hangs in my soul is to be reached there' (23 Feb. 1926, 3:59: emphasis added).[3]

Visiting Knole in January 1927, Woolf and Sackville-West flung open the doors of unused rooms, lifted the lids of mouldering trunks, and poured out the contents of brittle letters. So, too, did they expose to light the rocky shores of the past and the safe, deep harbour that awaited them together. How did they come to this place? What brought them to be walking together through Knole, throwing open shutters and spilling out the golden locks of hair hidden in 200-year-old love letters? Sackville-West, with her ability to desire, desired Woolf. In so desiring, she awakened Woolf's desires. These desires were both sexual as well as those of a child for comfort, unconditional love, attention, and security. 'Why do I think of you so incessantly, see you so clearly the moment I'm in the least discomfort?' Woolf wrote to Sackville-West. 'Like a child, I think if you were here, I should be happy' (23 March 1927, 3:352). Sackville-West provided the acceptance and emotional security that Woolf needed in order to work through, to some degree, the trauma of a past that included the loss of her mother and the loss of innocence.

Much has been written on Woolf as a survivor of childhood sexual abuse, largely thanks to Louise DeSalvo's important work on this subject. Many critics and biographers have speculated that Woolf's 'sexual frigidity' as well as her periodic depression and ultimate suicide resulted at least in part from these traumatic experiences. While sexual abuse is clearly one important factor in Woolf's struggle with depression, I am here concerned with its (not unrelated) impact on her sexuality. Specifically, I wonder why she was not sexually repressed with Sackville-West. What was different about that relationship that allowed her to experience desire and express it in her writing? This was the question that initiated this book.

In the posthumously published autobiographical essay 'A Sketch of the Past,' Virginia Woolf describes being sexually molested at age six by the younger of her two half-brothers, eighteen-year-old Gerald Duckworth. From the time of Gerald's violation Woolf became so 'ashamed and afraid' (68) of her own body that she could not even look in a mirror. 'I cannot now,' she wrote at the age of fifty-seven, 'powder my nose in public' (68). No touch, no gaze, no longing would ever again bring her pleasure – with the one brief exception of Vita Sackville-West's.

Throughout her adolescence Woolf was repeatedly sexually abused by her other half-brother, George Duckworth. Quentin Bell consistently describes Woolf as frigid (e.g., 2:5) and reports: 'Vanessa, Leonard, and, I think, Virginia herself were inclined to blame George Duckworth' (2:6). In the absence of their mother, Julia Duckworth Stephen, who died when Woolf was thirteen, George undertook the responsibility of introducing Woolf and her elder sister, Vanessa, to London society. Respectable, handsome, and emotionally demonstrative, George escorted his half-sisters to balls, plays, dinners, and dances, where they met the best people. After Julia Stephen's death, Woolf writes in 'A Sketch of the Past,' 'There were no more parties; no more young men and women laughing. No more flashing visions of white summer dresses and hansoms dashing off to private views and dinner parties, none of that natural life and gaiety which my mother had created' (94). This is the life George tried to recreate. This is what Woolf herself sought when she moved from Richmond to London many years later. Woolf was sixteen, George was thirty. After they returned home from the parties, George's attentiveness continued, now inappropriately, as George paid his final visit of the night to Woolf's bed.

When Woolf wrote of these incidents in '22 Hyde Park Gate,' an essay she read to the Memoir Club in 1920, her tone is very different from the one she uses to describe her experience of being molested as a child. In recreating a typical scene, her thoughts, feelings, and sensations end abruptly upon George's appearance in her bedroom: '"Who?" I cried. "Don't be frightened," George whispered. "And don't turn on the light, oh beloved. Beloved" – and he flung himself on my bed, and took me in his arms' (155). In the context of Woolf's witty essay, this is more like a description of a scene from the French bedroom farce she and George had seen earlier that evening than an account of abuse. The essay concludes with the dramatic declaration: 'Yes, the old ladies of Kensington and Belgravia never knew that George Duckworth was not only father and mother, brother and sister to those poor Stephen girls; he was their lover also' (155). When writing for the Memoir Club, Woolf could be expected to be more entertaining than reflective; nevertheless, there is a lack of detail and an element of melodrama that suggests Woolf is disassociated from the experiences she describes. What really happened when George flung himself into her bed and took her into his arms crying 'Beloved' (155) was surely more than a 'nasty erotic skirmish' (Bell 1:43). Throughout her life Woolf writes of no one with more hatred than her half-brother George. Her description of him in '22 Hyde

Park Gate' is a case in point: 'if you looked at him closely you noticed that one of his ears was pointed; and the other round; you also noticed that though he had the curls of a God and the ears of a faun he had unmistakably the eyes of a pig' (144). Her estimation of his intelligence is equally acerbic: 'It is true that he was abnormally stupid' (145). The sharp, sneering tone that accompanies George throughout this memoir signals Woolf's lasting abhorrence. The events she depicts justify her feelings. Woolf did not repress her memory of these events, but she nevertheless distanced herself from them. When George enters her bedroom, the complexity of her responses is gone. She is passive and silent. She becomes one of 'those poor Stephen girls,' about whom she can write in the third person. The essay ends without commenting on Woolf's response to George's intrusion. Her feelings about his actions are represented only in snide comments about his appearance and mental abilities. Displacing her emotional response onto seemingly objective observations, Woolf masks her own reactions. The physical and emotional pain she experienced as a result of his abuse is censored.

The pattern of Woolf's response – or lack of response – to George's abuse had already been created as a result of Gerald's earlier attack. Once again, a loving and trusted brother transformed affection into violence. Once again there was no defence, no protection, no way to prevent future abuse. Woolf was not able to defend herself from her half-brothers, who lived in the same house and with whom she had daily contact. Like many victims of abuse, Woolf would have had complex responses to the attacker, whom she had been taught to love and trust but grew to fear and hate. The irresolvable conflict makes it impossible to work through the experience. The result is self-blame and shame about one's own body, as if it had caused the attack. Woolf seems to have shut down physical sensation – pain as well as pleasure. This is a common response to sexual abuse, which has only relatively recently been documented. Because of the lack of early twentieth-century stud- ies, we must draw on recent clinical data in order to recognize typical patterns of responses to abuse. While one must be careful not to decontextualize such responses, Woolf's self-described response is like that of many abused children, for whom a separation between mental and physical consciousness blocks full recognition of abuse. Now de- scribed as dissociative identity disorder, shutting down physical re- sponses protects the child from the knowledge of the abuse by creating a mechanism whereby the child's consciousness becomes separate from her physical experiences. After the first incident of abuse, the child experiences a separation between his or her body (which is being abused) and a self that, whether or not the abuse is consciously remembered, does not have an emotional response to it.[4] For the rest of her life Woolf experienced sensual pleasure predominantly through what she read and what she wrote instead of through her body – except during her affair with Sackville-West.

When they met in 1922 the Woolfs were living in Richmond, but Woolf longed to return to London, where she imagined she would find more 'life.' Sackville-West satisfied Woolf's appetite for life by appealing to her 'social side' (*Diary*, 28 June 1923, 2:250) – the side she lost with the death of her mother. This was not the society, or life, of Bloomsbury. Sackville-West offered access to the aristocratic and literary life beyond Woolf's grasp and wrapped this gift in affection and maternal concern, a combination irresistible to Woolf, who associated all of these things with her mother, Julia Stephen. Her powerful attachment to Sackville-West was energized by the positive associations Woolf made between her mother and Sackville-West.[5]

Woolf's descriptions of her early attempts to introduce Sackville-West into Bloomsbury highlight the latter's status as an outsider, for instance, a 'Rocky steep evening' with Duncan Grant and Lytton Strachey (*Diary*, 17 March 1923, 2:239) and a 'thorny' dinner party with Roger Fry (21 Dec. 1924, 2:325). Bloomsbury did not bring out the best in Sackville-West: she seemed as a snob and a dilettante. Conventional in all but her most private life, she represented everything Bloomsbury – with its multifaceted critiques of art, literature, politics, and society – opposed.

Woolf, on the other hand, was predisposed to like Sackville-West. Four months before their first meeting, Woolf wrote in her diary: 'Mrs. Nicolson thinks me the best woman writer – & I have almost got used to Mrs Nicolson's having heard of me. But it gives me some pleasure' (3 Aug. 1922, 2:187).[6] A week later Woolf wrote to her sister: 'Would you be so angelic as to look in Clives room for The Heir, by V. Sackville-West, and bring it with you? She admires me; therefore I must try to admire her, which, of course, I shan't find difficult' (10 Aug. 1922, 2:544–5). The solution Woolf found to the conflict between her new friend and her old circle was to keep the two separate. She saw Sackville-West alone. The increased privacy of their contact encouraged their growing intimacy. By September 1924 Woolf was committed to their relationship: 'Oh yes, I like her; could tack her on to my equipage for all time; & suppose if life allowed, this might be a friendship of a sort' (*Diary* 2:313). Not entirely masculine but never passive, Sackville-West was like no one Woolf had ever met before – but she was also uncannily familiar.

On the night after their first meeting, after describing Sackville-West in her diary, Woolf digresses: 'Half past ten just struck on one of these fine December nights, which come after sunny days, & I don't know why, keep sending through me such shocks from my childhood. Am I growing old & sentimental? I keep thinking of sounds I heard as a child – at St Ives mostly' (2:217). After this paragraph Woolf returns to describing Sackville-West. Sandwiched between two descriptions of Sackville-West is St Ives, where Woolf spent the summers of her childhood. Elsewhere in Woolf's writing St Ives is associated with her mother and with a feeling of well-being. In 'A Sketch of the Past' she writes: 'last night I tried to sooth myself to sleep ... by thinking of St. Ives ... I could fill pages remembering one thing after another that made the summer at St Ives the best beginning to a life conceivable' (109). To help herself to sleep, Woolf used the strategy suggested by her mother: 'she came up at night to see if we were asleep, holding a candle shaded; this is a distinct memory, for like all children, I lay awake sometimes and longed for her to come. Then she told me to think of all the lovely things I could imagine. Rainbows and bells' ('A Sketch of the Past' 82).[7] Now the rainbows and bells and Proustian longing for the mother have been replaced by St Ives, and it is the soothing sounds of that place that intrude into her thoughts of Sackville-West.

Woolf's description of her next dinner with Sackville-West is once again dominated by thoughts of her childhood and her mother. After the dinner, hosted by Vanessa Bell and Duncan Grant, Woolf writes: 'We had the photographs out. Lytton [Strachey] said "I don't like your mother's character. Her mouth seems complaining"& a shaft of white light fell across my dusky rich red past' (Diary, 17 March 1923, 2:239). That evening the 'rich winy fluid' (2:325) of Sackville-West's character was similarly held up to the light. Earlier in the paragraph, Woolf comments: 'Exposed to electric light eggs show dark patches,' before recording the Bloomsbury verdict on Sackville-West and her husband as 'incurably stupid.' As though the 'shaft of white light' from Strachey's criticism of Julia Stephen shone equally on the patchy egg of Sackville-West, Bloomsbury criticized Sackville-West and Julia Stephen almost in one breath.

It is telling that Woolf was prompted to look at pictures of her mother after dining with Sackville-West. The associations that stimulated that desire are easy to guess. From their first meeting thoughts of Sackville-

West led Woolf to think of her mother. Her diary entries suggest many reasons for this association. Woolf wrote that on the night they met, Sackville-West made her feel 'virgin, shy, & schoolgirlish' (2:217), like the child she was before her mother's death. Additionally, both Sackville-West and Julia Stephen belonged outside the unconventional, intellectual world of Bloomsbury. Sackville-West's and Julia Stephen's beauty and social connections were not appreciated, even as their ideas were ignored. They represented a world apart from Bloomsbury, a dusky red world of parties and dinners lit with softly glowing candles far from the glare of electric lights that showed their dark patches. It was after this dinner party that Woolf began to think seriously of moving to London to find more life. She began to wish for more than the shaft of intellectual light that showed the flaw in the social life she describes as 'the piece of jewellery I inherit from my mother' (2:250). She wished for more occasions on which to see the wine red gems sparkling.

The early death of Julia Stephen would have rendered her thirteen-year-old daughter bereft not only of her mother but also of a part of herself. Again, in 'A Sketch of the Past,' Woolf describes this loss: 'If it were true, as I said above, that the things that ceased in childhood, are easy to describe because they are complete, then it should be easy to say what I felt for my mother, who died when I was thirteen ... But the theory ... breaks down ... I find it now so curiously difficult to describe both my feeling for her, and her herself' (80). Woolf's experience of her mother was not concluded by her mother's death, because she did not feel separate enough from her mother to mourn the loss of something outside herself. The death left her with a fragmented sense of self that made it as impossible to describe her feelings for her mother as it was to describe her mother herself.[8] In order to mourn her mother, Woolf first would have to recreate her.

From their first meeting, Woolf repeatedly described Sackville-West in her diary and in letters.[9] Sackville-West's fluid gender identity allowed Woolf to have both maternal and masculine associations to her. Initially masculine, almost comic, these descriptions ultimately transformed Sackville-West into a luscious text that suggests the return of Woolf's repressed desire, as Sackville-West provides her with another opportunity to experience – and thus recreate – the intensity of affection she felt for her mother. The evening after they first met, Woolf describes Sackville-West in her diary as 'florid, moustached, parakeet coloured, with all the supple ease of the aristocracy.' Two paragraphs later, Woolf returns to Sackville-West, as if already she cannot get enough: 'she is a grenadier; hard; handsome, manly; inclined to double chin' (15 Dec. 1922, 2:216–17). The image of Sackville-West as a member of the Grenadier Guards is especially appropriate, since, as the first regiment of the royal household infantry, the Guards suggest a connection to the aristocracy as well as masculinity: they are not only virile, but also defenders of the nobility. This metaphor would persist (e.g., 2:325), as would Woolf's attention to Sackville-West's body and class status. After visiting Knole for the first time, Woolf writes: 'All these ancestors & centuries, & silver & gold, have bred a perfect body. She is stag like, or race horse like, save for the face, which pouts, & has no very sharp brain. But as a body hers is perfection' (5 July 1924, 2:306). As their friendship developed, Woolf's descriptions of Sackville-West acquire ever greater sensuality: 'Vita ... is like an over ripe grape in features, moustached, pouting ... she strides on fine legs, in a well cut skirt' (15 Sept. 1924, 2: 313). The masculine characteristics Woolf ascribes to Sackville-West are connected to her bearing, for which she credits Sackville-West's aristocratic lineage. Indeed, Sackville-West was tall, large boned, and physically active. In contrast to Woolf, Violet Trefusis describes Sackville-West in conventional, feminine terms: 'She was tall and graceful. The profound, hereditary Sackville eyes were as pools from which the morning mist had lifted. A peach might have envied her complexion. Round her revolved several enamoured young men' (70).[10] Trefusis describes Sackville-West as the lovely young debutante, passively receiving the admiration of her male attendants. Woolf's view is markedly different. She sees Sackville-West as active – a stag or a racehorse. She does not retouch her portrait by, for example, turning facial hair into peach fuzz. She emphasizes sensuality over beauty. Woolf sees the Sackville heritage in the bearing of the body, not in misty eyes.

As their friendship intensified during 1924 and 1925, descriptions accompany references to Sackville-West in Woolf's letters. To Molly MacCarthy she is 'more than ever like a Guards officer in bearskin and breeches. Very Elizabethan too' (3:135). To Jacques Raverat she is called 'daughter of Knole,' whose 'real claim to consideration, is, if I may be so coarse, her legs. Oh but they are exquisite – running like slender pillars up into her trunk, which is that of a breastless cuirassier (yet she has 2 children) but all about her is virginal, savage, patrician' (3:150). To David Garnett she is 'of ravishing beauty' (3:153). The descriptions are variations on the same themes of aristocracy, masculinity, and sensuous physicality. In her diary and her letters Woolf recreates and savours Sackville-West's physical presence.

Unable to look at herself, she got enormous pleasure from looking at – or at least writing about looking at – Sackville-West. She also fantasized about Sackville-West's past and possible future: 'She is a pronounced Sapphist ... I trace her passions 500 years back, & they become romantic to me, like old yellow wine' (*Diary*, 19 Feb. 1923, 2:235–6). Visions of Sackville-West here begin to develop into more elaborate fantasies that implicate Woolf herself. She would eventually copy them down in *Orlando*, but they had a more immediate role to play in her own life.

In her diary Woolf raises an issue that is to take on increasing urgency during the next months and is, if not inspired by, then at least influenced by her friendship with Sackville-West. Woolf refers to it as 'the social question' (6 March 1923, 2:237). It eventually resulted in her determination to move back to London from Hogarth House in the suburb of Richmond, where she and Leonard had moved in 1914. Her wish to move was prompted by a desire for more social contact. She considers this repressed aspect of herself in her diary: 'There is, I suppose, a very different element in us [Leonard and herself]; my social side, his intellectual side. This social side is very genuine in me. Nor do I think it reprehensible. It is a piece of jewellery I inherit from my mother' (28 June 1923, 2:250). It was difficult to get agreement from Leonard, who 'instead of being ... sympathetic has the old rigid obstacle – my health' (2:250). Leonard was concerned that the excitement of a livelier social life would be too much for Woolf, but she herself felt that in the suburbs she was 'tied, imprisoned, inhibited' (2:250). Woolf prevailed, and in March 1924 they moved to Tavistock Square in the Bloomsbury district of London.

Happily back in Bloomsbury, Woolf wrote to Sackville-West: 'please come and baptise our rooms for us as soon as you can' (11 March 1924, 3:93). Sackville-West visited in the following week, lunching alone with Woolf for the first time. Afterward, Sackville-West wrote to her husband, 'I went on ... my head swimming with Virginia' (noted by Nicolson and Trautmann in Woolf's *Letters* 3:94 n3). Woolf's desire for more life and her move into town to find it opened up the possibility of increased intimacy with Sackville-West. Up to this point, the trauma of sexual abuse had prevented Woolf from fully experiencing pleasure in her own body; now she seems to have come to life. More life translated into more 'Vita,' which means 'life' in Latin, a joke she makes in *Orlando* (270). Woolf was open to receive whatever Sackville-West might offer, and Sackville-West offered what she had. To fill Woolf's lack Sackville-West offered the gift she herself had been given: fruit. On Tuesday, 27 January 1925 Woolf wrote to invite Sackville-West to tea, explaining that she could not extend a dinner invitation because she had influenza and headache: 'But if you would come and drink a mild tea cup with me on Friday it would be angelic and charitable and very very dull (for you)' (3:157). Sackville-West sent her acceptance accompanied by a basket of peaches. Woolf describes the peaches as 'heavenly, delicious,' when she responds: 'I accept peaches, kummel [a type of wine], everything, with complete gratitude and delight' (29 Jan. 1925, 3:159).

This was not the first or last gift Sackville-West would offer. She took up her grandfather's role, bestowing the ripest peaches on her beloved friend. Woolf's wounds were deeper than the injustice of inheritance laws; Sackville-West's use of the fruit might not be enough to repair the damage of years of physical abuse, but the gesture was as powerful as it was familiar. She passed on to Woolf the love and care she had received from her grandfather, and Woolf accepted all of it. In response to Woolf's desire for more life, Sackville-West created a sort of 'Virginia's Drawer' and filled it with the bounty from her own plate. With her gift of fruit she handed Woolf a promise of intimacy as sweet and juicy as a peach.

The day after first visiting Knole and Long Barn, Woolf wrote to Sackville-West: 'I have paralysed my own pen by telling you that you dont write intimate letters – which however you are going to reform in the Dolomites' (6 July 1924, 3:117). Sackville-West did reform. She wrote from Italy: 'I hope that no one has ever yet, or ever will, throw down a glove I was not ready to pick up. You asked me to write a story for you ... and to you alone shall it be dedicated. But of course the real challenge wasn't the story ... but the letter. You said I wrote letters of impersonal frigidity' (50). Sackville-West draws a connection between the request for a letter and the request for a story. Both are challenges, both responses are addressed to Woolf. Both increase the intimacy of the friendship.

The long story *Seducers in Ecuador* was dedicated to Woolf and published by the Hogarth Press in November 1924. *Seducers in Ecuador* is unlike Sackville-West's other work. *The Spectator* describes it as 'a slim, fantastic *conte* in the Bloomsbury manner' (Glendinning 141).[11] Associations with Bloomsbury are not difficult to discover. It is much like the sort of parable produced by Bloomsbury writers such as David Garnett, whose *Lady into Fox* (1922) and *A Man in the Zoo* (1924) share the same spare style and fantastic plot that Sackville-West experiments with in *Seducers in Ecuador*. Her characters don't actually turn into animals, but as in Garnett's long stories, the plot is quickly given away: 'It is now time to be a little more explicit on the questions of the companions of Lomax. Perhaps Miss Whitaker deserves precedence, since it was she, after all, who married Lomax. And perhaps Bellamy should come next, since it was he, after all, for whose murder Lomax was hanged. And perhaps Artivale should come third, since it was to him, after all, that Lomax bequeathed his, that is to say Bellamy's, fortune' (16). Thus we discover the fate of the main character, Arthur Lomax, whose need to believe in the outrageous fantasies of his acquaintances seals his doom. Seduced by their tales of exotic lands, passion, disease, and mysterious pasts, he is defenceless when faced with the truth. As Garnett does in his allegories, Sackville-West literalizes this message, hanging the blame for the main character's behaviour on his use of sunglasses, which distance him from reality.

Sackville-West knew from her experience with Violet Trefusis that fantasies can be seductive. More clearly than in her previous, suppressed novel, *Challenge*, *Seducers in Ecuador* tells of the consequences of believing in and acting out someone else's fantasy. As much as Sackville-West enjoyed playing 'Julian' for Trefusis, that persona played into Trefusis's fantasies even more than it did into Sackville-West's, whose cross-dressing was (so far as we know) confined to that relationship. Trefusis was raised from childhood to become, like her mother before her, the mistress of an aristocrat; Julian was a prize she eagerly sought. In the journal Sackville-West wrote at the end of that affair, she reconsiders Julian and her own masculinity, forging an internal sense of an androgynous self independent of the masquerades of cross-dressing or traditional femininity.[12]

Seducers in Ecuador demystifies the romantic dreams of Julian, played to the hilt in *Challenge*, by showing such fantasies to be play-acting designed to fill an otherwise empty life. Not only are such false dramas pathetic, but they are also dangerous. People get hurt. Sackville-West recognized in her journal that the affair with Trefusis damaged everyone involved. During the winter of *Seducers in Ecuador*'s publication, Harold Nicolson wrote to Sackville-West in a panic when he heard that she would be dining with Trefusis: 'Her very name brings back all the aching unhappiness of those months: the doubt, the mortification, and the loneliness. I think she is the only person of whom I am frightened – and I have an almost superstitious belief in her capacity for causing distraction and wretchedness' (4 Dec. 1924, 126). Julian's rebellion over, *Challenge* was withdrawn from the publisher, and Sackville-West's cross-dressing was at an end. The execution that ends 'Seducers in Ecuador' proclaims the end of playing out Trefusis's fantasy and the beginning of Sackville-West's sense of herself undisguised by dark glasses or a bandaged head. From now on she would act according to her own fantasies and desires, not as the facilitator of someone else's.

Sackville-West took off her dark glasses in another way in *Seducers in Ecuador*. While the title might refer to the fantasies one believes at one's peril, the book also contained an actual message of seduction in its dedication. Sackville-West typically dedicated her work to her most intimate attachment at the time of writing: Violet Trefusis, Harold Nicolson, her mother. The dedications are in-jokes, coded messages, references to shared experience, or a sign of current passion. The accounts of her travels in what was then Persia, *Passenger to Teheran* and *Twelve Days*, are dedicated 'To Harold Nicolson,' who was her travelling companion during much of that time. *The Heir* is dedicated to her mother, who understood more acutely than anyone Sackville-West's pain at not inheriting Knole. *Challenge*'s original dedication to Trefusis under the code name 'Eve' was replaced with the even more obscure gesture of a Turkish love poem (see ch. 2, n32). For Sackville-West, dedications were like kisses; indicative of intimacy, they crossed the distance between two people and signalled a passionate connection. Sackville-West's books have a different, more personal meaning for the dedicatee than for any other reader. Dedicating a book to a new friend like Woolf was highly unusual for Sackville-West and suggests a fantasy of future intimacy.

That this was the case is corroborated by Sackville-West's response to the parallel challenge of writing an intimate letter to Woolf, which she takes up in the same letter in which she announces the dedication. *Seducers in Ecuador* is a coded invitation to intimacy; the letter is more overt: 'I told you once that I would rather go to Spain with you than with anyone, and you looked confused, and I felt I had made a gaffe, – been too personal, in fact, – but still the statement remains a true one, and I shan't be really satisfied till I have enticed you away' (16 July 1924, 51). Having been too personal once, Sackville-West invokes that earlier moment as testimony to her past and continued receptivity to increased intimacy. Indeed, more than receptive, Sackville-West suggests elopement when she writes: 'Will you ever play truant to Bloomsbury and culture, I wonder, and come travelling with me?' Even with the immediate qualifier, 'No, of course you won't,' Sackville-West's proposition is reminiscent of her travels with Trefusis, but she is not proposing the return of Julian. Instead, the fantasy she suggests in this intimate letter is one that Woolf will ultimately create for both in *Orlando*: 'Will you come next year to the place where the gipsies of all nations make an annual pilgrimage to some Madonna or other? ... next year *I am going*. I think you had much better come too. Look on it, if you like, as copy, – as I believe you look upon everything, human relationships included. Oh yes, you like people through the brain better than through the heart, forgive me if I am wrong' (51; emphasis original). Her letter is prophetic. Woolf does turn Sackville-West's fantasized trip into copy when Orlando lives with the Gypsies, and in the following year Woolf did accept Sackville-West's invitation – although they did not travel abroad together until some time later. Sackville-West asks Woolf to leave 'Bloomsbury and culture' to travel with her, and this Woolf did, metaphorically, when she entered Sackville-West's cultural sphere. As their relationship developed, Woolf left Bloomsbury to explore homoerotic practices, with Sackville-West as her guide.

Woolf's response to the letter replayed her response to Sackville-West's earlier, too-personal comment about travelling to Spain. Focusing on the comment about turning the fantasized trip into copy, Woolf transformed the seduction into a criticism, which she tongued like an aching tooth over the next three months: 'I enjoyed your intimate letter from the Dolomites. It gave me a great deal of pain – which is I've no doubt the first stage of intimacy – no friends, no heart, only an indifferent head. Never mind: I enjoyed your abuse very much' (19 Aug. 1924, 3:125; for recurring references see 3:138, 3:140). While Woolf admits the intimacy of Sackville-West's letter, and her response could be read as a tease, there is a hint of pique that is reinforced by the lack of intimacy in this brief letter, which concludes: 'But I will not go on else I should write you a really intimate letter, and then you would dislike me, more, even more than you do' (3:126).

What Woolf did not know was that for Sackville-West it was natural to imagine turning experiences into copy. The suppressed dedication of *Challenge* proudly announces this: 'Dedicated with gratitude for much excellent copy to the original of Eve.' Just as the affair with Trefusis made for good material, so too can Sackville-West imagine her relationship with Woolf feeding their hungry pens. Perhaps this expectation had its origins in the early 'intimate' letters Sackville-West exchanged with her schoolmates. Their lives and characters were the subject of analysis, fantasy and textual elaboration: 'I think you are *very very passionate* and *loyal* and *generous*! but that you can hate as much as you can love!' begins a character analysis a seventeen-year-old Sackville-West had requested from her friend Irene Hogarth (Glendinning 33; emphasis original). This personal and dramatic style of writing persisted, characterizing her later correspondence with Trefusis. It is natural that Woolf's request for an 'intimate letter' would be met with the character analysis Sackville-West provides.

For her part, Sackville-West recognized neither the accuracy of her analysis nor the sensitivity of the nerve she hit. Moving to London to find more life, Woolf had hoped to leave behind the feeling of being 'tied, imprisoned, inhibited.' It was Leonard who was 'intellectual' at the expense of a 'social side' (*Diary*, 28 June 1923, 2:250). That Sackville-West's invitation into life should be qualified by the suggestion that Woolf 'like[d] people through the brain better than through the heart' – that she was like Leonard instead of her mother or Sackville-West – was hurtful indeed.

When their relationship became too painful, Woolf did turn it into copy. At its beginning, the offence Woolf seems to have taken provides the subject for their first extended textual flirtation. 'My Dear Virginia,' Sackville-West replies, 'Aren't you a pig, to make me feel one? I have searched my brain to remember what on earth in my letter could have given you "a great deal of pain." Do you just enjoy baffling the people who try to creep a little nearer?' (22 Aug. 1924, 52). Undaunted by Woolf's snub, or still emboldened by the request for intimacy, Sackville-West once again comments on a quotation from Woolf: '"Dislike you more, even more." Dear Virginia, (said she putting her cards on the table,) you know very well that I like you a fabulous lot.' Woolf responds by quoting Sackville-West's comments about copy from memory before announcing that she had forgotten them 'and so we'll consider it cancelled' (26 Aug. 1924, 3:127).

Forgiving but clearly not forgetting, in her next letter Woolf is concerned with arranging the details of Sackville-West's visit to the Woolfs' house in Sussex, at which time *Seducers in Ecuador* was delivered to its publishers. On reading it, Woolf wrote her first intimate letter to Sackville-West. After a paragraph praising the manuscript, with a few pointed criticisms, Woolf writes: 'I am very glad we are going to publish it, and extremely proud and indeed touched, with my childlike dazzled affection for you, that you should dedicate it to me' (15 Sept. 1924, 3:131). The kiss was accepted and returned. Now, instead of feeling like a pig, Sackville-West writes to say Woolf's letter made her feel 'like a stroked cat' (17 Sept. 1925, 56). When Woolf finds the original offending

letter a few weeks later, she writes, quoting it once more and concluding: 'So there. Come and be forgiven' (4 Oct. 1924, 3:138).

Sackville-West was not alone in stimulating Woolf's affectionate responses for her lost mother. Violet Dickinson and Janet Case before her
and Ethel Smyth after her also were recipients of Woolf's strong feelings
of attachment. As far as we know, her feelings for Sackville-West were
unique in being accompanied by erotic fantasies and activities. What
made this friendship so much more? Certainly, what Woolf calls
Sackville-West's 'proclivities' encouraged Woolf's fantasies. In a letter
to Jacques Raverat, Woolf pronounces Sackville-West 'violently Sapphic' and gives an inaccurate synopsis of her elopement with Trefusis,
after which Woolf playfully declares: 'To tell you a secret, I want to
incite my lady to elope with me next' (24 Jan. 1925, 3:156). Sackville-
West was notorious not simply because she had an affair with another
woman but also because she had that affair openly and unashamedly.
She acted on her desires at a time when for a woman to have desires at
all was practically a scandal.

The relationship with Sackville-West was different from Woolf's previous infatuations in another way. Woolf discerned Sackville-West's
fluid gender identity and found the commingling of masculine and
feminine traits in her overwhelmingly sensual. Sackville-West was like
Julia Stephen, but she was also decidedly not like her. This, I believe,
was key to their relationship and to their shared goal of making up
women, which, as we shall see in chapter 5, found its fulfilment in print
even after the passion with which they invented one another had waned.

In her aristocratic bearing, cross-dressing, and creation of the houses
and gardens of Long Barn and Sissinghurst, Sackville-West developed
an erotics of private space that, like her writing, was also publicly
accessible. In the hothouse environment of Knole, the Spanish Gypsy's
granddaughter had flourished. Fed on ripe fruit and disappointment,
Sackville-West wrote her own story and defied the existing categories
of gender and sexuality. She was not a mannish lesbian. She had her
own theory of gender and sexuality that defied easy categorization. She
exaggerated her femininity, wearing her signature ropes of pearls even
when gardening in tight trousers and high boots. She exaggerated her
masculinity, wearing broad-brimmed hats and breeches. She refused to
conform to traditional gender type. She refused to repress her sexuality.
She acted on her desires. While the aristocracy traded on their hyper-
privileged status to indulge whims, flings, and eccentricities, Sackville-
West's behaviour and appearance would have been scandalous in

respectable middle-class dining rooms, and even bawdy Bloomsbury was not amused.

Sackville-West's open sexuality and fluid gender identity coupled with Woolf's positive associations between her and Julia Stephen made her an irresistible alternative to Bloomsbury and marriage and sexual repression, which formed Woolf's life. From the start their relationship was textual as well as sensual. Even before they met they had read each other's fiction. In the end, it was the textual side of their relationship that endured. They shared a private and public literary partnership that began with the promise to make one another up and extended into making up other women writers. After their affair cooled, it was in this written conversation that they sought expression for their desire. They found that expression in the creation of a narrative voice that had all of the fluidity they sought in one another. Their narrators resist the constraints of genre expectations even as they themselves resisted social constraints. In this narrative voice they found the expression of desire.

Before Woolf turned Sackville-West into copy – first as Orlando and then as an always absent longing – the flirtation bore fruit. Sackville-West blew Woolf the kiss of *Seducers in Ecuador*'s dedication and then on Wednesday, 16 December 1925 Woolf went to Long Barn to spend several days with Sackville-West.[13] It is likely that during this visit Woolf confided to Sackville-West the story of the sexual abuse she had suffered throughout her childhood and adolescence; it was a story she typically shared with her intimate confidantes.[14] 'Talked to her [Woolf] till 3 a.m. – Not a peaceful evening,' Sackville-West wrote in her journal (Glendinning 149). 'Not a peaceful evening' is Sackville-West's code for an emotional and erotically charged evening. It was during this visit that the ceilings of Long Barn first swayed above their heads. Something, perhaps something in their conversation, lifted the veil of Woolf's repressed body awareness to reveal desire.

In accepting Sackville-West's gift of fruit, Woolf was experiencing – however briefly – an integration of her own sensual responses and desires: she was discovering her own ripe fruit. It would be consistent with the experiences of other incest survivors if confessing the secrets of her step-brothers' abuses relieved Woolf of the body shame that had prevented her from experiencing erotic pleasure. Woolf's desire for her mother's attention was satisfied by Sackville-West, who, wrote Woolf, 'lavishes on me the maternal protection which, for some reason, is what I have always most wished from everyone' (*Diary*, 21 Dec. 1925, 3:52). Secure in her 'mother's' love, Woolf could feel whole and thus able to connect to another. This is the reparation of the fruit Sackville-West offered.

Sackville-West's offerings continued, and Woolf ate readily. After her first nights at Long Barn, Woolf wrote in her diary: 'I like her & being with her, & the splendour – she shines in the grocers shop in Sevenoaks with a candle lit radiance, stalking on legs like beech trees, pink glowing, grape clustered, pearl hung ... there is some voluptuousness about her; the grapes are ripe' (21 Dec. 1925, 3:52). More fruit was to follow. 'I have brought 2 bottles of Allella,' Sackville-West wrote to her husband while staying alone with Woolf at Monks House, 'and a box of cherries' (13 June 1926, 146). She gave and gave some more until Woolf put a moratorium on gift giving. But first came the gift of the dedication, their longing letters during Sackville-West's trips to Persia, and, finally, Woolf's transformation of the affair into *Orlando* after Sackville-West betrayed her by falling in love with Mary Campbell. Again betrayed, abandoned, unable to protest, Woolf writes the comedy of Orlando, not so much in revenge as in displacement. Writing once more becomes, and now will remain, the site of passion. Virginia Woolf could eat the fruit from her lover's plate, but she could not keep it for her own, despite her entreaty to Sackville-West to come, and be forgiven.

4 *Orlando*: A Biography of Desire

I feel like a moth, with heavy scarlet eyes and a soft cape of down – a moth
about to settle in a sweet, bush – Would it were – ah but thats improper.
Virginia Woolf to Vita Sackville-West (6 March 1928, 3:469)

I prefer to write to Virginia – not that I have anything to say except that I love
her and wish she were not ill ... Do you know what I believe it was, apart from
'flu? it was SUPPRESSED RANDINESS. So there –
Vita Sackville-West to Virginia Woolf (6 Feb. 1929, 318)

When Virginia Woolf and Vita Sackville-West first met, Sackville-West
had just completed *Knole and the Sackvilles*.[1] The final story of hidden
fruit makes for a surprisingly personal conclusion to this history of a
family and their estate. The story allows Sackville-West to write a
narrative that places her permanently inside the house she could not
inherit. At the end of her story of Knole, she is always the little girl
running through the halls in search of her secret fruit. In this way
Sackville-West's own writing table replaces her grandfather's. His table
produced the fruit of Knole, hers a fantasy of Knole. When Lord Sackville
ignored his guests' looks of amazement in order to hide fruit from the
banquet table in his table drawer, he was showing his granddaughter
that ignoring convention can lead to transformation. Just as a writing
table becomes a cornucopia, so too can a book about a house become a
portrait of one's beloved.

Knole and the Sackvilles is perhaps the first example of Woolf and
Sackville-West's biographies of desire. *Knole and the Sackvilles* is the
biography of a house that has the presence of a person, and Sackville-

West's desire for it is denied and rediscovered in unconventional, even subversive, practices. When she writes her history of the house, she rewrites the line of succession to conclude with herself as Knole's rightful heir. (Re)writing history is another way to fulfil desire.

'Come and see for yourself,' Sackville-West wrote to Woolf in a roguish invitation into the bed Sackville-West slept in at Knole (25 Dec. 1926, 157). Woolf accepted this invitation, and, when she arrived, she and Sackville-West explored the acres of rooms and miles of hallways of Knole.[2] Woolf wrote: 'All the centuries seemed lit up, the past expressive, articulate' (*Diary*, 23 Jan. 1927, 3:125). In this moment, we see one of the first glimpses of *Orlando: A Biography*, which Woolf began planning six weeks later (3:131).

As much about Knole as it is about Sackville-West, *Orlando* tells the story of Knole and the Sackvilles. It draws from, and also parodies, *Knole and the Sackvilles*, a copy of which Sackville-West sent Woolf, at Woolf's request, soon after they met (letter to Sackville-West, 3 Jan. 1923, 3:1). Woolf recognized Knole as Sackville-West's metaphorical safe house. Knole was both a locked safe holding treasure and a protected place where Sackville-West could feel secure enough to desire what she could not have, whether Knole itself or Virginia Woolf. Sackville-West's fantasy of Knole was the key to an internal treasure chest of security, and she created that fantasy through writing even as that fantasy inspired her to write. At one point, she asked the new heirs for an actual key to the house. Upon receiving it, she wrote to her husband: 'I am so happy, *writing*, with the key to Knole in my pocket' (Dec. 1950, quoted in Glendinning 368; my emphasis). Sackville-West wrote to Woolf, inviting her into a bed she could describe but not own. Woolf responded with a description of the bed and of Sackville-West in it as Orlando. Woolf's portrait of Sackville-West at Knole was particularly important, since, while she was writing *Orlando*, Sackville-West's father died (28 Jan. 1928) and the estate passed to her cousin Eddy. When she received *Orlando* from Woolf, Sackville-West no longer had open access to Knole: *Orlando* is a different sort of key.

Written as their affair was ending, *Orlando* is another heaping plate of ripe fruit from a writing table. Sackville-West wrote of this to Woolf: 'Do you know, I never read Orlando without tears pricking in my eyes? ... Whether it is the mere beauty of the book, or whether it is because it is you, or because it is Knole, or because it is all three, I don't know' (317). *Orlando* certainly is all three, and more besides. When it pokes fun at Sackville-West's obsession with her family estate, Woolf is making a joke she hoped Sackville-West would miss. She sent a copy to Sackville-West on the day of publication. Sackville-West apparently responded with a telegram indicating her pleasure in the book. Woolf betrays the double nature of the novel as both homage and parody in her response: 'What an immense relief! ... It struck me suddenly with horror that you'd be hurt or angry' (12 Oct. 1928, 3:544). Sackville-West did not notice anything to be angry about. After reading it, she wrote to Woolf: 'It is like being alone in a dark room with a treasure chest full of rubies and nuggets and brocades' (11 Oct. 1928, 288).

Woolf's narrative sleight of hand is not directed solely at Sackville-West: *Orlando* is replete with double messages. Despite its jokes (which are many and directed variously), it also participates in what had become a shared fantasy of restoring Knole to Sackville-West. *Orlando* recovers the mother's protective body in a symbolic manner for both Woolf and Sackville-West. At the end of the book, Sackville-West has Knole and Woolf has had her vision of Sackville-West. Just as Lily's painting leads to both a vision of Mrs Ramsay and an artistic accomplishment, *Orlando* is also a multiple creation as it recoups Knole for Sackville-West and Sackville-West for Woolf. Woolf recognized the complex mixture of influences from the start, writing to Sackville-West:

> Look, dearest what a lovely page this is, and think how ... it might all be filled to the brim with lovemaking unbelievable: indiscretions incredible: instead of which, nothing shall be said ...
>
> But listen; suppose Orlando turns out to be Vita; and its all about you and the lusts of your flesh and the lure of your mind ... suppose, I say, that Sibyl [Colefax] next October says 'Theres Virginia gone and written a book about Vita' and Ozzie [Dickinson] chaws with his great chaps and Byard [of Heinemann] guffaws, Shall you mind? ... as I told you, it sprung upon me how I could revolutionise biography in a night: and so if agreeable to you I would like to toss this up in the air and see what happens.
>
> I am reading Knole and the Sackvilles. (9 Oct. 1927, 3:427–9)

While reading *Knole and the Sackvilles*, Woolf found herself wishing to revolutionize biography. She responded by writing a portrait of Sackville-West as Orlando and a letter that represses the love letter she wished to write, since 'nothing shall be said' of lovemaking. *Orlando* accommodates all of these impulses – biography, lovemaking, and repression – and accomplishes the double restoration of Sackville-West and Knole through an indeterminate narrative voice that Woolf and Sackville-West created between them.

Orlando is the literary centrepiece of the Woolf/Sackville-West affair, in Joanne Trautmann's phrase, 'its chief literary fruit' (*Jessamy Brides* 37). As such, it deserves to be considered at some length to better understand the complex and multifaceted expression of desire that weaves its way through their relationship. Most obviously, *Orlando* expresses Woolf's desire for Sackville-West through homoerotic allusions that are simultaneously revealed and concealed. Ultimately, I will argue, *Orlando* transforms desire into writing (see ch. 7). Before we arrive at that conclusion, however, I want to consider the connections Woolf makes in this book between sexual, social, and literary transgressions. *Orlando* breaks the rules of all three.

Orlando operates on multiple, interconnected levels to serve the goals of a feminist politics that resists restrictions of sexuality, gender, and literary form. In *Orlando* writing and desire are inextricably intertwined and both are vulnerable to patriarchal censure. Repressing one has a chilling effect on the other: when nineteenth-century social pressure ('the spirit of the age') questions Orlando's sexuality, for example, she is unable to write: 'For it would seem – her case proved it – that we write, not with the fingers, but with the whole person. The nerve which controls the pen winds itself about every fibre of our being, threads the heart, pierces the liver. Though the seat of her trouble seemed to be the left finger [absent a wedding ring], she could feel herself poisoned through and through, and was forced at length to consider the most desperate of remedies, which was to yield completely and submissively to the spirit of the age, and take a husband' (243). Until Orlando can demonstrate her respectability, she is brought to a halt. She cannot express herself until she complies with social expectations. Similarly, a successful challenge to one set of laws lifts repression elsewhere: when Orlando finally completes her poem, she rediscovers her desire for her long-lost lover, Sasha (303).[3] *Orlando* alludes to homoerotic desire, and it disentangles sex, gender, and sexuality. It defines gender as a socially constructed category that serves the interests of the patriarchy.

Woolf and Sackville-West struggled to articulate desire in their letters and in the literary texts they were writing during their affair. As the affair ended, they turned from making up one another to making up women writers in biographies that narrate the repression of women's desire in the lives of the subjects and develop narrators who evade this repression. Biography at first seems an odd genre for them to have chosen to work in, since it is not a form with which either is typically associated. That makes the choice all the more intriguing. The history of their affair continues in these biographies, first in *Orlando*, then in Sackville-West's *Aphra Behn*, followed closely by Woolf's *A Room of One's Own*. These three interrelated biographies tell the same story of the repression and emergence of desire.

Woolf began planning *Orlando* in March 1927: 'Suddenly between twelve & one I conceived a whole fantasy to be called "The Jessamy Brides" – why, I wonder?[4] ... Sapphism is to be suggested. Satire is to be the main note – satire and wildness' (*Diary*, 14 March 1927, 3:131). *Orlando* was published nineteen months later, as the last words of the book proclaim, on 'Thursday, the eleventh of October, Nineteen Hundred and Twenty-eight' (329). It was certainly both satirical and wild. Considered a novel by most critics and readers, *Orlando: A Biography*, along with its structure, photographs of the main players, index, and discussions about proper biographical practices, deliberately calls straightforward classification into question. Indeed, when it first appeared, London bookstores displayed it with the biographies, much to Woolf's chagrin, since she feared that such a label would lower its sales. *Orlando* preceded Woolf's other satirical biographies, *Flush* (1940), a biography of Elizabeth Barrett Browning's cocker spaniel, and her only play, *Freshwater* (performed privately in 1935), as well as her only serious, full-length biography, *Roger Fry* (1940).

In *Literary Biography*, biographer Leon Edel devotes considerable attention to *Orlando*, which he describes as a 'fable for biographers' and credits with influencing his own biography of Henry James (94).[5] Genre instability is only the beginning of the ways in which *Orlando* evades restrictive expectations. The subject of the biography, Orlando, is not fixed in history, sex, or gender. The book opens with Orlando's youth during the reign of Elizabeth I in 1586 (236) and concludes with a thirty-six-year-old Orlando in the present moment of the book's completion, 1928. About halfway through this 342-year-long romp, Orlando, initially a young man, awakens from a week-long sleep to discover himself a woman. The newly female Orlando must learn to act feminine in order not to wreak social havoc, but she soon discovers that crossdressing facilitates a myriad of gender transformations. *Orlando* connects sexual desire with writing; indeed, conception of the poem Orlando writes is wildly erotic, and, when it is completed, 'The manuscript which reposed above her heart began shuffling and beating as if it were a living thing' (272). Throughout the book only desire – as evidenced in sexual object choice – and the (related) urge to write remain constant. *Orlando* demonstrates that in order to desire, in order to write, and even in order to genuinely live, one must ignore the rigid categories that restrict and repress and censor – but one must ignore them carefully.

As Woolf was writing *Orlando*, Radclyffe Hall's novel *The Well of Loneliness* was being prosecuted for obscenity.[6] The trial itself took place on 9 November 1928, a month after *Orlando*'s publication. Radclyffe Hall appealed the decision on 14 December, but to no avail. Leonard Woolf, who had reviewed the novel in the *Nation* the previous summer, and E.M. Forster collected signatures protesting the ban. Virginia Woolf signed this list, but (as noted in chapter 1) Sackville-West was deliberately excluded from participation. She wrote to her husband, Harold Nicolson, that she herself would like to write about lesbianism: if it were possible to take it as a topic, 'the field of fiction is immediately doubled' (Glendinning 199). Woolf attended the first trial and described it in her diary (3:206–7).

Jane Marcus reads *A Room of One's Own* in the context of the trial (*Language* 163–87) and convincingly argues that *Orlando* carefully raises issues of lesbian desire without courting censorship. Julia Briggs argues that the repression of female sexuality is, in fact, Woolf's subject: 'The writer's proper task, Woolf had recognized from the outset [of her career], was to investigate "the things people don't say" [204]: Terence Hewet in *The Voyage Out* had wanted to write a novel about silence. This issue assumed a central importance in her novel *Orlando* and [in] *A Room of One's Own*: in both, it is associated with women's love for women, and the ways in which literary traditions have ignored or cast a veil over this aspect of women's physical experiences, as well as others' (xxvi). According to Briggs, Woolf's reticence came from her 'delicate sense of what it was acceptable for women to say' (xxvi–xxvii), a sense that was in conflict with 'her urgent desire to speak openly about the position of women within society' (xxvii). Briggs and Marcus agree that in *Orlando* Woolf is walking a fine line.

But how does Woolf keep her balance – or rather, how does she keep readers off balance? Pamela Caughie argues that Woolf uses 'equivocation' in order to resist certainty and as 'a guard against the desire to prevail' (*Virginia Woolf and Postmodernism* 8). Equivocation, at least in *Orlando*, also avoids censorship. The slippery narrator (about whom more later) is here the key to what Caughie, using Jane Gallop's phrase, describes as Woolf's 'double discourse.' The Biographer offers frequent comments, interpretations, and editorial asides while recounting of the events of Orlando's life. We know nothing of the Biographer beyond his profession, although when referring to himself, he uses the Royal 'we,' and all other biographers are referred to as 'he.'[7] His intrusive presence deliberately complicates the narrative as he both exposes, hides, hints at what has been hidden, and undermines the hiding. Just as Woolf could make a joke in *Orlando* calculated to go over Sackville-West's head, so too were there messages Sackville-West alone would understand. *Orlando* is a book in which multiple discourses merge to provide very different readings, none of which can easily be pinned down.

Orlando's narrative instability is exemplified by Orlando's sexes and genders, both of which are key plot points. When, a little less than halfway through *Orlando*, the main character, male up to this point, suddenly becomes a woman, the Biographer is careful to specify that this change of sex does not produce any other changes: 'Orlando had become a woman – there is no denying it. But in every other respect, Orlando remained precisely as *he* had been' (138; emphasis added). There is no change in Orlando's identity, face, or memory. Even the pronouns referring to Orlando resist transformation as the Biographer announces: 'he was a woman' (137). If the transformed Orlando remains the same in every respect except for sex, her gender and sexuality should remain unchanged as well.

Orlando's gender (masculine) and sexual object choice (Sasha) do remain unchanged, although the Biographer warns the reader that there will be scant evidence to support any claim regarding Orlando's sexuality: 'let other pens treat of sex and sexuality; we quit such odious subjects as soon as we can' (139). The line is an allusion to the first sentence of the last chapter of Jane Austen's *Mansfield Park*: 'Let other pens dwell on guilt and misery. I quit such odious subjects as soon as I can' (474). It is tempting to speculate on the associations that lead to the connection of guilt and misery with sex and sexuality. It is commonplace for the Biographer to rehearse the rules of biographical propriety before proceeding to break them. In this case, however, the Biographer actually treats sex and sexuality as the odious subjects they are said to be by moving swiftly on. To quit these odious subjects does not help the Biographer to avoid the guilt and misery that they replaced. The Biographer's satiric dismissal, although similar in style and tone to scores of others, reveals real anxiety. Has Orlando's sexuality emerged intact from the transformation? What would that mean? The Biographer does not discuss it outright; however, there are clues scattered throughout the last half of the novel that suggest that Orlando has indeed 'remained precisely as he had been': even after he changes sex, desire remains unchanged.

After Orlando changes sex, her sense of self, despite the Biographer's initial assertion to the contrary, does change as a result of her response to social expectations: 'what was said a short time ago about there being no change in Orlando the man and Orlando the woman, was ceasing to be altogether true. She was becoming a little more modest, as women are, of her brains, and a little more vain, as women are, of her person' (187). Orlando is being recast as she becomes gendered, but the Biographer makes it clear that this change is not inherent but the result of experience.[8]

The male Orlando is apparently heterosexual. As a man, Orlando has any number of sexual encounters with women, with no evidence of any desire for or sexual experimentation with men.[9] The same is true for the female Orlando; she is also sexually active and (even though she marries) exhibits little erotic interest in men: 'as all Orlando's loves had been women, now, through the culpable laggardry of the human frame to adapt itself to convention, though she herself was a woman, it was still a woman she loved; and if the consciousness of being of the same sex had any effect at all, it was to quicken and deepen those feelings which she had had as a man' (161). This is a powerful statement that defines Orlando as what Woolf would call a sapphist.

The reader's attention is diverted from the announcement of Orlando's sapphism by the context of the statement. Submerged among Orlando's conflicted thoughts about femininity and her new place as a woman in a society she now recognizes as sexist, the stability of her sexual desires are less urgent than the wild swings in opinion she has about gender: 'she was horrified to perceive how low an opinion she was forming of the other sex, the manly, to which it had once been her pride to belong' (158). It is understandable that such a radical change in opinion would occupy Orlando's attention more than any lack of change. Be that as it may, the issue of Orlando's desire, however bravely raised, is quickly replaced by gender issues.

Resisting convention and the pressure of social expectations, Orlando openly admits to herself that her change of sex has not produced an alteration in her sexuality. However, even as she sorts through the experience of being a woman who feels like the man she once was, she finds herself behaving increasingly as society expects a woman at her most ladylike to behave. Hanging on the arm of the ship's captain, she allows herself to be escorted, pampered, served, and teased. It is hard to

Konyos's desire theory is not as easy to support as she makes out (goto p. 80)

imagine such a creature acting on the desires she realizes she has, and, indeed, we do not see her acting on any sexual desires whatsoever for some time to come – just like a lady. She becomes the passive recipient of male attention. This is part of the point: as Orlando learns to be feminine, her sexuality is repressed.

Nevertheless, the female Orlando does have sexual desire, and women are her object choices. This assertion is supported by the text and by Woolf's own admission. Even in her earliest ideas about *Orlando*, Woolf planned to include what she described as a sapphist theme, as even Quentin Bell concedes: '*Orlando*, of all Virginia's novels [is] the one that comes nearest to sexual, or rather to homosexual, feeling' (2:118). Most of the female Orlando's sexual activity occurs during the eighteenth century, in keeping with the broad depiction of history, much of it drawn from literature, that characterizes *Orlando*. During this period, Orlando is able to resist both internalized and external patriarchal Law. Her escapades bear a striking resemblance to those of fellow writer and adventurer, the Restoration playwright Aphra Behn (1640?–89), about whom both Woolf and Sackville-West wrote during and immediately following the publication of *Orlando*. Orlando is even ridiculed in verse by Alexander Pope, just as Behn was (*Orlando* 214). Behn's career was earlier than this period in *Orlando*, but she is a likely influence, not only because she was on the minds of Woolf and Sackville-West at the time, but also because in her life and writing she had come to represent sexual licentiousness (this point is further discussed in chapter 6): as Pope wrote, using her pen name, 'Astrea': 'The stage how loosely does Astrea tread, / Who fairly puts all characters to bed' (3:366; lines 290–1).

Like Behn, Orlando's defiant awareness of the Law is facilitated by cross-dressing, which enabled her 'adventures,' including, apparently, sexual encounters with women: 'she found it convenient at this time to change frequently from one set of clothes to another ... She had, it seems, no difficulty in sustaining the different parts, for her sex changed far more frequently than those who have worn only one set of clothing can conceive; nor can there be any doubt that she reaped a twofold harvest by this device; the pleasures of life were increased and its experiences multiplied. From a probity of breeches she turned to the seductiveness of petticoats and enjoyed the love of both sexes equally' (220–1). Dressing the part of man or woman allows Orlando to behave as she pleases without openly challenging patriarchal Law.[10] Regardless of the sex of her lover, she stages heterosexual desire. She can 'pass'

as lady or rake as long as the clothes fit. She moves through society like a subversive chameleon:

> one may sketch her spending her morning in a China robe of ambiguous gender among her books; then receiving a client or two (for she had many scores of suppliants) in the same garment; then she would take a turn in the garden and clip the nut trees – for which knee breeches were convenient; then she would change into a flowered taffeta which best suited a drive to Richmond and a proposal of marriage from some great nobleman; and so back again to town, where she would don a snuff-coloured gown like a lawyer's and visit the courts to hear how her cases were doing ... and so, finally, when night came, she would more often than not become a nobleman complete from head to toe and walk the streets in search of adventure. (221)

Impersonating lawyers, gardeners, and gentlemen, Orlando represents a fluidity of subject position of the sort children experience when playing dress up. When Orlando acts on her fantasies, changing clothes becomes more than a child's game – even as participating in the symbolic order is shown to be little else.

Orlando's heterosexuality is also a false front – sometimes literally. When dressed as a lady, Orlando pretends to be interested in the advances of male suitors. The gown of flowered taffeta is as much a disguise as any other costume, perhaps more so, since it effectively masks Orlando's sexuality. She is possibly being even more misleading about her identity while dressed as a woman (which she is) than when passing as a man (which she no longer is). As a nobleman looking for adventure, Orlando openly represents her desires. As a lady, she courts proposals she has no interest in accepting.

Receiving a proposal, which will be refused, does not seem like a manifestation of sexual desire, at least not on Orlando's part. The desire she expresses as a woman especially pales when compared with her adventures after she has 'become a nobleman complete from head to toe.' The deliberate language here is intriguing. What would it mean to actually 'become' a nobleman – particularly 'from head to toe'? Could Orlando be wearing more than simply clothes? The catalogue of her adventures as a man includes a story that she 'was seen to dance naked on a balcony' (222), which suggests that her alteration must have been convincing. Another story that is repeated is that she 'fled with a certain lady to the Low Countries where the lady's husband followed them' (222).[11] This is the strongest suggestion given that Orlando actually engaged in a love affair with another woman. It certainly indicates a more active physical relationship than does the rejection of a proposal.

These examples also illustrate the Biographer's willingness to rely on rumour to flesh out the details of Orlando's life during the eighteenth century. While the Biographer expresses the traditional concern for precise identification of Orlando at any given moment in her life, he does so without anxiety. During this period of frequent cross-dressing, superficial appearance is unavailable as a marker of the conventionally recognized unified subject. Sexual and gender flexibility undermine biographical authority that rests on facts and documentation.

The description of Orlando's typical day during the eighteenth century is given as evidence that she 'enjoyed the love of both sexes equally' (221). But the love she receives from men is different from the love she enjoyed with women. There is no explicit evidence that Orlando is hetero- or bisexual. Orlando may receive the love of both sexes – and enjoy it – but her own sexual desires seem to remain consistent: she is physically attracted to women, whereas her relationships with men are purely ceremonial. Orlando plays the social games that result in receiving the approval of men. 'Love' can perhaps be understood to describe relationships in which climaxes occur in conversation rather than sexual activity. Because she flatters men by entertaining their proposals, Orlando's masquerade as a heterosexual woman is successful.[12] Having male approval permits Orlando to follow her desire for women uncensored. During the eighteenth century she is allowed to pursue her own interests without arousing suspicion.

The most detailed description of Orlando's sexual interest in women is given when, on the first occasion of cross-dressing, she picks up Nell, a prostitute:

> Orlando swept her hat off to her in the manner of a gallant paying his addresses to a lady of fashion in a public place ... The young woman raised her eyes ... Through this silver glaze the girl looked up at him (for a man he was to her) appealing, hoping, trembling, fearing. She rose; she accepted his arm. For – need we stress the point? – she was of the tribe which nightly burnishes their wares, and sets them in order on the common counter to wait the highest bidder. She led Orlando to the room in Gerrard Street which was her lodging. To feel her hanging lightly yet like

a suppliant on her arm, roused in Orlando all the feelings which become a man. (216–17)

Orlando soon admits to Nell that she is a woman and Nell laughs. Before she discloses her sex, however, Orlando enjoys the prospect of a sexual encounter. Orlando is aroused by Nell physically, both by looking at her and by touching her. The long description of their meeting also allows the reader to become tantalized by the encounter. We are reminded in the last sentence that we are witnessing foreplay between two women: 'To feel *her* hanging lightly ... on *her* arm, roused in Orlando all the feelings which become a man.' Orlando is 'roused' by this woman just as a man would be. Orlando's sexual desire is described in terms of a heterosexual model; but the scene, and the desire, are explicitly between two women.

Orlando and the reader are denied consummation of this passion. When Orlando's sex is revealed, Nell does not fall into her arms but 'told Orlando the whole story of her life' (218) and introduces her to her friends, who 'had a society of their own of which they now elected her a member' (219). Sexual activity is replaced by conversation. It is in this way suggested that Orlando's friendship with Nell and the other prostitutes, Prue, Kitty, and Rose, is purely platonic. The description of their evenings together perpetuates this notion: 'So they would draw round the Punch bowl which Orlando made it her business to furnish generously, and many were the fine tales they told and many the amusing observations they made' (219). An association that begins in the model of heterosexual exploitation is replaced by homosocial attachment.

While this provides an important opportunity for the Biographer to make fun of male notions about the inability of women to have rewarding friendships, it also gives rise to comments on female desire, which, the Biographer suggests, exists by being kept secret: 'for it cannot be denied that when women get together – but hist – they are always careful to see that the doors are shut and that not a word of it gets into print. All they desire is – but hist again – is that not a man's step on the stair? All they desire, we were about to say when the gentleman took the very words out of our mouths. Women have no desires, says this gentleman, coming into Nell's parlour; only affectations. Without desires (she has served him and he is gone) their conversation cannot be of the slightest interest to anyone' (219). The pleasure in ridiculing the gentleman, who insults women verbally after using Nell physically,

may distract from the logical conclusion gained by refuting his offen-
sive assertions. We have just seen that women are interested in each
other's conversation. We have also seen that they have desires. When
they first met, Orlando substituted desire for Nell with conversation.
Desire and conversation – two things men insist women don't have –
are here connected. The reader glimpses Orlando, Nell, Prue, Kitty,
and Rose sharing conversation and desire as long as they are not
interrupted.

Minow-Pinkney, evoking Lacan, sees Orlando's friendship with Nell,
Prue, Kitty, and Rose as an exemplification of women's inability to
articulate their desires in a patriarchal society that is structured upon
their repression. While it is true that *Orlando* censors the desires and
conversation of these women (substituting the gentleman's comments
instead), we are told that they talk to each other and that these conversations are satisfying. I take this to indicate that they can express their
desires to each other – as long as no man (or reader) is listening, as in
Luce Irigaray's concept of '*parler femme*' (*Ce sexe* 141). In such moments
Orlando challenges the patriarchal repression of women by evoking the
presence of lesbian desire (if not activity). These moments are few, and,
when they do occur, they are (perhaps deliberately) muddled or, as
Woolf said they would be, only suggested.

Minow-Pinkney suggests that the 'society of their own' that Orlando
and the prostitutes form is 'a phrase which glances back to the short
story "A Society" and points to a parallel with *A Room of One's Own* and
Three Guineas, which advocates "the Society of Outsiders"' (133). Susan
Squier proposes that *Orlando* tries out the 'outsider' position later defined in *Three Guineas* 'not only in the person of her protagonist, but also
in the novel's very form and style' (124). Woolf's 'Outsider's Society'
exemplifies what Lacan calls 'the feminine position,' the place the abstract concept of 'Woman' would occupy if there were a place for her in
patriarchy. Absent that place, there is a gap, or lack, a marker of the
impossibility of Woman to exist in and of herself in the symbolic order
(*Feminine*). Yet, as Simone de Beauvoir shows, patriarchy depends on
the notion of woman in order for there to be man, so the lack must
remain as a trace of her absence. In *Orlando* 'hist' is the trace, the
warning that the door is about to be opened and the feminine position
must vanish, as 'the gentleman took the very words out of our mouths'
(219). Thus, there can be no evidence to support the notion that Orlando's
relationship with Nell, Prue, Kitty, or Rose is sexual, even though her
initial meeting with Nell was highly sexualized. However, at the end of

the novel, when Orlando is reviewing her life, her association to love is 'But Nell, Kit, Sasha?' (311). The only serious loves she names are women, but her love for them is continually revealed and repressed by the Biographer's interruptions.

With the exception of the briefly described period of cross-dressing, the female Orlando engages in little sexual activity. Orlando does have male suitors, but she does not show any sexual desire for them. She is never serious about the Archduke Harry, whose own sex change is more comic than provocative. Her marriage to Marmaduke Bonthrop Shelmardine is prompted by social pressure: Orlando marries not because she feels heterosexual desire but because she feels coerced by Victorian society's suspicions of single women. What women might be suspected of is erotic activity, which marriage does not prevent but only appears to do so. Orlando uses marriage to shield herself from scrutiny, just as Harold Nicolson and Sackville-West did. The Biographer is delightfully sarcastic on the point that to marry is to assert the absence of heterosexual desire and activity. The model presented is Queen Victoria, who wears a crinoline 'the better to conceal the fact; the great fact; the only fact; but, nevertheless, the deplorable fact; which every modest woman did her best to deny until denial was impossible; the fact that she was about to bear a child' (234–5). Orlando responds to the pressure of these conventions by participating in form but not in spirit: she and Shelmardine marry only to part. Even though Orlando admires Shel, there is no evidence that she feels sexual desire for him.

Their initial contact parodies romantic conventions, with Orlando as the damsel in distress,[13] but most of the focus of their relationship is on their conversations, which (unlike the conversations with Nell, Prue, Kitty, and Rose) we actually get to hear. Shel's 'voyage round Cape Horn in the teeth of a gale' (252) is the sort of adventure Orlando fantasized about when she was a boy. Their conversation represents not heterosexual desire, but the highly sublimated desire of adolescent adventure fantasies specifically located in a homosocial environment. Orlando identifies with Shel, and, like Shel's voyage, the description of his travels serves to avoid (hetero)sexual contact while establishing (homo)social camaraderie.

If Shelmardine and Orlando find each other's conversation so sympathetic that they believe the other to be of his or her own sex, then perhaps this indicates a smothering of sexual difference that represses adult sexuality: '"You're a woman, Shel!" she cried. "You're a man, Orlando!" he cried. Never was there such a scene of protestation and demonstration as then took place since the world began' (252). This playful scene evokes childhood exhibitions that stem from curiosity – and incredulity – about sexual difference. Orlando and Shel engage in a version of 'if you show me yours, I'll show you mine,' which has its charm, but lacks a certain erotic potential. Their investigations could lead to the development of heterosexual erotic practice, but at this stage there is evidence of little more than show and tell.

Shel is the youth Orlando can no longer be – not so much because she is female but because she has grown up. While Shel satisfies his sweet tooth with strawberry jam, Orlando fantasizes about his adventures: 'The vision which she had thereupon of this boy (for he was little more) sucking peppermints, for which he had a passion, while the masts snapped and the stars reeled and he roared brief orders to cut this adrift, to stow that overboard, brought the tears to her eyes' (252–3). This scene from childhood play indicates how immature Shel appears to Orlando. As Orlando sees him, Shel is a young man interested in candy and boats. Even when her feelings for him cause her to reassess her sense of herself as a woman, she is stimulated not by sexual desire but by maternal instincts. The fantasy of him sucking peppermints amid snapping masts 'brought tears to her eyes, tears, she noted, of a finer flavour than any she had cried before. "I am a woman," she thought, "a real woman, at last"' (253). The 'finer flavour' of her tears suggests not erotic but maternal passion. Orlando lives vicariously through Shel as he describes his adventures, but her response is one a mother might have for her son.[14]

Orlando's apparent lack of sexual desire for Shel supports the notion that her desire has remained constant. As was true of Sackville-West and Harold Nicolson, Orlando's marriage is socially convenient.[15] It is a cover under which she conceals her true nature. For the Victorian Orlando, a husband is useful for fending off social criticism, and by taking a husband she avoids censorship. This seems to describe the book's strategy also. A heterosexual object choice is a screen that hides not only same-sex object choice but also the inability to confront sexuality more openly.

Orlando's marriage might have been enough to throw the suspicious off the track even as it is presented as just such a ploy to evade censorship. Shelmardine leaves almost immediately on another voyage around the Cape, and Orlando 'plunged her pen neck deep in the ink. To her enormous surprise, there was no explosion' (264). The strategy works, and Orlando writes. She writes four lines from the 'Spring' section of

Vita Sackville-West's poem 'The Land,' including: 'the snaky flower,/ Scarfed in dull purple, like Egyptian girls –' (265). The spirit of the age, Orlando's internalization of social censorship, intrudes to examine her work, commenting: 'the snaky flower – a thought strong from a lady's pen, perhaps, but Wordsworth, no doubt, sanctions it; but girls? Are girls necessary? You have a husband at the cape, you say? Ah, well, that'll do. And so the spirit passed on' (265). A married, respectable woman, Orlando can write what she likes (if she is careful), and the spirit of the age will approve. Even comments about girls are excused from a woman whose sexuality is in the control of a man, albeit an absent man. Marriage gets Orlando and *Orlando* off the hook.

Orlando illustrates the constancy of desire by its suggestions of same-sex object choice. This is ultimately obscured by a conflation of female sexual desire into patriarchally constructed feminine sexuality. Orlando marries to avoid social condemnation, and the 'spirit of the age' allows her to write, but the expense is high. At the end of the novel, repressed desire returns in the form of Sasha, the long-mourned object of constant desire. When the re-appearance of Sasha gives Orlando a chance to confront her enduring passion, she turns away.

Sasha's physical attractiveness is apparent in the description of her as 'marvellously well preserved, seductive' (303). The assumption that she is 'a Grand Duke's mistress' defines her in terms of illicit sexual activity. Is it for this reason that the respectably married Orlando does not want to be seen with her?: '"Oh, Sasha!" Orlando cried. Really, she was shocked that she should have come to this; she had grown so fat, so lethargic; and she bowed her head over the linen so that this apparition of a grey woman in fur, and a girl in Russian trousers ... might pass behind her back unseen' (303). The implication is that Sasha's obvious sexuality is somehow her undoing.

But there is a conflict between the description of Sasha as well preserved and seductive and Orlando's sense of her as lethargic and grey. Orlando tries to avoid being seen by Sasha, and since Orlando is elsewhere able to confront the pain she still feels over the loss of Sasha, it would seem that what is frightening is Sasha as she is now – an adult woman whose sexuality is alive and well and who rekindles Orlando's past – and possibly present – desires. What Orlando scorns in Sasha is the very thing that was originally (when Orlando was a boy) attractive about her. Perhaps Orlando is afraid to be approached by Sasha because it would be too difficult to resist her.

Like Clarissa Dalloway, who is evoked throughout the book's final section by the references to the chiming of clocks, Orlando remembers loving a woman. Also like Clarissa, the adult Orlando disregards any abiding passion. Both women remember; both women betray their memories. Desire is beaten back like a blowing curtain.[16] Hidden by marriage, forced to remain in the past, the energy of desire is redirected into conversation, among other connections. Clarissa gives parties. Orlando writes. So does Woolf. This, despite the recognition of constant desire, remains unchanged.

5 Genre Instability and *Orlando*: Biography as a Feminist Practice

How delicate, how decent is English biography, bless its mealy mouth! *ha-wowf*
                                                    Carlyle, *Critical Essays* 4:29

For Virginia Woolf and Vita Sackville-West the struggle against the repression of sexual desire is bound up with the struggle against larger social restrictions. *Orlando* demonstrates the coercive pressure the 'spirit of the age' exerts to enforce the respectability of marriage (and thus the outward show of patriarchal control of sexuality) before a late nineteenth- and early twentieth-century woman is free to write. For Sackville-West, restrictions were culturally produced by the absence of sexual knowledge. For Woolf, restrictions were overdetermined by her cultural and familial environments. Like Orlando, Woolf and Sackville-West forged marriages that protected them from social pressure and camouflaged their desires. Their marriages also fostered them as writers. In their pact to imagine one another, desire and writing are inextricably intertwined. In *Orlando* the delicate and decent mealy-mouthed English biography is transformed into a biography of desire. Woolf understood that this was not only a political but also an expressly feminist act.

Orlando's insistent distinction between sex, gender, and sexuality is deliberately subversive. More revolutionary still, I will argue, is its literary challenge to the authority of biography as a coercive form of normative social control. Through its examination of sexuality, gender, and the representation of the subject, *Orlando* questions the very nature of subjectivity. The radical intervention proposed by its multiple challenges is easily overlooked. It is particularly easy to diminish the importance of the subversion of the subject in a text presented in the form of a biography, since biography is not typically recognized as having the political potential I believe (and I believe Woolf believed) it has. As a genre through which we imagine people and their lives, biography straddles literature and history. In many respects, the traditional 'life and letters' established in the nineteenth century still guides twenty-first-century biographies. Biography's influence extends beyond formal tomes to permeate society in ways as varied as social introductions, job interviews, political campaign speeches, and obituaries. Biographical information is used to make judgments and is indicative of the way in which people imagine themselves and others. As Woolf's father, Leslie Stephen, realized, it is an enormously powerful tool of social control. Following Carlyle, nineteenth-century biography defined what it was to be a great man and thus set the standard against which greatness was measured. In Woolf's words, 'the Victorian biographer was dominated by the idea of goodness. Noble, upright, chaste, severe; it is thus that the Victorian worthies are presented to us' ('The New Biography' 231). With a subject – Sackville-West/Orlando, who is a noble, but certainly is neither chaste nor severe – *Orlando* undermines the central tenet of 'goodness' that Victorian biographies reinforced. Just as *Orlando* shows gender to be a coercive construct, the book deconstructs biography by revealing the process of its creation and uncovering the fictitious nature of the facts upon which it rests. *Orlando* subverts the authority of biography in a homoerotic, feminist satire.[1] *Orlando* expresses the vision they created together. Its main character embodies, in the guise of Sackville-West, their partnership. In form and content, *Orlando* challenges the patriarchal forces of repression that bore down upon them as lovers and as writers.

As *Orlando* illustrates, in order to express desire (rather than be only the object of desire), one must be able to express oneself in general. Thus, in *Orlando*, as well as in the other biographies Woolf and Sackville-West wrote, the expression of desire is bound up with resistance to cultural and psychological conventions that restrict women's expression. In Judith Butler's reading of Joan Riviere, in order to speak her mind a woman usurps 'the place of the father in public discourse as speaker, lecturer, writer – that is, as a user of signs rather than a sign-object, an item of exchange. This castrating desire might be understood as the desire to relinquish the status of woman-as-sign in order to appear as a subject within language' (*Gender Trouble* 51). Expression of desire and of everything else is a struggle with the father, as the representative of the symbolic order. Desire is thus central to the very creation – and representation – of subjectivity ('a subject within language').

For Woolf, the struggle to speak her mind was pre-eminently a struggle to write. It was also a struggle with the legacy of her actual father, the eminent Victorian biographer Leslie Stephen. Biography, already a particularly traditional and normative genre, was especially challenging for her, since in late nineteenth-century England Leslie Stephen dominated the field as well as his family. It took Sackville-West's invitation to bed and gifts of fruit to coax Woolf out of her safe, stifling Bloomsbury enclave. In the previous chapter, I argue that *Orlando* breaks sexual, social, and literary rules. Since for Woolf these were not simply external conventions but family expectations, in *Orlando* the personal is political. Sackville-West's comfort with transgression gave Woolf a model that was neither a reproduction of Victorian biography nor the ambivalent Oedipal rebellion of Lytton Strachey. As Sackville-West transformed biography and Knole into a fantasy of desire, Woolf transformed biography and Sackville-West into her own version of that fantasy. In *Knole and the Sackvilles* Sackville-West rewrote the line of succession so that Knole could be hers in fantasy and in print. In *Orlando* Woolf rewrote the conventions of desire so that Sackville-West could be hers – reinvented, adored, and faithful – in fantasy and in print. *Orlando* is homage to Sackville-West and a joke on her at same time, and it is also Woolf's way of taking care of her own family business in a manner she learned from Sackville-West.

Nineteenth-century English biographies often served as normative social tools. A popular series such as George Lilie Craik's *The Pursuit of Knowledge under Difficulties illustrated by Anecdotes* preached hard work and clean living as the keys to success. Leslie Stephen, editor of *The Dictionary of National Biography* (*DNB*) during Woolf's early childhood, established the *DNB*'s emphasis on public service and private morality.[2] Biography functioned collectively as a sort of multivolume instruction manual in how to behave, what to aspire to, how to be successful, and even, one might say, how to be. Biography represented the nineteenth-century English subject. These subjects were rarely women, but when they were, even if they were also writers, they were first and foremost good wives, mothers, and daughters (as we shall see in the next chapter). The late nineteenth-century English biographical tradition did not include desiring women.

Biographers surrounded Virginia Woolf. From Leslie Stephen to Lytton Strachey and the other members of the Bloomsbury Group, Woolf's intimate relationships were dominated by people writing about the lives of other people and about the proper way to write those lives.[3] Her own contribution to this debate was the direct result of her more private conversations with Sackville-West. Influenced and inspired by Sackville-West, Woolf produced not the serious historical studies that occupied her nearest and dearest but a fierce and funny satire of the genre, *Orlando: A Biography* (1928). *Orlando* thus takes on biography and biographers in more ways than one.

Orlando begins, appropriately, with the eponymous hero slicing with a sword at a severed head: 'Orlando's fathers had ridden in fields of asphodel, and stony fields, and fields watered by strange rivers, and they had struck the heads of many colours off many shoulders, and brought them back to hang from the rafters. So too would Orlando, he vowed' (13). Orlando swings, simultaneously imitating the father and challenging him through this metonymic replacement. Orlando finds that it can be hard to strike out at the absent father, but it is too easy when he is present. Even when the string holding the head is severed, there is nothing to do except 'string it up again, fastening it with some chivalry almost out of reach' (14). The father needs to be almost out of reach for the game to continue. No matter how many times the head is cut down, Orlando comes back unchanged to the same place in the attic where he practises for his future role in the empire.[4]

Like its hero, *Orlando* is also both an imitator and a challenger, but after Woolf swings this biographical sword of a book, she does not come back unchanged to the same place. Nurtured by her relationship with Sackville-West, Woolf's confidence in herself as a writer and a daughter had increased enough to allow her, finally, to take on the father. She swings, like Orlando, only to string the head back up and take aim again. This fight is the playful game she has learned from Sackville-West in which the stakes are high, the sword is sharp, and the reward is in the pleasure of the attack. But all the while Woolf is very much aware that this is a game, and that when she has finished, she can just walk away.

Having worked through her relationship with her parents in *To the Lighthouse*, now Woolf's ambivalent identification with her writer-father is transformed through the persona of *Orlando*'s narrator, the Biographer. The Biographer is a constant, often intrusive, presence in the book. This voice represents an alternative relationship to the Law, much like Sackville-West's. Instead of seeing imitation and challenge as the only two options, the Biographer offers a third, in which the Law can be acknowledged at the same time as its power of enforcement is ignored. The Law exists, but it does not restrict. The Biographer can take it or leave it. This position vis-à-vis Law is one that allows for the expression of desire – that allows for expression itself – regardless of the speaker's gender, sexuality, or object choice. It is a position Woolf and Sackville-West search for in their letters to one another and a position they succeed in representing in their interconnected biographies of women writers.

Woolf was not making an idle threat when she wrote to Sackville-West that *Orlando* would 'revolutionise biography in a night' (9 Oct. 1927, 3:429). In challenging biography, she set out to revolutionize the representation of the subject. As biography is a tradition that attempts to reconstruct the life of an individual, and as biography is a genre that has remained formally conservative, resisting most attempts at experimentation,[5] it is an appropriate site for Woolf's ongoing experimentation with the tension between the Cartesian subject and the (repressed) instability of the subject.[6] Dealt with internally in her previous novels through silence (*The Voyage Out*), absence (*Jacob's Room* and *To the Lighthouse*), and memory (*Mrs. Dalloway* and *To the Lighthouse*), the instability of the subject is made manifest in *Orlando*. This externalization of an internal state brings *Orlando* directly up against the conventions of nineteenth- and early twentieth-century biography, which typically did not engage the inner life of its subject. It is this tension that makes *Orlando* so funny, so difficult,[7] and so challenging. These are also reasons to dismiss, repress, or misread this astonishing book.

One of the ways in which the Biographer calls attention to himself and to his licentious relationship with the Law (in this case as manifested through genre identity) is to frequently discuss the rhetorical devices of biography and consciously parody the most common habits of biographers: 'Up to this point in telling the story of Orlando's life, documents, both private and historical, have made it possible to fulfil the first duty of a biographer, which is to plod, without looking to right or left, in the indelible footprints of truth; unenticed by flowers; regardless of shade; on and on methodically til we fall plump into the grave and write *finis* on the tombstone above our heads' (65). This description of the tedious task of biography in following its subject from birth to death also implies that any biographer who walks the straight and narrow path will also end up dead and buried. With that final '*finis*,' such a biographer writes his own epitaph. In the revolution in biography that Woolf announces (*Letters* 3:429), heads will roll. This is a declaration her family and friends could have taken personally.

The motivation for examining biography critically – and even for killing off traditional biographers – is not hard to find in the daughter of the editor of the *Dictionary of National Biography*. Woolf made no secret of her feelings that her father was an oppressive force and that his death liberated her to live her own life. Soon after the publication of *Orlando* she described in her diary the process of working through that occurred as a result of writing *To the Lighthouse*: 'I used to think of him & mother daily; but writing The Lighthouse, laid them in my mind. And now *he comes back sometimes, but differently*. (I believe this to be true – that I was obsessed by them both, unhealthily; and writing of them was a necessary act)' (3:208; emphasis added).[8] After confronting the impact her father had had on her emotional life, Woolf proceeds to confront his literary influence. If *To the Lighthouse* laid her father to rest in her mind, *Orlando* drove him out of her pen. In *Orlando*, the father-biographer 'comes back ... differently.'

Leslie Stephen's life had a powerful effect on his daughter, as did his work as a literary critic and biographer. It is not surprising to find her exorcising the ghost of his literary, as well as personal, influence within her work. Woolf wrote in her diary that 'the D.N.B. crushed [her bother Adrian's] life out before he was born. It gave me a twist of the head too. I shouldn't have been so clever, but I should have been more stable, without that contribution to the history of England' (3 Dec. 1923, 2:277). To satirize that crushing and destabilizing form would be a fitting gesture of rebellion to make towards a biological and literary father. To revolutionize the form would be even fitter; in *Orlando* Woolf does both.[9]

A biographer-father would pass on the rules of biography to his biographer-daughter with all the weight of tradition to support him – and biography has a long and seemingly stagnant tradition.[10] As Ira Bruce Nadel points out, for a biographer like Leslie Stephen 'the importance of history in the period ... emphasized documentation, industriousness, fact-gathering and objectivity' (185). Within the genre, formal traditions function, like the Law of the Father, as rules internalized within every biographer. *Orlando*'s self-conscious Biographer refuses to submit to that biographical tradition. Woolf's challenge to the traditional biography, then, defies the literary and biological father internalized together as the superego. After Woolf is finished with it, biography feels no guilt over its transgressions.

As a modernist biography, *Orlando* is concerned less with the facts of history than with investigating psychological reality. Eschewing facts and objectivity, Orlando is presented using every means available to fiction to allow readers to build a coherent fantasy world in which the characters live and breathe, while, at the same time, readers are asked to contemplate the artificial structure of the book and the instability of the subject presented. By asserting that each person has many selves (308), *Orlando* defies the narrative convention of the unified self and calls for a radical change in the way character is represented in fiction and non-fiction alike.

In 'The Subversion of the Subject,' Lacan posits that it is desire that is constant, while the ego is intermittent. Our lack of recognition of ourselves as a unified subject blocks the horrible dual knowledge of unending desire and unstable subjectivity.[11] *Orlando*'s challenge to the illusion of stable identity is raised, in part, through an attack on the biographical reliance on documented fact to support every point, as though truth could be discovered and proved. Facts make up the seamless illusion of the unified biographical life, and it is this belief in facts that *Orlando* finds preposterous. *Orlando* is the return of the repressed biography that comes back differently. Facts, like the subject, are unstable. Facts, like subjectivity, are fiction. Desire, however, is another matter. Sackville-West, the subject of Woolf's biography, is needed to raise that aspect of the riddle of subjectivity.

Orlando's formal resistance to the factual tradition of biography is paralleled by the Biographer's irreverent attitude to great literary figures: 'the very thought of a great writer stirred [Orlando] to such a pitch of belief that she almost believed him to be invisible. Her instinct was a sound one. One can only believe entirely, perhaps, in what one cannot see' (197–8). Orlando is disillusioned time and time again by contact with men of letters, until she finally joins the Biographer in rejecting the notion of genius. A genius, Orlando discovers, is not all-powerful, but a fallible man whom she generally does not like very much: Orlando 'began to live much in the company of men of genius, yet after all they were not much different from other people' (208). The reputations of men of genius are revealed to be constructs reproduced in the *DNB* as a seamless narrative of greatness. Like the notion of a unified subjectivity, these notions reinforce patriarchal power and resist interrogation. Recognizing their power as real and external reveals the individuals as empty structures who support social stability; they are no longer able to dominate. Orlando realizes that she need neither bow down to men of genius nor attack them: it is easy enough simply to ignore them, exercising revolutionary indifference in place of violence or submission. After dispatching the men of genius, Orlando 'was hugely relieved to find herself alone' (214). Having begun by striking out at the suspended heads of authority, Orlando comes to realize that she need only put down the sword and walk away. *Orlando* challenges literary and biographical traditions by offering an alternative relationship to patriarchal authority, externalized as men of genius and internalized as the superego.

Orlando also calls it quits with the tradition that values documentation over imagination. Woolf mocks biographical fact finding by way of the Turkish Insurrection, which destroys the documentary evidence of Orlando's life in Constantinople, including her sex change. After this revolution, facts (along with the biographical genre, the patriarchy, and the empire) have suffered a severe blow. The Biographer explains: 'We have done our best to piece out a meagre summary from the charred fragments that remain; but often it has been necessary to speculate, to surmise, and even to make use of the imagination' (119). Documentation as proof of authority forces attention exclusively on the external social world, where patriarchy and logic are in control, repressing internal psychic experience, where the possibility of political resistance lies. The Turkish Insurrection results in a revolutionary biography: the 'charred fragments' of *Orlando* resist traditional expectations about fiction and biography by blurring genres. Imagination is needed to write biographies after the revolution.

The sword of imagination that Woolf swings at the head of the father is supplied by Vita Sackville-West's succulent alternative to actual violence. Privately enjoying a juicy ripe peach is a form of resistance. Just as Sackville-West embodies an alternative model of sexuality, so too does her acceptance of Law permit an escape from an ongoing struggle with literary fathers. She suggests this structure in the self-conscious narrator of *Aphra Behn* (discussed further in chapter 6), a model Woolf develops in *Orlando*'s extended satire of the traditional biographical form.

As an intrusive narrator, the Biographer comments continually on the action, the characters, and the genre of biography itself, beginning with the suggestive opening sentence: 'He – for there could be no doubt of his sex' (13). *Orlando*'s Biographer picks up the sarcastic tone that appears intermittently in *Aphra Behn*, which begins: 'Aphra Behn ... was born at Wye near Canterbury in the summer of 1640, and disappears at an early age from the shores of England and the pages of reputable biography' (11). The tone Woolf and Sackville-West employ is distinct from that of Woolf's more obvious influence in writing biographies, Lytton Strachey, whose irony is directed at the subject of the biography rather than the biographical project.[12] *Orlando*'s irony is aimed at the traditional narrative strategies of biography. The meticulous documentation, confusion over data, absence of evidence, quarrels with previous biographers, and the very nature of biographical research that structure *Aphra Behn* are the object of *Orlando*'s relentless satire. And *Orlando* is relentless, not only because it never gives in to the urge to narrate the reputable life Woolf and Sackville-West try to make up for Behn, but also because its ironic tone is not intermittent but sustained by the fully developed, self-aware narrative voice of the Biographer.

Orlando has lately been celebrated for its feminist content;[13] the structural feature of the intrusive Biographer has received scant critical attention, however, presumably because it is considered an unproblematic literary device. Critics treat this aspect of the novel in diverse, if implicit, ways. The Biographer is variously presumed to be 'Woolf,' a dupe set up by Woolf as an element of the satire, or a hybrid of the two – sometimes Woolf and sometimes a target of Woolf's wit. In neither of these conceptions is the Biographer considered to be the perpetrating agent of the satire in which he participates. Whatever self-reflexivity exists in *Orlando* is assumed to be located outside the book in Woolf rather than in her presumably unselfconscious narrator. In most accounts of *Orlando*, the Biographer is either unaware of the mockery Woolf is making of him as a representative of biographers, or the critic is unaware of the Biographer.

Critics who do not engage the Biographer tend to refer to him as 'Woolf,' eliding any distinction between the narrator and the author.[14] Excluding the Biographer from critical consideration tends to keep the issue of self-consciousness (and where it is located) from emerging. While some critics simply see the Biographer as a fool, set up by Woolf to demonstrate the stupidity of the fact-obsessed biographers,[15] other critics add to this a discussion of Woolf's participation in the narrative. Her presence adds an element of self-consciousness to the text – or at least to the author – but it entails a delicate splitting of the task of narrating between author and Biographer.[16] The tricky division between Woolf as narrator and Biographer as narrator is typically asserted rather than analysed. Sandra Gilbert refers to Woolf (not the narrator) 'as a sort of metabiographer – a writer who both deploys and criticizes the form in which she is working' (206).

John Graham separates the Biographer from the style of the book, which he takes to be Woolf's (107). The energy and imagery, presumably, are Woolf's not the narrator's. According to Madeline Moore, 'there are actually two biographers telling Orlando's story: one is the naive biographer and one is Woolf herself' (102). This approach imagines a division between narrators that, although interesting in the conflict it suggests of an author openly at odds with her narrator or of two narrators fighting it out, is not evident in the text. Instances of 'momentary detachment' (Graham 101) are ascribed to Woolf, while the Biographer is taken to be responsible for the rest. Graham attempts to define this division as an intricate splitting of the narrative: the archaic words and syntax are the Biographer's; the engaging style of the same sentences is Woolf's (108). This elaborate explanation does little to contribute to an understanding of the satirical or narrative structures of the book. Reading the narration as schizophrenic ingeniously preserves Woolf from criticism, since whatever the critic does not like about the book can be blamed on the Biographer. Ultimately, however, at least in Graham's analysis, even this approach does not work: 'Virginia Woolf's mask [the Biographer] is never firmly in place, and her tentative use of it is characteristic of this exploratory and uncommitted book' (116). An analysis of Orlando that considers the Biographer as the producer of his own narrative, self-consciously constructing the satire instead of its target, avoids the unproblematic conflating of narrator into author and frees us from the acrobatics entailed in separating the narrative into two parts.[17] Such a reading uncovers the brilliance of Woolf's text: more than a parody, Orlando does indeed revolutionize not only biography but also the representation of subjectivity in a night.

Recognizing the distinction between Woolf and the narrator exposes the critical function of the Biographer within the text: the work, not only its author, is self-conscious. A more conservative reading, which locates the satirical function of Orlando in Woolf, instead of in the Biographer, avoids the need to confront the self-reflexive function of the text. The repression of self-consciousness works to stabilize the social order by maintaining rigid obedience to internalized patriarchal Law.[18] By denying the Biographer's self-consciousness, critical practice represses Orlando's revolutionary potential. Its challenge is not merely to the form of biography as a literary convention, but to the construction of the unified biographical subject as a model for subjectivity. This is a challenge Sackville-West earlier (and privately) articulated in her journal, where she attests to the oscillation of gender within her own sense of

Peta Nagourney on the protocols of biography [handwritten annotation]

self. Woolf literalizes and publicizes this insight into the instability of the subject as central to her portrait of Sackville-West as Orlando.

The repression of self-consciousness within *Orlando* parallels Lacan's critique of Freud's creation of the tripartite model of identity in the ego–id–superego formulation as a repression of the unconscious. *Orlando*, as I read it, consistently illustrates Lacanian insights. In my use of the concept of the superego, I follow Lacan in recognizing that this unconscious function represents limits as well as enforces them. In this way the 'critical function,' originally theorized in 'On Narcissism' (9:96) and subsequently repressed by Freud in 'The Ego and the Id,' is recovered. *Orlando*'s Biographer exemplifies the 'critical function,' which points out limits (e.g., of the biographical form) without enforcing boundaries. The Biographer understands what he is supposed to do as a biographer, but that does not mean he will conform to expectations. Whereas Orlando must perform heterosexuality in order to write, the Biographer is exempt from any regulatory pressure.

In his essay 'The Basic Assumptions of Literary Biography,' Peter Nagourney posits three enabling biographical assumptions: 'the premise of a unified life' (92), 'the use of anecdotal evidence' (93), and 'the assumption of development and growth' (97). The form of biography, Nagourney argues, creates these assumptions about how a biographic subject must be presented, so that even as our conception of the subject changes, readability requires the stagnation of the biographical project: 'We can state these assumptions about literary biography fairly easily, and recognize in them cultural biases which are so basic as to seem inevitable to us: a biography should present a unified life, should reveal this unity with specific anecdotal evidence and should demonstrate change, development and/or growth with the passage of time. The question we are considering now is whether these prominent characteristics of literary biography derive from the nature of life or from the nature of writing about life' (88). Nagourney concludes that it is the biographical form itself that frustrates change for both the biography and our conception of the subject: 'There is no expectation that the writing of biographies will decline, even if this discussion has illuminated some of the inherent contradictions of the genre' (102). The most Nagourney can hope for is that the repetition of traditional biographies will fail to satisfy their readers: 'Older biographers could simplify their subjects to satisfy their audience's expectations; modern biographers will never be able to make their works sufficiently complex' (100).

Mistakes / Talks

The assumptions Nagourney outlines are the very ones under attack in *Orlando*.[19] By failing to comply with the strategy of simplifying the subject used by the 'older biographers' *Orlando* does become 'sufficiently complex.' As Nagourney suggests, this greater complexity is available because *Orlando* defies the traditional form of the biography. Intruding the subjectivity of the Biographer into the narrative creates an awareness of the constructed nature of the biography and the biographical subject. When the Biographer reminds us at the turn of every page that what we are reading is a construct instead of a Life, he frees *Orlando* from the 'enabling assumptions' that constrain attempts to create a 'sufficiently complex' narrative. Woolf and the Biographer are in a partnership, like the partnership between Woolf and Sackville-West, to reinvent one another outside expected social restrictions and literary conventions.

Unable, perhaps for the reasons Nagourney maintains, to make her attack in an actual biography (e.g., *Roger Fry*), Woolf's two biographical farces, *Orlando* and *Flush*, take on the father/biographer from outside the arena of battle. As a more typical parody, *Flush* (published in 1933, five years after *Orlando*) directly attacks the silliness of rigid historical documentation. A biography of Elizabeth Barrett Browning's cocker spaniel (Sackville-West's dog was her model), *Flush* cites other dogs, for example, as sources. That the biography tells the story of Browning's escape from her loving but tyrannical father is not beside the point. The slim book acidly and joyfully follows the daughter's flight from oppression to a husband of her own.

Orlando certainly paved the way for the tour de force of *Flush*, but it does much more as well, extending the exaggeration of parody into, as Woolf wrote, 'satire and wildness' (*Diary*, 14 March 1927, 3:131). *Orlando* presents an alternative to biography as well as to the biographer-father's authority. In justifying one of its more obvious rebellious moves, creating a character that lives for over 300 years, Woolf makes the only direct reference in *Orlando* to her father's great work: 'The true length of a person's life, whatever the *Dictionary of National Biography* may say, is always a matter of dispute. Indeed it is a difficult business – this time-keeping; nothing more quickly disorders it than contact with the arts' (305–6). Disputing the reliability of facts, however cross-checked, the Biographer suggests that not only is there more to biography than the sorts of dates one can find in the *DNB*, but also that those facts themselves are misleading.

In essays such as 'Mr. Bennett and Mrs. Brown' and 'Modern Fiction'

(1925) Woolf presents this position more fully: 'It is because they are concerned not with the spirit but with the body that they [in this case H.G. Wells, Arnold Bennett, and John Galsworthy] have disappointed us' ('Modern Fiction' 104). To represent characters by attending to the buttons on their coats is to miss the internal, and to Woolf more significant, aspects of life: 'The writer seems constrained, not by his own free will but by some powerful and unscrupulous tyrant who has him in thrall, to provide a plot, to provide comedy, tragedy, love interest, and an air of probability embalming the whole so impeccable that if all his figures were to come to life they would find themselves dressed down to the last button of their coats in the fashion of the hour ... Is life like this? Must novels be like this? Look within and life, it seems, is very far from being "like this"' ('Modern Fiction' 106). The hidden emotional experience of life is the focus of Woolf's attention, and this is the subject of the modern novel as she defines it. In order to represent internal experience, the writer must rise up against the 'powerful and unscrupulous tyrant who has him in thrall.' The sword must be swung hard at the father who safeguards traditional literary assumptions.

However directly influential psychoanalysis was on Modernism, the circumstances that influenced Freud to turn his attention to internal life as a source for explaining physical responses were also present for Modernist artists. Like Freud, Woolf's concern is for the psychical context of the character. Her criticism of the DNB expands this attention to include not only the invention of fictional characters but also the representation of the subjects of biographies. As an experimental biography, Orlando might be seen as extending the goals of Modernism into that genre. It is also a work in the service of feminism, and, as such, it reveals the sword of Modernism as simply another weapon in the patriarchal game. When you win that game, your head becomes the next target. Orlando exemplifies Woolf's developing brand of feminism by refusing to reinforce coercive structures in representations of sexuality, gender, subjectivity, history, or even time.

The quality of life, the experience of the progress of time – these are not captured by a history that refuses to allow such things to be relative. For Orlando's Biographer all facts are open to dispute. Even time, when it comes in contact with the arts, can become disordered, and the art of Orlando disorders all that one would expect to find represented as stable in the DNB. When Orlando lives for over 300 years and changes from male to female, the disorder is obvious. This character cannot be pinned down in any of the ways the DNB would require. But it is not merely the facts of Orlando's life that are put into disorder by the novel but also the way in which such slippery facts are presented. Orlando challenges the absolute stability expressed by the authority of the Biographer. Contact with the arts also has disordered this stability.

Embracing Sackville-West's relationship to Law, the Biographer is aware of the rules of biography without feeling constrained by them. The Biographer *presents* the formal structure and expectations of the genre instead of *enacting* them. Early on he calls attention to the rules of biography and to his intention to operate outside these rules. During the obligatory physical description of Orlando the Biographer defines his position: 'The red of the cheeks was covered with peach down; the down on the lips ... But, alas, that these catalogues of youthful beauty cannot end without mentioning forehead and eyes. Alas, that people are seldom born devoid of all three ... Directly we glance at eyes and forehead, we have to admit a thousand disagreeables which it is the aim of every *good biographer* to ignore' (15; emphasis added). The Biographer here presents a conflict between exposing what is admirable in the subject and repressing what is troubling. The 'good biographer' attempts to ignore what is disagreeable. He presents the sort of description of Orlando that is begun here, in hyperbolic purple prose of the sort the Biographer criticizes Orlando for using in his juvenilia: 'He was fluent, evidently, but he was abstract' (16). The tone of the passage pokes fun at the 'good biographer,' but the conflict that results from the attempt to enumerate Orlando's physical characteristics and the desire to ignore any problem areas presents a more serious criticism. To be a 'good biographer' means omitting what is disagreeable. To present a biographical portrait that does not flatter, then, is to fail to follow the path of the 'good biographer.'[20]

Orlando's Biographer could perhaps be labelled a 'good enough' biographer, following Donald Winnicott's notion of the 'good enough mother,' who nurtures her child without making individuation impossible by her suffocating attention. The 'good biographer' stifles his subject with praise while burying any aspect of his character that does not live up to such accolades. Orlando's good enough Biographer is not unwilling to 'admit a thousand disagreeables' into his description of Orlando. Indeed, this moment provides an opportunity to make a distinction between 'the aim of every good biographer' and the practice of this particular biographer. He knows the expectations of his profession and, even as he presents them, he refuses to follow them blindly. Called upon to look at Orlando, he looks. Called upon to describe Orlando, he describes. He presents the conventions of biographical description instead of obeying them and, in presenting them, he looks at them, too. For what is 'disagreeable' is telling.

The description of Orlando continues: 'Sights disturbed him, like that of his mother, a very beautiful lady in green ... sights exalted him ... all these sights ... began that riot and confusion of the passions and emotions which every good biographer detests' (15–16). What is distressing about Orlando's eyes is not any physical flaw: a good biographer would be distressed by 'the passions and emotions' that arise in Orlando when he sees his mother. As in the *DNB*, the 'good biographer' would stick to delineating observable details that contribute to the subject's worthiness for biographical consideration. The 'good biographer,' one could speculate, is determined by how 'good' his subject is – or can be made to appear. To embellish the stature of one's subject is good biographical practice, since it results in the increase of the biographer's own stature. Orlando's Biographer alerts us at once that this he will not do. He will not use the biography eulogistically. He will not be motivated by self-interest to repress the disturbing fact that Orlando, after slicing at the father-head, is 'disturbed' by the sight of his beautiful mother. The 'good enough' Biographer makes room for all facets of the Oedipus complex, hinting even in these first pages that the Oedipal resolution will not result in Orlando's putting out his eyes as Oedipus did, whose story cannot bear to witness the discomforting gaze of its hero upon his mother. A biography that can include disturbing sights and the 'riot and confusion of the passions' they produce is a biography struggling to include (however cryptically, however disturbingly) desire.

Even before the Biographer announces his intention of departing from the rules of biography, he has done so by situating his description of Orlando in a specific situational context of the sort that no biographer could access. By recreating a particular day in Orlando's life and including as part of a physical description his internal response (being disturbed by the sight of his very beautiful mother), the Biographer treats his subject as though he were a fictional character. The creation of dramatic scenes is not uncommon in biography. Indeed, as Nagourney points out, the key to writing a good biography is to present characteristic anecdotes, telling phrases, and idiosyncratic mannerisms that make the subject come alive to the reader. In her essay 'The New Biography' (1927), Woolf criticizes Sir Sidney Lee, who succeeded her father as editor of the *DNB*, for failing to do just that: 'Truth being thus efficacious and supreme, we can only explain the fact that Sir Sidney's life of

Shakespeare is dull, and that his life of Edward the Seventh is unread-
able, by supposing that though both are stuffed with truth, he failed to
choose those truths which transmit personality' (229). It is not uncommon to use the methods of fiction in biographies, and Woolf recom-
mends it: 'in order that the light of personality may shine through, facts
must be manipulated; some must be brightened; others shaded; yet in
the process, they must never lose their integrity' (229).

'The New Biography' posits *Some People*, a memoir by Sackville-West's
husband, Harold Nicolson, as an example of the current trend in biographical writing to mix fact and fiction: 'here he has devised a method
of writing about people and about himself as though they were at once
real and imaginary. He has succeeded remarkably, if not entirely, in
making the best of both worlds' (232). *Some People* has been suggested as
an influence on *Orlando*,[21] although Woolf concludes that even though
'Mr. Nicolson has proved that one can use many of the devices of fiction
in dealing with real life' (232), his mingling of the two is not entirely
successful. Nicolson's ironic treatment of his subjects, which is modelled, she implies, on Strachey's, 'stunts their growth' (232). And the
balance between fact and fiction is too precarious: 'Mr. Nicolson makes
us feel, in short, that he is playing with very dangerous elements. An
incautious movement and the book will be blown sky high. He is trying
to mix the truth of real life and the truth of fiction. He can only do it by
using no more than a pinch of either. For though both truths are genuine,
they are antagonistic; let them meet and they destroy each other' (232).
While this may sound like the conservative caveat of the biographer of
Roger Fry, it can also be seen as a challenge: Nicolson 'makes us feel' that
what he is doing is dangerous. *Orlando*'s reader is unaware of any
danger as a result of mixing a pinch of fact with a pinch of fiction. In
Orlando the antagonistic truths of fact and fiction are mixed in great
handfuls, and the novel is blown sky high by its exaggeration of both.
Orlando elaborates Nicolson's more cautious experimentation and, as
such, throws down a gauntlet that is perhaps more than literary. In
acknowledging Nicolson's contribution to biography, Woolf is not only
praising and criticizing him, she is also acknowledging him as a literary
and personal rival. Which of them will slice down the head of the
ancestral father and win the love of the disturbingly beautiful Lady
Vita? Woolf may have hoped that *Orlando* would be the winning stroke.
In terms of their relationship, however, *Orlando* functions more like
Sackville-West's journal, which expresses her jealousy of Violet Trefusis's
husband even as it works though her desire for Trefusis. Woolf's *coup de
grâce* is to swing not only at the father but at biography itself.

Orlando's Biographer claims that art disorders biography (306) and, in Woolf's hands, art also comments on biography. As the Biographer points out, because art does not ignore the disagreeable internal workings of its subject, it can create a biography in which the character, like Mrs Brown of Woolf's essay, is alive. In 'Mr. Bennett and Mrs. Brown' Woolf describes what she wants to know about character as consistent in a novel, in fantasy, and in real life. In *Orlando* those observations are applied to the biographical subject, where they are perhaps more revolutionary than in any of the other categories, because to argue for more art and more life in biography blurs the boundaries of the genre until one has a novel like *Orlando: A Biography* or a biography like, for example, *To the Lighthouse*, a novel.

Orlando's Biographer's specificity and vividness of detail set him apart from other biographers and serve as constant reminders that this book is a novel, not a biography, and that this Biographer works like a novelist. We are also reminded of the material fact of the book in the frequent, self-referential discussions of writing, which are evidence of the self-conscious nature of the Biographer. A description of Orlando's struggles as a writer is preceded by the comment: 'Anyone moderately familiar with the rigours of composition will not need to be told the story in detail' (82). Who could be less remote or more familiar than the Biographer himself?

As part of their project to imagine women writers, Woolf and Sackville-West pay close attention to the writing process (and the obstacles to it) for women. *Orlando* is part of this project. The self-conscious Biographer documents Orlando's writing process as well as demonstrates the process of producing the book we are reading. The decisions the Biographer makes along the way are made obvious, as are his research difficulties: 'It is, indeed, highly unfortunate, and much to be regretted that at this stage of Orlando's career ... we have the least information to go upon' (119). This comment is reminiscent of statements Sackville-West makes in her biographies of Aphra Behn and, later, of Joan of Arc. Like Sackville-West, *Orlando*'s Biographer makes no attempt to let the facts speak for themselves or to submerge his opinions in careful presentation and omission. At every point the Biographer calls attention to himself and to the constructed nature of biography.

The Biographer's reminders that he is a writer and that the biography is a construct expose the potential identification between the Biographer and his subject. Both are writers, and the Biographer highlights that commonality. This suggests a connection with yet another writer involved in producing the book: Virginia Woolf. Woolf makes her presence felt by the inclusion of her personal life in *Orlando*'s references. The preface lists family and friends. Madame Lopokova, the wife of Woolf's long-time friend Maynard Keynes, is mentioned in passing (315) and included in the index (332). Woolf's niece, Angelica Bell, posed for the photograph of the Russian Princess (54). And ever present is another writer, Vita Sackville-West, who, if she is not recognizable in the character and details of Orlando's life, most certainly is as the actual subject of several of the photographs of Orlando (158, 246, 318).[22] Just as the Biographer does not allow the reader to forget his shaping hand, neither does Woolf allow us to forget that she is behind everything. In the preface, the dedication ('To V. Sackville-West'), and the photographs, the novel's extratextual references escape even the Biographer and suggest that something larger is at play – or is being played.

More conventional perhaps, is the way in which *Orlando* is a *Bildungsroman* that models the maturation of a writer, but a writer with a difference. Orlando eventually becomes the sort of writer the Biographer is; indeed, the Biographer measures Orlando's progress towards this ideal position in which the praise of famous men is of no consequence. The Biographer indicates that a similar process is required for the reader, since a reader who holds the traditional conceptions of literary success lampooned by the book will not get the joke but become the butt of it. The question is not whether we are man enough to strike down the father's already severed head but whether we see how silly we look in trying to do so. This question goes deeper than our ability to laugh. It asks how flexible we are, how tolerant of complexity and indeterminacy, how capable of dancing in the gaps in the text.

While Orlando is engaged with the works of Sir Thomas Browne, the Biographer describes the ideal reader in such a way as to allow a more rigid reader to miss the point, so that, once again, the joke could end up being on him (or her): 'Orlando ... opened the works of Sir Thomas Browne ... For though these are not matters on which a biographer can profitably enlarge it is plain enough to those who have done a reader's part in making up from bare hints dropped here and there the whole boundary and circumference of a living person ... *and it is for readers such as these alone that we write* – it is plain then to such a reader that Orlando was strangely compounded of many humours – ... To put it in a nutshell ... he was a nobleman afflicted with a love of literature (72–3; emphasis added). A reader does not have to intuit from hints that Orlando likes to read; for the passage begins with a description of Orlando in the act of reading. The Biographer's tone and circumlocutory style reflect Browne's but they also suggest that something more is going on in this passage, and, knowing this Biographer, it is probably a joke.[23] On one level, the joke is simply that insofar as Orlando is based on Vita Sackville-West – and we have the photographs to prove it – we do know exactly what Orlando looked like 'without a word to guide' us. And if we ignore the words in the book we can safely assume that our conclusions are correct. Correct as they may be, however, they are not complete, as the tone of the passage makes (un)clear.

The obvious point of this passage (Orlando loves to read) is linked to the more subtle message that Orlando is a close and careful reader. He 'investigates ... contorted cogitations' (72–3) not unlike the Biographer's. Throughout the book the Biographer's tone is too sly to be safely ignored. He does not always say what he means. His jokes are often subtle. This said, can we be certain that the Biographer is serious when he says that he writes for the reader who can make 'up from bare hints dropped here and there the whole boundary and circumference of a living person'? Orlando is not a living person, and the reader who presumes otherwise will have his or her expectations sorely challenged when Orlando changes from man to woman. The Biographer is not writing for a reader who jumps to conclusions or relies on easy stereotypes. This is not a book, in other words, for a reader who doesn't read carefully. The Biographer's reminder that Orlando's 'contortions and subtleties of temper' were 'indicated on the first page' cautions us that we must, in fact, read this book in order to develop a full picture of the main character, and he further reminds us that this is a character constructed by a text. Orlando began on page one. S/he is not the 'living person' that 'readers such as these' imagine; furthermore, the Biographer lets us know that he knows this.

Throughout the book the Biographer demonstrates the unstable, multifaceted nature of the subject, culminating with the discussion of Orlando's different selves ('as many as a thousand') and a biography's ability 'to find room for' only six or seven (309). The reader for whom the book is written is the reader who must learn that Orlando's appearance, as with his/her sex, is indeterminate, even when – or perhaps especially when – photographs of various other people are given as illustrations.

The creation of the ideal reader starts even before the book proper begins, in Woolf's preface, where the 'gentleman in America, who has generously and gratuitously corrected the punctuation, the botany, the entomology, the geography and the chronology of previous works' (ix) is not thanked because his name is forgotten. This unnamed critic marks the sort of audience for which this book is not intended: it is not for one who harps on insignificant details and points out errors. *Orlando* will make no sense to a rigid critic concerned with following the rules instead of enjoying the flexibility of a text that breaks them all. To hope that the American will 'not spare his services on the present occasion' (ix) is repayment indeed, since to correct *Orlando* at that level would be a task well deserved by any reader who attempts it.

The Biographer addresses a reader who can play the textual games of the novel, neither missing nor getting caught up in the details. It is just as important to remember that Orlando is a textual construct, begun on page one, as it is to recognize Vita Sackville-West in the photographs. No doubt the audience Woolf's preface enumerates would have been able to recognize much more than the physical resemblance between Orlando and Sackville-West. But the presence of the Bloomsbury Group at the outset calls up not only in-jokes but also a loving, yet critical, readership. In evoking nearly all of her friends by name (Leonard Woolf is a notable exception) at the start suggests the need to begin the book by imagining an audience who would be tolerant, playful, and demanding. Such expectations can be imagined to be free from traditional constraints, as opposed to *Roger Fry*, which, composed as it was for an intolerant and uncritical audience (i.e., Fry's family, who requested the biography), does not overtly challenge the assumptions of biographical form.

While it is not necessary to have access to the personal information that undoubtedly made the novel funny – or not – to Woolf's family and friends, their invocation in the preface and the photographs prevents us from treating the novel as a strictly textual game. The warning that to know exactly what Orlando looks like is to be deluded also reminds us that readers do imagine characters as if they were real people whose appearance can be known. Indeed, the book consciously encourages – even as it plays with – such a reading. The preface and photographs are jokes that remind us that Woolf was a real person who had a life and a lover. *Orlando*'s references are always intra-, inter-, and extratextual. That is the slippage at the heart of the novel: *Orlando* cannot be pinned down, not even to words, and the subject it represents cannot be fixed.

It is the joyful undecidability introduced at each stage of the novel and by each level of the novel that keeps it going. The slippage of signifiers in the text of *Orlando* is not confined to the language. The preface, the photographs, and the intertextuality of the jokes intrude the real world into the fictional. Such oscillation is in constant play in biographies. One may risk a naive reading by pretending a character is like a real person, but, when reading a biography, one knows that the character, although a product of the biographer, is supposed to represent someone who was (or is) alive. To consider the subject of the biography only as a linguistic construct is as ridiculous as to ignore the way in which what one reads is a linguistic construct. Both are the case in this textual game, which is refereed by a biographer who may or may not be playing by the rules.

Orlando's Biographer, in playing *with* the rules, creates in Orlando neither only a character about whom we read as though s/he were a real person, nor an attempted portrayal Vita Sackville-West, nor a set of characteristics grouped around a proper name. Orlando is always all of them. The Biographer criticizes Orlando and readers who rigidly follow the rules, and, just as the book narrates Orlando's development into a more flexible character, it also puts in motion the reader's process towards a similar flexibility.

Orlando goes beyond parodying biography to theorizing it. Enacting the very criticisms Nagourney articulates, *Orlando* urges a poststructuralist-feminist reading by rejecting the unity of time and the stability of the subject that support patriarchy. But it does not stop there. Just as the Biographer supports Orlando's transformation from compliant youth to self-aware defiance, so too does the book stimulate change in its readers by challenging expectations. Once representational conventions have become defamiliarized, it is a challenge to think of Orlando as if s/he were a real person or to think of Woolf's relationship to this text as straightforward. These are habits of mind *Orlando* encourages readers to outgrow, and, when another novel requires us to try them on again, we might discover that they are no longer the seamless garments we discarded when we changed our critical clothes.

Orlando is a game that goes flat when any one register is dismissed. Reading it, we are taught to laugh at *all* the jokes or risk missing the point(s). The referee-Biographer occupies all registers, since this narrator does have a certain status as a character in his own right even as he introduces the textual play that demands a self-conscious reading of the text. The Biographer, it might be imagined, keeps score: How is the book being read and how well? His intrusions are often aimed at adjusting the reader's perceptions – or rather, at multiplying them. By thus undermining biographical assumptions, Woolf exemplifies the New Biography her essay only begins to hint at. Recognizing the self-consciousness with which the Biographer functions allows us to recognize the position Woolf herself is taking and the ways in which *Orlando* is indeed a revolutionary act: sapphism and wildness give rise to a feminist biographical practice that imagines women (Orlando, Sackville-West, Woolf) writing and desiring.

6 Making up Women: Revolutions in Biography

[handwritten: this ch. is on aphra Behn]

Sackville-West's Respectable Aphra Behn: Performative Biography and Revised Desire

A course of Mrs. A.B. [Aphra Behn] has turned me into the complete ruffling rake. No more than Mrs. A.B. do I relish, or approve of, chastity.

> Vita Sackville-West to Virginia Woolf (4 Aug. 1927, 220)

would you lend me whichever is in your opinion the most romantic novel of Mrs Behn's?

> Virginia Woolf to Vita Sackville-West (22 Aug. 1927, 3:412)

All women together ought to let flowers fall upon the tomb of Aphra Behn for it *[handwritten: wow]* was she who earned them the right to speak their minds.

> Virginia Woolf, *A Room of One's Own* (69)

Virginia Woolf and Vita Sackville-West joined together to imagine women writers by creating biographies that use many of the same strategies Woolf used in *Orlando*. Like *Orlando*, these narratives challenge late nineteenth-century biographical conventions even as they carefully evade censorship in order to represent desiring women. Sackville-West's *Aphra Behn* (1927) and Woolf's *A Room of One's Own* (1928) combine literary criticism and biography to reinvent history for women writers. More direct than *Orlando*, both *Aphra Behn* and *A Room of One's Own* are, in different ways, feminist polemics that employ disruptive narrative strategies that challenge gender, sexuality, the unified subject, biography, and history, all the while celebrating women writers.

[handwritten: how "on" or "challenge" sexuality?]

A Room of One's Own is not usually cited for its use of biography, yet it does effectively rewrite the biographies of women writers in order to support its larger feminist goals, as I will argue in the second section of this chapter. Sackville-West is not usually thought of as a feminist writer, yet her work celebrates feminine desire and exemplifies a type of feminist practice. Sackville-West led a life consistent with feminist goals, even though she did not consider herself a feminist – a refusal to be categorized that parallels Woolf's rejection of categories of sexuality. Sackville-West's refusal to accept the feminist label is in keeping with her rejection of gender, sexuality, and other categories of identity. She was infuriated, for instance, at being defined by her marriage, as she wrote to her husband: 'I've been absolutely enraged by a book about Knole, in which ... I am described as "the wife of the Hon. Harold Nicolson, C.M.G." ... I do resent being dismissed as merely somebody's wife – with no existence of my own ... Very, very cross about this. You know I'm not a feminist, but there are limits' (7 Feb. 1945, 361). In the margin of her copy of sexologist Otto Weininger's *Sex and Character*, Sackville-West wrote 'I disagree' next to the assertion 'When [women] marry they give up their own name and assume that of their husband without any sense of loss' (Glendinning 405). Although she did not directly write about it, she made sure that Harold Nicolson was fully aware of her support for equality for women. After a conversation on the subject, he wrote in his diary that her position 'saddens me. I know that there is no such thing as equality between the sexes and that women are not fulfilling their proper functions unless subservient to some man. But I do not say so, as it would hurt Vita's feelings' (23 Feb. 1934; quoted in Glendinning 270). Sackville-West's support for women's equality was clear to her husband, and it comes through in her biography of Behn, where she champions a woman who also spoke her mind.

A Room of One's Own, Rachel Bowlby writes, calls for a reconsideration of women and writing: 'Not only is fictional writing considered historically important [according to Woolf], but "rewriting" history now appears not so much as a rectification in the light of new evidence but as the telling of a different story, elicited by new questions asked of the evidence' (*Virginia Woolf* 30). In Bowlby's reading, this revision of history depends on women's ability to escape thinking along the tracks historians have been trained to follow. Arguing that Woolf uses deconstruction as a feminist methodology, Bowlby sees her suggesting a strategy in which 'the woman reader can begin to break down the apparent coherence of that writing by questioning it on its own terms,

by writing her own marginal comments, revealing the limits of logic
there all the time but never before shown up' (34–5). According to
Bowlby, as well as to Marianne Hirsch, Peggy Kamuf, and Toril Moi,
Woolf models this disruptive narrative strategy *In a Room of One's Own*
through the use of multiple perspectives (Moi 9), evasive narrators
(Mary Beton, Seton, or Carmichael), interruptions (Kamuf), digressions
(Bowlby 35), and oscillations (Hirsch 93). The strategies at work in *A
Room of One's Own* are also used in *Orlando* and in Sackville-West's
Aphra Behn to the same ends. In addition to promoting Woolf's and
Sackville-West's particular brands of feminism, these strategies under-
mine the authority of history by deconstructing biography and promot-
ing women's sexuality through a discourse that evades censorship.

Toril Moi concludes that Woolf's self-consciously destabilized use of
language in *A Room of One's Own* 'reveals a deeply sceptical attitude to
the male-humanist concept of an essential human identity' (9).[1] We
have seen this scepticism illustrated in *Orlando*, which I have argued
challenges biography's reinforcement of the unified subject (see chapter
4). I have also argued that *Orlando* illustrates Woolf's call, in 'The New
Biography,' for history to free itself from its worship of great men (231)
and servitude to facts in order to represent life as 'that queer amalga-
mation of dream and reality' (234–5). Despite its subtitle, however,
Woolf did not intend *Orlando* to be taken as a serious biography. What,
then, would a biography that revised history look like and how would
it represent (or at least resist repressing) sexual desire? I suggest that
Sackville-West's *Aphra Behn* is one answer to that question and that *A
Room of One's Own* is another.

Jane Marcus argues that *A Room of One's Own* is Woolf's attempt to
convince Sackville-West to become a feminist (166). We have seen that
Sackville-West influenced Woolf more than has been supposed, and I
suggest that this is particularly apparent in *A Room of One's Own*, which
draws on Sackville-West's theory of sexuality and her biography of
Aphra Behn. *Aphra Behn* reveals her feminist practice, an important
part of which is the refusal to be labelled, which we saw developed in
her theory of sexuality. Like her sexuality, Sackville-West's feminism
was performative.

Aphra Behn was published as part of a series of biographies edited by
Francis Birrell entitled 'Representative Women,' an early attempt to
expand the literary canon through the inclusion of women writers.[2]
Birrell describes the project, in a page-long note included at the back of
the book, as an attempt to 'give in biographical form a picture of female

accomplishment throughout the ages.' This list, according to Birrell, challenges the suggestion that 'women after centuries of claustration are at last coming into their own' (95). Birrell's argument, one taken up again by feminists in the 1970s and 1980s, is that women have been accomplishing great things, which have been shamefully ignored. Birrell concludes that the series will demonstrate 'that no period in the world's history has lacked women of energy and character able to leave a mark on their times' (95). In *A Room of One's Own* Woolf also celebrates the women writers (including Behn) who have succeeded against the odds, complementing this retrieval of women with the argument that material constraints have made it nearly impossible for women to write.[3]

Sackville-West wrote *Aphra Behn: The Incomparable Astrea* during the summer of 1927.[4] It was published on 9 October 1927, the very day Woolf wrote to tell Sackville-West she had begun writing *Orlando* (3:428). Before she had read *Aphra Behn*, Woolf wrote to Sackville-West: 'I think its a very good plan to have some straightforward work like Aphra to keep one's machinery engaged' (21 Aug. 1927, 3:409). They saw each other frequently during this time, when the 'machinery' of Woolf's imagination was just beginning to engage the prospect of *Orlando*. It is impossible to tell how much their conversation about *Aphra Behn* influenced Woolf's conception of her project, but the problems of writing biography evidently occupied both of them. As a component of their literary exchange on the subject of biographies, *Aphra Behn* is significant not only for its subject and its engagement with the problems of documentation and undecidability but also for the intrusive narrator, who prefigures *Orlando*'s self-conscious Biographer.

To rescue a woman writer from the neglect of history and tell her story in a way that shows her to be both compelling and powerful is a fantasy shared by biographers and feminists. Rachel Bowlby credits Woolf with initiating the rescue of women writers ('Trained' 180), but, while Woolf wrote in glowing terms of Aphra Behn in *A Room of One's Own* in 1928, the first rescue attempt was made a year earlier in Sackville-West's *Aphra Behn*. Woolf's condensed version of Behn's life differs in emphasis, as we shall see, but all of the details she includes, even the quotations, appear in Sackville-West's earlier book, suggesting that it was the primary source for Woolf's comments. Since their initial efforts, Aphra Behn has been the object of a continuing rescue attempt by feminist biographers and scholars, who have reintroduced her into the canon by including her work in their classes and research.[5] Opening the canon to Aphra Behn not only reintroduces an excluded woman but not just "Dreams"

also, because of the content of her work and the facts of her life, compels attention to female sexual desire. There has been, not surprisingly, a certain resistance to the latter consequence. Desiring women are not easily included in the male-dominated literary canon. Unless they come in the guise of Eve-figures, fallen women whose notoriety provides a model for Behn's own reputation, women in literature are angels in the canonical house. Sackville-West's biography rejects the traditional polarization of women into saints or whores, rewriting Behn's story in a different voice, a voice characterized by self-conscious multiplicity of subject, biographer, and history instead of unified authority.

A seventeenth-century playwright, poet, novelist, spy, and libertine, Behn was the first woman in England to support herself as a professional writer. Under the pen name 'Astrea,' her most popular works, such as the Restoration comedy *The Rover* (1677) and the novella *Oroonoko* (1688), garnered her a reputation during and immediately after her lifetime equal to that of Dryden and Rochester. Her literary status changed dramatically in the eighteenth and nineteenth centuries, when her life and work came to be considered indecent. Richardson and Fielding, writes Janet Todd, 'vilified her as unwomanly' (2). Her plays, as Angeline Goreau points out, were comparable in licentious content to those of her male contemporaries, but, when written by a woman, expressions of sexual desire and erotic activity typical of late seventeenth-century literature were considered obscene by the Victorian standards Sackville-West sought to transform.[6] Similarly, Behn's life itself contributed to her reputation – or lack thereof. After her husband died, she neither remarried nor returned to her family, but made her own way, first as a secret agent for Charles II and then as a successful writer, with a stint in debtors' prison in between. She disregarded conventional standards of behaviour for women by writing professionally and by the conduct of her private life. She went about freely in public, drank, and had love affairs with men (and perhaps women)[7] in which she behaved much as any man in her position might be expected to behave.

Readers of *Orlando* would recognize in Behn's life a model for Orlando's own amorous adventures prior to the chilling of desire in the nineteenth century (226). In short, she acted in keeping with the standards imposed upon any other professional (i.e., male) writer of the time; for a woman this behaviour was scandalous. Behn worked for money, placing herself on the open market as a writer. A professional writer, involved with the theatre no less, she was looked upon as little more than a prostitute – an opinion her behaviour corroborated.[8] Promiscuity in a man is called something else in a woman. Caring as little for regulations as Sackville-West did, Behn was apparently undisturbed by being labelled a whore. Her work was considered a corrupting influence. She shamelessly made public her words and her sexual desires, and for this she was silenced. To rescue Aphra Behn from obscurity is, as Woolf claims Behn herself did, to earn for women the right to speak our minds.

Aphra Behn was published a year before *The Well of Loneliness*, and even before that caveat Sackville-West is careful in her attempt to reconstruct Behn as a respectable writer. Omitting any reference to poems such as 'To the Fair Clarinda, Who Made Love to Me, Imagined More than Woman' (6:363), 'To My Lady Morland at Tunbridge' (6:175) or 'On her Loving Two Equally' (6:189). Sackville-West knew better than to call attention to the homoerotic content of Behn's work. However, she does not disguise the fact that her defence of Behn is also a defence of women's sexuality. A neglected, disreputable figure when Sackville-West was writing, Behn had been the subject of inaccurate, disreputable biographies. Sackville-West's biography was a direct response to the *Dictionary of National Biography (DNB)* entry on Behn, written by Edmund Gosse, which laments: '[Mrs Behn] deserves our sympathy as a warmhearted, gifted, and industrious woman, who was forced by circumstances and temperament to win her livelihood in a profession where scandalous writing was at that time obligatory' (2:130). By insisting that readers respect rather than pity Behn, Sackville-West rescues her from the effects of history by interpreting her behaviour and her writing as lively and spirited. Sackville-West calls Behn's reputation as a pornographer exaggerated (49), arguing instead that she was 'an exceedingly moral and idealistic writer' (50). Sackville-West makes this argument by placing Behn's work in context: 'Let it be clearly understood that I am making no attempt to whitewash her, or to represent her as other than she was. She meant to enjoy herself, and she meant to be a popular writer; she was an attractive woman, so she found plenty of men ready to make love to her; her tastes were naturally coarse, the tastes of her day were coarse, so she gratified both herself and her audience by indulging in coarseness' (49). Sackville-West defends Behn against the imposition of nineteenth-century prudishness on a late seventeenth-century sensibility. She also cautions against confusing the details of Behn's literature with the facts of her life. Explaining that her own conclusions about Behn are derived from the general tone and theme of her written work, Sackville-West is careful to insist that literary and biographical interpretations are simply that: 'How dangerous, however are these literary exercises! How fatally easy to construct a case, almost any case, by a little adjustment of the data!' (47). Calling attention to the constructed nature of biography and literary criticism, Sackville-West reinvents Behn by disrupting facts, biographical authority, and the repression of women's sexuality.

Sackville-West's treatment of Behn's life is structured around direct confrontations with the inaccuracies previously perpetrated about Behn. The biography begins with a rehearsal of the points of contention in the narrative of Behn's life: 'Her parentage, the place of her birth, the status of her father, the spelling of her name, the scenes of her childhood and adolescence, the spelling of her husband's name, the very existence of her husband, all have been subjects of dispute. It makes matters ticklish and exciting for her biographer' (11). By this account, Sackville-West could hardly have chosen a more uncertain subject, yet she faces the plethora of conflicting evidence with obvious enthusiasm. In fact, she organizes her biography around the disputes she enumerates, substituting attention to factual lack for documented certainty. The biography alternates between two narratives: the story of Behn's life is interspersed with the story of the impossibility of determining the facts of her life. Even Sackville-West's opinion of Behn and her work is in conflict.

According to Sackville-West, Behn 'disappears at an early age from the shores of England and the pages of reputable biography. From the moment when she was carried, an infant in arms, past the hop gardens and into the church under the green hill at Wye, she set out on a career rich in contradiction and controversy' (11). The disputes over the facts of her life, then, parallel the life itself. Both are fraught with 'contradiction and controversy,' and Behn, disappearing from 'the pages of reputable biography,' is found only in a disreputable life unreliably reported.

The scene Sackville-West imagines of Behn being carried into church is significant because it is over the data generated by this event – Behn's baptism – that the first dispute arises. Sackville-West begins by telling the story of parish records consulted and misread, misinformation disseminated, facts checked, interpreted, and ignored. Indeed, the story Sackville-West tells throughout is the story of the construction of Behn's life in writing, and that story begins not with her birth but with the creation of the first piece of biographical data: the entry of her baptism in the Wye parish register. Behn enters and leaves the certainty of recorded history at one and the same moment. The disputed record of her baptism at once marks the beginning of her biography and her disappearance from 'reputable biography.' Truly under erasure, Behn is absent because no fact about her can be authenticated and because the unauthorized story is disreputable: 'There was a time when the name of Aphra Behn might scarcely be mentioned, or mentioned only apologetically; it was synonymous for all that was bawdy both in life and literature' (12). Sackville-West rescues Behn from disrepute by examining the disruption of the facts of her life. Sackville-West will settle the score by rereading Behn's life and work and the disreputable biographies that arose from both. Sackville-West searches out the source of the rumours and the generation of the false biographies, permitting the troubled data that result to remain unsettled and unjudged. She does not forge a coherent narrative from the gaps and conflicts in the evidence, and she calls attention to the false stability of interpretation: 'I have myself devised at least three theories, all based on her own writings, to explain Astrea's morals. All are equally satisfactory, all equally untrustworthy' (48).

In *Aphra Behn* Sackville-West deals with questions of doubt in a lucid, straightforward, and expedient manner, even making it clear that she understands the need to avoid 'examinations too minute to be anything but wearisome to the general reader' (12). Difficulties of identity are raised at once: 'Is he [Behn's biographer] to call her Aphra, Ayfara, Aphara, Aphora, Afra, Apharra, Afara, or, more fantastically, Aphaw or even Fyhare? Is he to call her Amis or Johnson? Is he to write Behn, Bhen, or Behen? Is he to keep her at Wye or send her off to Surinam? If he is to send her to Surinam, is he to send her there once, or twice? Is he to believe in Van der Albert and Van Bruin? She lies under a black slab in Westminster Abbey, and cannot answer these questions' (11). These are the questions that will structure Sackville-West's investigation into Behn's life, and they are presented in the context of the traditional biographer's desire to construct a stable narrative in the face of the absence of all but the single fact of Behn's death and burial in Westminster Abbey. Instead of puzzling out a coherent narrative, she emphasizes, instead, the inconclusive research process in a biography that is performative rather than authoritative.

Sackville-West refuses to come to unjustified conclusions simply for the sake of expediency, and she is untroubled by the lack of closure this produces. Even when she does come to reasonable conclusions, she deliberately reopens issues that might otherwise be considered settled.

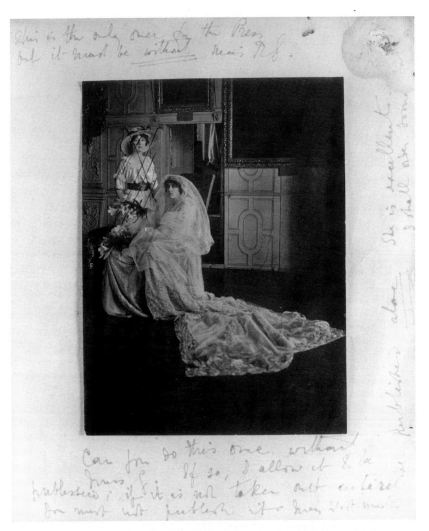

1. Proof of Vita Sackville-West's wedding portrait with Rosamund Grosvenor. Sackville-West's mother, Lady Sackville, has crossed through the image of Grosvenor and written in the margin: 'This is the only one for the Press but it must be *without* Miss R G. Can you do this one without Miss G. If so, I allow it to be published; if it is not taken out entirely you must not publish it. Miss West must be published *alone*. She is excellent I shall order some too' (1 Oct. 1913; see Glendinning [following 106] for the retouched photograph in which Grosvenor has been removed and Sackville-West's nose has been shortened).

2. The garden side of Knole, the estate where Vita Sackville-West grew up but which she could not inherit. Sackville-West describes it in *Knole and the Sackvilles*: 'The other side is the garden side – the gay, princely side, with flowers in the foreground; the grey walls rising straight up from the green turf; the mullioned windows, and the Tudor gables with the heraldic leopards sitting stiffly at each corner' (1–2).

3. Vita Sackville-West's sitting room at Long Barn (her home with Harold Nicolson from 1915 until they moved to Sissinghurst in 1932). 'And to think,' Sackville-West wrote to Woolf, 'how the ceilings of Long Barn once swayed above us!' (19 Dec. 1938, 417).

4. Virginia Woolf with Vita Sackville-West's sons, Nigel and Benedict Nicolson, photographed by Sackville-West at Knole (1927). In anticipation of Woolf's visit to Knole, Sackville-West wrote to her: 'I've got a lovely full moon (or nearly) for you – I've just been out looking at the court; it's now midnight; I like the battlements in the moonlight and the frost. You *will* stay over Tuesday night, won't you? And I'll motor you up to London on Wednesday morning. Do remember what a dreadfully long time it will be before I see you again' (15 Jan. 1927, 162).

5. Vita Sackville-West sitting on a ship's railing en route to Persia (Jan. 1926). Sackville-West wrote to Woolf from somewhere off the coast of Greece: 'You must imagine me please, as sitting up in a small bunk, at an angle of 45, with my suit-case tobogganing up and down the floor, and all my possessions disappearing under my bed; the ship filled with the clatter of crockery at every lurch; and me trying to write to you. But you see one's whole system of values changes, and the important thing is merely to keep one's balance—' (23 Jan, 1926, 91).

6. Virginia Woolf photographed by Sackville-West at Rodmell (June 1926).
After this visit Sackville-West wrote to Woolf: 'I must tell you how much I
enjoyed my weekend with you … Darling Virginia, you don't know how
happy I was' (ellipsis original; 17 June 1926, 128).

7. Vita Sackville-West with dog (1928). Sackville-West wrote to Woolf: 'This letter is principally to say that Potto is not very happy; he mopes; and I am not sure he has not got the mange; so he will probably insist on being brought back to Mrs Woof on Wednesday ...' (5 Oct. 1928, 286).

8. Virginia Woolf photographed by Vita Sackville-West on their trip to France (September 1928). After their return Sackville-West wrote to Woolf: 'I've returned home a changed being. All this summer I was as nervous as a cat, – starting, dreaming, brooding, – now I'm all vigorous and sturdy again, and ravenous for life once more. And all thanks to you ... My dearest I do love you' (5 Oct. 1928, 286). Woolf responded: 'I shant say anything: not a word of the balm to my anguish – for I am always anguished – that you were to me ... somewhere I have seen a little ball kept bubbling up and down on the spray of a fountain: the fountain is you; the ball me. It is a sensation I get only from you. It is physically stimulating, restful at the same time I feel suppled and anointed now' (7 Oct. 1928, 3:540).

9. One of the photographs of Vita Sackville-West with her dogs taken by Leonard Woolf for *Orlando* (29 April 1928). Woolf wrote to Sackville-West: 'I wanted to ask you if it would be convenient should we call in on Sunday on our way back [from Rodmell]; at Long Barn. It has now become essential to have a photograph of Orlando in country clothes in a wood, to end with' (27 April 1928, 3:488).

Appendix I is dedicated to this process, beginning: 'What was the date of Mrs Behn's visit to Surinam? We have a number of conflicting statements to consider' (87). In the last paragraph of the appendix, the initial question of Behn's maiden name is thrown open once again: 'I am not at all satisfied in my own mind that the problem of her birth and parentage has been really solved. The persistence of the name Johnson, to my mind, has not been really explained away, even by the evidence of the parish register at Wye' (89). Revisiting in its final pages the disputes that introduced the book indicates not only a willingness to hold open questions but an insistence on indeterminacy.

Even when Sackville-West engages in narrative reconstructions of key events she maintains contradictions. Describing the events following Behn's husband's death, in what can only be an invented scene, she first depicts Behn's mother refusing to take in her widowed daughter. In an equally lively picture, Behn is imagined choosing independence over a return to her loving family. After filling in this gap in the story with two conflicting possibilities, she concludes: 'it is all conjecture. At all events it is certain that it was not to her family that she turned, but to the [royal] court' (33). Sackville-West emphasizes the slippery nature of biography, particularly when documentation is scarce. She complicates this point further for literary biographies by asserting that relying on what a writer wrote to inform her biography is dangerous: 'though it would be a possible contention that Mrs Behn's pen wrote, and wrote with gusto, words which Mrs Behn's tongue would have refused to utter, the converse might equally have chanced to be true' (48).

Aphra Behn exemplifies a strategy more fully developed by Woolf in *Orlando*, in which the narrator assumes a presence in the text and a critical distance from both the subject and the biographical project itself. These are rhetorical strategies, very much in opposition to traditional English biographies of the late nineteenth and early twentieth centuries. Such strategies allow the biographer to criticize as well as admire the subject, and, more significantly, to indicate a level of self-awareness about the constructed nature of the subject in biography. The structure of *Aphra Behn*, organized as it is around disputes about the subject, certainly, allows us to read the book as a self-conscious performance of the task of biography. The narrator's own awareness of this act, however, is an additional element in the disruption of the traditional method of biography as the seamless presentation of a unified subjectivity. Distinguishing herself from the traditional biographer who asks – and answers – factual questions about Behn's life, Sackville-West does not present the facts uncontested, and she does not stick to the facts once they are presented. She comments on Behn's life with a self-consciousness that allows both critical commentary on and wry irreverence for the serious task of biography.

When the narrator refuses to come to the sorts of conclusions traditional biographies lead us to expect, *Aphra Behn* sounds remarkably like *Orlando*. After presenting one of Behn's poems as evidence that Behn had writer's block, Sackville-West comments, 'It is a somewhat ambiguous verse, which may be interpreted according to the taste of the reader, and is here offered without comment' (32). At the end of a story of Behn's romantic exploits with two Dutchmen, Sackville-West calls the tale into question by saying the incident 'bears, to say the least of it, a suspicious family likeness to the regular stock-in-trade of Restoration comedy and the Italian novella' (39). Then she dismisses her own dismissal: 'It is all good farce, and whether it is true or not does not, after all, very much matter' (39). Such comments throw the narrative open to interpretation and undermine any attempt to establish a single truth by making a joke of the biographical demand for accuracy. The dismissal of the importance of truth value allows Sackville-West to include sexually suggestive material, even though it is only speculative, even as she undermines it by questioning its veracity.

When referencing Behn's past biographers, Sackville-West proposes compromise and suggests various acceptable conclusions. Opinions differed, for example, on the question of whether or not Behn had actually been to Surinam. Behn herself is not credited as a trustworthy witness, and her accounts are not always historically or geographically accurate. Consistent with her own fluid attitude towards facts, Sackville-West suggests that Behn's work is a mixture of truth and invention, a solution that made earlier biographers uneasy. Addressing herself specifically to Dr Bernbaum, whose 'destructive arguments' (9) she notes throughout, Sackville-west comments, 'it may seem strange that so obvious a compromise should not have occurred to him' (25). She is willing to suppose that Dr Bernbaum might be correct in his assertion that Behn had never gone to Surinam and that the tales of her travels were mere inventions, in which case 'the fact would emerge that she [Behn] was a far finer novelist than has hitherto been supposed. She would leap at once in our estimation from the respectable class of the realist to the giddier heights of the imaginative writer' (28). In either case, Behn's reputation is exonerated, and Sackville-West's flexibility is demonstrated.[9]

Sackville-West's references to prior biographies provide her with opportunities to consider directly the position of the biographer and the biographer's relationship to the subject, even though this digression takes her narrative far afield. She pursues Dr Bernbaum's theory that the 1696 *Life and Memoirs* 'written by one of the fair sex' was actually written not by Behn (as was previously supposed) or by a female friend, but by Charles Gildon, a 'literary hack' (31) 'adept at literary hoaxes' (30). Gildon's supposed hoax leads Sackville-West to speculate on his position as a literary cross-dresser who gained authority to speak about the life of a woman by passing as one himself: 'it had already occurred to him [Gildon] in his own avowed *Account* [*of the Life of the incomparable Mrs Behn* (1690)] that: "To draw her to the life, one must write like her, that is, with all the softness of her sex and all the fire of ours"' (30). Sackville-West reads this sentence as a declaration of Gildon's desire to become, at least on paper, a woman, as well as a description of Behn's bi-gendered writing. Writing and gender identity become intertwined as Gildon imagines Behn as a textual cross-dresser whose feminine appearance and rhetorical style camouflage the masculine content and passion of her work. She appears passive but is, in fact, active as a writer and a passionate woman. This mixture of masculine and feminine characteristics resembles Sackville-West's own gender position. Her digression on biographers and the veracity of Behn's supposed memoir lead circuitously towards a disruption of Behn's gender identity and an assertion of the sexual content of her life and works. As usual, Sackville-West throws the entire discussion into the air with the conclusion: 'The authorship of the *Life and Memoirs* is not perhaps a very interesting question' (30). Ultimately, it does not matter to her who wrote the work, whether it is autobiography or biography, or whether the author was a man or a woman, and none of these issues has any bearing on whether or not it tells the truth.

In *Aphra Behn* uncertainty is of no consequence. Factual debates are entered and abandoned without anxiety. This critical distance is extended to Behn herself. Sackville-West begins the biography with a critical judgment, 'let us say straight away that Aphra Behn is no Shakespeare' (11–12). She returns to her evaluation of Behn at the conclusion: 'it is Aphra the woman of whom I have grown fond, to the extent of forgiving Aphra the writer the tedious hours she has compelled me to spend over her volumes' (84–5). Neither pretentious nor daunted, Sackville-West unhesitatingly says what she thinks, and she has no qualms about dividing her opinion of the writer from her feelings for the person about whom she has written. Nor is she concerned to assert biographical authority; indeed, she suggests that she is merely a reader responding to a writer, rather than a Victorian-style biographer holding up the larger-than-life model for adulation. In Sackville-West's hands, Aphra Behn is not disreputable, but neither is she the 'Noble, upright, chaste, severe' subject Woolf ascribes to Victorian biographies ('The New Biography' 231).

Sackville-West presents Aphra Behn as a role model, but she is not the model one would expect to find in a biography of its time: 'Sensible Astrea. Miss Julia Kavanagh, writing in 1863, thought otherwise. But Astrea, living in 1670, knew that her two greatest assets were her charm and her pen, and she had no scruples about using both to procure for herself the comfort, fun, and popularity, that she desired. "Give me but love and wine," she exclaimed' (45). By celebrating Behn's *joie de vivre*, she implicitly encourages her readers to emulate Behn's life even as they rediscover Behn's work. This was not Woolf's father's idea of biography. Sackville-West shuns the biographical tradition with her intrusive narrator, digressions, conflicting evidence, undermining of the biographer's authority, attention to biography as a construct, insistence on the unknowablity of history, criticism of the quality of Behn's work, and frequent references to Behn's masculinity, femininity, sexuality, and sexual conduct. Her concluding portrait of Behn retains the conflicts but prescribes admiration: 'Gay, tragic, generous, smutty, rich of nature and big of heart, propping her elbows on the tavern table, cracking her jokes, penning those midnight letters to her sad lover by the light of a tallow dip, – this is the Aphra of whom one cannot take leave without respect' (85). Sackville-West rewrites history and Behn's reputation by asserting unknowablity and redefining respectability.

Instead of blindly following the rules of traditional biography, Sackville-West presents data as fallible in itself and as leading to erroneous – and irrelevant – conclusions. Questioning and dismissing the structure and assumptions of traditional biography parallels Sackville-West's wilful flaunting of convention in her personal life. A biography that represents, instead of reinforces, patriarchal Law is also able to resist the similar demand for maintenance of the illusion of the unified subject. The ironic tone that emerges in her *Aphra Behn* suggests the beginnings of self-consciousness as an aspect of the narrative. This self-consciousness about the constructed nature of the biographical form – a form that typically dictates the structure of a narrative that produces a coherent, unified subject – parallels her simultaneous recognition and defiance of the dominant culture as it is governed by the Law of the Father.

Sackville-West thus couples the reformation of the feminine biographical subject with a transformation of the biographical form. Along with feminine sexuality comes uncertainty and instability; along with feminine sexuality comes the exposure of the illusion of the unified subject position. The emergence of feminine sexuality exposes the split subject – two absences upon which patriarchy depends – since feminine sexuality challenges male reproductive dominance.

Unlike Woolf's *A Room of One's Own*, Sackville-West's biography of Aphra Behn is not thesis driven, even though its role in the *Representative Women* series defines its feminist agenda. Like Woolf, Sackville-West is determined to recover Behn as a model for all women with ambition and spirit – especially for women who want to write. But just as she does not manipulate evidence to create a coherent version of Behn's life, neither does she alter her own appraisal of Behn in order to reclaim her as a long-lost literary genius. Less interested in the quality of Behn's work than in the injustice of its repression, she champions the genius of Behn's unrepressed life and uncensored work. Behn becomes a model of a desiring woman and Sackville-West's biography exemplifies how to imagine one. In *Aphra Behn* she makes up a woman complete with gaps and guesses and contradictions and desires.

In her biography of Behn, Sackville-West introduces Woolf not only to the first professional woman writer, but also to the self-conscious narrator who recognizes the gaps in historical knowledge and the desires of the biographical subject. The development of a self-conscious narrator in biography exemplifies the reciprocal nature of the Woolf/Sackville-West collaboration. Woolf's interests in women writers and the constructed representation of identity may very well have inspired Sackville-West in the writing of *Aphra Behn*, and the self-conscious narrator emerges fully formed in *Orlando* and Aphra Behn herself appears in *A Room of One's Own*.

Liking Women in *A Room of One's Own*: Coded Desire and Gender Instability

If one could be friendly with women, what a pleasure – the relationship so secret & private compared with relations with men. Why not write about it? truthfully?

Woolf, Diary (1 Nov. 1924, 2:320)

[*The Well of Loneliness*] is a perfectly serious attempt to write a quite frank and completely unpornographic book about [homosexuality] ... Of course I simply *itch* to try the same thing myself.

Vita Sackville-West to Harold Nicolson (4 Aug. 1928,
emphasis original, quoted in Glendinning 199)

If Chloe likes Olivia and Mary Carmichael·knows how to express it she will light a torch in that vast chamber where nobody has yet been.

Woolf, *A Room of One's Own* (88)

On 20 and 26 October 1928, nine days after the publication of *Orlando*, Woolf lectured on 'women and fiction' first at Newnham and then at Girton, women's colleges at Cambridge University. She subsequently revised the lecture for publication as *A Room of One's Own* (1929). In this complex and ambitious essay, one of Woolf's projects is to create a canon of women writers. Using information provided by Sackville-West, Woolf hails Aphra Behn with unqualified acclaim. In *A Room of One's Own* Woolf gives only the briefest outline of Behn's life and provides no details about her work. Like Sackville-West, Woolf emphasizes Behn's place in history as the first professional woman writer, being careful to applaud Behn as an important and industrious writer: 'Mrs. Behn was a middle-class woman with all the plebeian virtues of humour, vitality and courage; a woman forced by the death of her husband and some unfortunate adventures of her own to make her living by her wits. She had to work on equal terms with men. She made, by working very hard, enough to live on. The importance of that fact outweighs anything that she actually wrote, even the splendid "A Thousand Martyrs I have made," or "Love in Fantastic Triumph sat" for here begins the freedom of the mind, or rather the possibility that in the course of time the mind will be free to write what it likes' (67). Here, Woolf condenses Sackville-West's portrait of Behn, suggesting that Behn's difficulties could have happened to anyone, and that in the face of them she drew on her talent and courage to produce not only a living but masterpieces. The two poems Woolf refers to are reproduced in their entirety in Sackville-West's biography and are the only works of Behn that Sackville-West praises. The titles are thoroughly wholesome, making it difficult to imagine why one would object to a poet who writes of love or martyrdom as indecent. Woolf makes no mention of Behn's bawdy, comic plays or the complex issues of race and imperialism raised by *Oroonoko*. Like Sackville-West, Woolf omits references to poems that smack of homoeroticism. She gives us a sanitized version of Behn well suited to support the thesis that given time and money women *can* write.

To defy the refrain 'women can't write, women can't paint' that haunts artist Lily Briscoe (*To the Lighthouse* 75), Woolf presents a Behn who was significant because of her life and her work. Instead of repeating Sackville-West's assertion that these two poems are the only good things Behn wrote, Woolf refers to them as though they are universally admired, the bright spots in a glorious career dimmed only by Behn's even greater accomplishment of having a career at all. Woolf paints Behn in the most flattering light possible. In so doing, she answers Sackville-West's initial call to respect Behn by making up a Behn who is respectable. Woolf is satisfied to save the creation of desiring women for the present, in which 'Chloe liked Olivia' (*A Room of One's Own* 86), in order to make a stronger case for the success of women writers in the past. Woolf's political instincts were clearly on target, and it is she, not Sackville-West, who is credited with recovering Behn, along with other women writers, by reworking their biographies and rewriting literary history.

As a feminist, Woolf challenges the past – both historically and personally – by rewriting the lives of women writers in *A Room of One's Own* (61–81). In chapter 4, she presents a history of English women writers, beginning with Anne Finch (Lady Winchilsea) and including Margaret Cavendish (Margaret of Newcastle), Aphra Behn, Fanny Burney, Eliza Carter, Jane Austen, Charlotte and Emily Brontë, and George Eliot. (Note that the first letters of all the last names fall between A and F.) Rachel Bowlby writes that Woolf: 'pioneered the work of making known the writing of women whose existence had previously been obscured, covered over, by the weight of the masculine canon' ('Trained' 180). While this assertion is certainly true, these women had not in fact, been entirely forgotten.

The first completed issue of the *DNB* ran to sixty-three volumes. The first twenty-one volumes, A through GLA, were completed under the editorship of Woolf's father, Leslie Stephen (1885–90). All of the women Woolf mentions in her revision of literary history in *A Room of One's Own* are included in those first twenty-one volumes of the *DNB*. Stephen himself wrote the entries for Fanny Burney, the Brontës, Jane Austen, and George Eliot.[10] Woolf did not 'discover' the women writers she extols; they would have been well known to her from her father's work. Nor does she look beyond his work to the rest of the alphabet to discover, say, Mary Shelley or Fanny Trollope.

Woolf does keep the work of alphabetically privileged women alive, as Bowlby suggests, but I would argue that her more radical act is in the attitude she takes towards them. She treats them as serious writers impeded by familial expectations and social restrictions. More important, she treats them as intimates, as women with whom she – and by extension her audience – could identify. She presents them as role models. This is not a relationship encouraged by Leslie Stephen's focus on facts and strict judgments of literary and personal merits. His extensive entry for Charlotte Brontë (2:1314–21), for example, is more family portrait than biography. The fifteen-column entry begins with three columns on the father, Patrick Brontë, and even includes a history of Emily Brontë's dog. There is no separate listing for Emily or Anne Brontë, who are treated under their sister's heading along with their father and brother. Leslie Stephen's attention to the literary work of the Brontë sisters focuses on the history of their publications and culminates in pronouncements such as, 'In point of style [*Wuthering Heights*] is superior [to *Jane Eyre*], but it is the nightmare of a recluse, not a direct representation of facts seen by genius. Though enthusiastically admired by good judges, it will hardly be widely appreciated' (2:1319).[11]

Woolf's revision of her father's biographies focuses on the material conditions of the subjects' lives as writers rather than on their family relations. Leslie Stephen, for example, gives particular attention to the thoughtful way in which Charlotte Brontë arranged her marriage so as not to disrupt her father's comfort.[12] Woolf, however, speculates on the potential success Brontë would have had under more favourable circumstances: 'One could not but play for a moment with the thought of what might have happened if Charlotte Brontë had possessed say three hundred a year' (73). This comment evokes the legacy that enabled her (and the narrator of *A Room of One's Own* 37) to become independent and reminds us that she was forcefully aware of the ways in which fathers impede their daughters. A month after giving the lectures that were to become *A Room of One's Own*, Woolf wrote in her diary: 'Father's birthday. He would have been ... 96, yes, today; & could have been 96, like other people one has known; but mercifully was not. His life would have entirely ended mine. What would have happened: No writing, no books; – inconceivable' (28 Nov. 1928, 3:208). In drawing this direct comparison to her own happier circumstances, she not only makes her point about the ways in which Brontë's material conditions crippled her work and the close call she herself had had, but she also engages her audience in a sympathetic identification with Brontë and, indeed, with all women writers.[13]

Woolf's speculation is a variation on the New Biography's mingling of fact and fiction. At the beginning of *A Room of One's Own* she warns: 'Fiction here is likely to contain more truth than fact ... it is for you to seek out this truth and to decide whether any part of it is worth keeping' (4). It is for the reader to choose, because the function of her biographical revision is not just to set the record straight but also to intervene in our ability to imagine the past. Woolf both rescues women writers from potential obscurity and transforms our relationship to them. She rewrites the *DNB* by celebrating women as writers rather than as daughters, and in this way she does not merely invite us to think back or think ahead to the new Judith Shakespeares, she also rewrites biography so that we have mothers to whom we can think back. She models a way of thinking about the past that frees her audience from the restraints imposed by Victorian biography by guiltlessly celebrating the death of the biographer-father.

I see *A Room of One's Own* not so much as an Oedipal challenge to patriarchal authority (which I do see in *Orlando*'s irreverent Biographer's refusal to follow the rules of biography) as an alternative biographical practice that emerges out of a redefined relationship to the authority of history. It models a new role for the biographer. No longer the authority on the facts of his subject's life, Woolf's Mary Seton, Mary Beton, or Mary Carmichael is a biographer who enjoys imagining her subjects and invites us to do the same. As much figures of fantasy as historical subjects, anecdotes capture her imagination far more than dates do. Truth is in the fiction she creates around her subjects, not in the verifiable facts of their sad lives.

In rewriting the biographies of these women, Woolf models a relationship that invites intimacy, opinion, fantasy, and affection – ingredients left out of the *DNB*. *A Room of One's Own* is history that allowed the women students of Newnham and Girton who made up Woolf's original audience to imagine themselves as writers in 1928 because they could imagine women writers in the past. It allowed them to imagine a future for women writers to come, and it allowed them to imagine literature in which 'Chloe liked Olivia' (86). For without the social restraints that prevented women from speaking their minds, they could also freely express their desires. As *A Room of One's Own* demonstrates, we need mothers *in* the past and mothers *of* the past. Woolf demonstrates a mothering biographical practice in which subjects are nurtured and embraced rather than scolded and judged.

For Sackville-West, Aphra Behn's attraction was her life, not her work. For her purposes in *A Room of One's Own*, Woolf imagines a Behn who was significant for her life's work. Woolf revises Sackville-West's judgment about Behn's talent, but both were in agreement when celebrating Behn as the first professional woman writer. Woolf and Sackville-West revolutionized biography not by writing about women but by liking the women about whom they wrote. The room that Woolf built is one in which women can love and women can write – and she gives us portraits of women doing exactly that, including the narrator and, when the essay was presented as a lecture, herself. Woolf's sister, Vanessa Bell, attended the lecture Woolf gave at Newnham on 20 October 1928, and, as Jane Marcus notes, Sackville-West went with Woolf to the Girton lecture on 26 October 1928 (*Languages* 166). So there she was: Virginia Woolf, a woman who loved women as sisters and lovers reading what she, a woman writer, had written. She was asked to speak about women and fiction. She showed that it is through fiction that women can find, and love, and celebrate women. It is in fiction that we find the truth, Woolf says at the beginning of her essay, and at the end she reveals it: 'The truth is,' she writes, 'I often like women. I like their unconventionality. I like their subtlety. I like their anonymity. I like – but I must not run on in this way' (115).

Aphra Behn and *A Room of One's Own* share the feminist mission of restoring women writers to the literary canon, and they do so by coming to the same conclusion: Sackville-West and Woolf like Aphra Behn. Indeed, as Woolf concludes, they like women. As careful as they are to avoid censorship, both projects nevertheless restore desire to women. The Aphra Behn they recreate is crucial to their endeavour because during her lifetime her work was applauded rather than banned. She was not forced to self-censor or resort to code to express desire. This is why she was found disreputable during the nineteenth century, and why she is so important to Woolf and Sackville-West in imagining desiring women. She was a woman who spoke her mind. In *A Room of One's Own* Woolf's narrator says that women writers need a tradition of women writers: 'For we think back through our mothers if we are women' (79). As they imagined mothers for one another, in Aphra Behn Woolf and Sackville-West imagined a mother for all women.

Aphra Behn spoke her mind, and at the end of *A Room of One's Own* Woolf charges her audience to imagine a future in which women will be able to do so again. She was well aware, however, that in 1928 that time had not arrived. Three months earlier, on 2 July 1928, Parliament had passed into law the Equal Franchise Act, giving women the same voting rights as men.[14] But this was not the end to Woolf's fight for women's rights to self-expression. In order to speak of desire, especially homo-

*how 'androgyny'
was a false promise*

erotic desire, she would still need to speak in metaphors and codes. One of her most discussed references to sexuality is her allusion to androgyny in *A Room of One's Own* (102–3); discussions of her attitude towards and depiction of sexuality are often connected to this difficult and variously explicated passage.[15]

Critical interpretations of Woolf's notion of androgyny frequently replicate the repression of female sexuality Woolf and Sackville-West struggle to circumvent. Androgyny is a subject that has the appearance of addressing sexual desire, since it is often connected to Woolf's same-sex erotic practice and emotional attachments. However, such discussions of androgyny commonly follow the practice reproved by Valerie Traub of conflating gender and sexuality. Initially giving the appearance of avoiding this misrepresentation by allusions to lesbianism, such discussions nevertheless avoid engaging questions of sexuality and erotic practice after suggesting that they will address them.[16]

This pattern is also discernable in discussions of androgyny that deal specifically with *Orlando*: self-knowledge is substituted for sexuality, and emotional ties take the place of erotic practice. Joanne Trautmann's intuitive discussion of androgyny in *Orlando* is more extensive than most. While I do not wish to be critical of Trautmann, whose pioneering work on Woolf and sexuality has been undervalued, this early comment nicely exemplifies the difficulties many Woolf scholars have faced: 'In her treatment of Orlando as an androgynous figure, Virginia Woolf is clearly glorifying those androgynous elements we have seen in Vita Sackville-West's appearance and values ... Virginia Woolf investigates the emotional aspects of Vita's lesbian interests, and shows Orlando capable of knowing both men and women better ... through *Orlando* Virginia Woolf illustrates how one woman may understand her full, androgynous self by coming close to another. The women to whom Orlando feels close – Sasha and the prostitutes – help her find a wider definition of her own womanliness' ('*Orlando* and Vita Sackville-West' 91–2). Trautmann does not claim to be addressing female sexuality, which is, in effect, my point. She is careful to say that Woolf is investigating the '*emotional* aspects' of lesbianism, but exactly what these aspects are and how they can be separated from erotic practice is unspecified. She also implies that the goal of an erotic attraction is self-knowledge and that Orlando's relationships with other women result in the fact that now she can 'understand her full, androgynous self,' which somehow becomes wider without challenging 'her own womanliness.' Orlando's sexual desire and erotic practice is obscured behind terms like 'coming close to,' and the result of her relationships with women gives her a 'definition' rather than a sexual practice.

As it has been constructed by Woolf scholars, androgyny allows Trautmann to focus on emotions and self-knowledge while avoiding contact with sexuality. A vague treatment of gender identity replaces any treatment (even emotional) of 'Vita's lesbian interests.' How a 'wider definition of ... womanliness,' which one assumes includes 'the necessity for women to recognize their masculine qualities' ('*Orlando* and Vita Sackville-West' 91), comes from contact with women is unclear. The very term 'womanliness' threatens to reinforce patriarchal notions of passive femininity while simultaneously conflating gender with sexuality, conveniently forgetting, as Traub argues, erotic practice (*Desire and Anxiety* 20).

Elizabeth Meese contends that androgyny is used by Woolf and her critics alike to repress specifically lesbian desire: 'In a sense, critical interest in androgyny in Woolf's work prepares us for and distracts us from as it disguises her lesbian interests – a diversionary tactic she deploys' (103). This problem is even greater, I believe, if androgyny diverts attention from all female sexuality and erotic practice. According to Meese: 'The androgyne, as a gap, an excess, resembles the lesbian, but without community, without the socio-politics of identity and the history of movement and struggle, and is still caught within the oppositional categories of gender' (36). This is an extremely important point. The androgyne combines masculine and feminine qualities, thus reinforcing, even as it reconfigures, patriarchal categories of gender identity. And, again, I would go further than Meese in critiquing androgyny as a potentially repressive tool, since along with community and sociopolitics, the androgyne lacks sexual desire. The androgyne has no erotic practice. To speak of androgyny is to avoid the very issues – emotional or otherwise – that lesbianism raises.

But Sackville-West's exploratory androgyny most emphatically includes sexuality, sexual desire, and erotic practice. In the journal she uses to conduct a sexual self-analysis, she examines her sexual history and gender identity in order to decide whether to continue her relationship with Violet Trefusis (see chapter 2). Her conclusion that Trefusis brings out the masculine side of herself and that her husband brings out the feminine results in the acknowledgment of a dual, or androgynous, sense of self that affected everything from how she dressed (or crossdressed) to who excited her erotically. In Sackville-West's sense of self, the 'feminine and the masculine elements alternately preponderate' (Nicolson 105–6). In the character of Orlando (who literalizes this shift by changing sex) and in the much discussed metaphor of the man and woman sharing a cab in *A Room of One's Own*, Woolf illustrates Sackville-West's theory of sexuality: 'The sight of the two people getting into the taxi and the satisfaction it gave me make me also ask whether there are two sexes in the mind corresponding to the two sexes in the body, and whether they also require to be united in order to get complete satisfaction and happiness' (102). Reading this metaphor back to Sackville-West's position, Woolf seems to be suggesting that gender oscillation is, as Edward Carpenter insists, an advantage of members of the 'intermediate sex,' who possess an 'extraordinary gift' in their 'double point of view, both of the man and of the woman' (quoted in Doan 142). Laura Doan argues that Radclyffe Hall gives this position to Miss Puddleton, who offers it as a way of assisting another woman writer to imagine herself: 'You may write with a curious double insight – write both men and women from a personal knowledge' (205). Woolf seems to be echoing Hall when she says that for a writer 'It is fatal to be a man or woman pure and simple; one must be woman-manly or man-womanly' (*Room* 108). Woolf suggests, then, that oscillation between genders described by Sackville-West, for whom it is characterized by bisexuality, is a goal to strive for. This is the gender instability Woolf gives to her portrait of Sackville-West in *Orlando*: 'it was this mixture in her of man and woman, one being uppermost and then the other, that often gave her conduct an unexpected turn' (189). Like Sackville-West, Woolf generalizes from this 'unexpected' individual to characterize men and women as unstable in gender: 'In every human being a vacillation from one sex to the other takes place, and often it is only the clothes that keep the male or female likeness, while underneath the sex is the very opposite of what is above' (189). Sackville-West's journal, *Orlando*, and *A Room of One's Own*, taken together, deconstruct the dichotomy between masculine and feminine. In these three texts, androgyny is a representation of gender as an unstable and entirely metaphysical construct.

Woolf's two published versions of Sackville-West's private position are understandably vague (and thus particularly open to interpretation), considering the hostile climate of the time. Woolf delivered the lectures that would be published as *A Room of One's Own* in October 1928; Radclyffe Hall's *The Well of Loneliness* was scheduled to be tried for obscenity the following month. Woolf refers to the upcoming trial when she playfully interrupts her list of the ways in which she likes women: 'I like – but I must not run on in this way. That cupboard there, – you say it holds clean table-napkins only; but what if Sir Archibald Bodkin were concealed among them?' (115). Bodkin, the director of public prosecutions, would have been a familiar name to the women in Woolf's audience who had been following the allegations of obscenity that led up to the trial. Similarly, the audience would have taken the hint, when she earlier asked if Sir Chartres Biron, the magistrate presiding over Hall's trial, was hiding behind a curtain, before realizing that, in the fictitious novel by Mary Carmichael that Woolf uses to illustrate the current state of writing by women, 'Chloe liked Olivia' (86).[17] Woolf's references to Biron and Bodkin at two points in the lecture in which 'liking' women is mentioned emphasize the homoerotic subtext that requires self-censorship. Her references to the censors of *The Well of Loneliness* are the nudge and the wink that say: when I say 'I like women,' I mean 'I *like* women.'

The women that Woolf and Sackville-West make up together are women who like women. They are also women who write and who, unlike Aphra Behn, have had to learn to express desire metaphorically. A car with two occupants does not seem to be a passionate metaphor for sexuality and, as such, it is perhaps an ideal cover for a coded message. Sackville-West was regarded by her friends as an expert driver, and *Orlando* ends with a solitary drive as Orlando leaves London and her glimpse of Sasha for her country estate. But there was a private code available to Woolf and Sackville-West in addition to Sackville-West's theory of androgynous sexuality and their shared rejection of categories. They shared a memory of two people together in a car; for it was Sackville-West who – literally – had taught Woolf how to drive.[18]

7 Love Letters and Feminine Sexuality

I never realised that ink could be so ubiquitous.
> Vita Sackville-West to Virginia Woolf (23 Nov. 1933, 288)

What bosh letters are, to be sure!
> Virginia Woolf to Vita Sackville-West (17 Feb. 1926, 3:42)

Copy It Down

'To tell you a secret, I want to incite my lady to elope with me next,' Virginia Woolf wrote of Vita Sackville-West to Jacques Raverat (24 Jan. 1925, 3:156). She had already received an invitation to that effect (followed by a barb she found especially painful) when Sackville-West invited her to go to Spain: 'Will you ever play truant to Bloomsbury and culture, I wonder, and come travelling with me? ... *Look on it, if you like, as copy,* – as I believe you look upon everything, human relationships included. Oh yes, you like people through the brain better than through the heart' (16 July 1924, 51; emphasis added). An elopement of Woolf and Sackville-West would have made good copy, but Sackville-West implies a more complex transformation of experience into narrative, a transformation that tames and controls by replacing desire with language. She understood the transformative power of writing about one's love affairs. Her *roman-à-clef*, *Challenge*, turned her affair with Violet Trefusis into good copy (see chapter 2) – so good that Harold Nicolson and the mothers of the two women banded together to convince her not to publish the book in England.

When Woolf wrote to Jacques Raverat that she fancied replicating

Sackville-West's affair with Trefusis, she was prophetic in more ways than one. Woolf replicates it, first, by having an affair with Sackville-West and then by turning both affairs into copy in *Orlando*. Sackville-West's liaison with Trefusis becomes Orlando's constant love for the faithless Sasha, and *Orlando* becomes one more of the many love letters Woolf and Sackville-West exchanged as part of their agreement to make each other up. In the last way, *Orlando* (differently from *Challenge*) may have succeeded too well. Woolf wrote to Sackville-West just after completing the first draft: 'The question now is, will my feelings for you be changed? I've lived in you all these months – coming out, what are you really like? Do you exist? Have *I made you up?*' (20? March 1928, 3:474; emphasis added). Woolf made good on her promise to Sackville-West – 'I'll make you' (*Letters* 3:214) – by inventing her so completely that she seems more real to Woolf in the book than in life. By writing *Orlando* Woolf has turned desire into copy, and Sackville-West's prediction has come to pass: 'think of it as copy' is what Woolf eventually did.

Sackville-West's invitation was more than an escape from 'Bloomsbury and culture' to the lawless Basque country, where they travelled only in Woolf's imagination when Orlando frolics ungendered with the Gypsies (141–52). Sackville-West offered more than a powerfully positive association to the lost Julia Stephen. Neither a turn away from wordy and social Bloomsbury nor a turn towards the prelinguistic maternal connection of childhood, she meant something to Woolf in and beyond language. Sackville-West restored Woolf to herself like the lighthouse that forms a connection with Mrs Ramsay when she 'looked up over her knitting and met the third stroke [of the lighthouse] and it seemed to her like her own eyes meeting her own eyes' (97). 'I do miss you,' Woolf wrote to Sackville-West, 'There's no fishmonger and porpoise in my life without you. All's grind over cobbles' (6 March 1928, 3:468). After their affair began, Woolf turned to symbols and images that went beyond her initial appreciation of Sackville-West's body to suggest that Sackville-West offered an escape from the repressive everyday contact Woolf bumped over like cobblestones. In contrast to the 'dull green' and 'unattractive duffle grey' that characterized the other days of her week, she wrote: 'Fridays Vita: orange and rose, tipped with amethyst – Please see to it that it's a fine day, that there's a bun for tea, a porpoise in the fishmongers: and darling, write me something' (21 Feb. 1928, 3:462). In the midst of all the demands of her life, she writes, 'I could only think of you as being very distant and beautiful and calm. A lighthouse in clean waters' (31 Jan. 1927, 3:319). Thinking of Sackville-West is healing, centring, completing. The thought of her fulfils an essential need, or lack, in Woolf. This was the outcome of their agreement: 'What I am,' Woolf wrote to Sackville-West; 'I want you to tell me' (26 Jan. 1926, 3:233).

In her provocative theory of lesbian sexuality, Teresa De Lauretis argues that 'the threat that confronts the female subject ... is not the lack or loss of a penis but the lack or loss of a libidinally invested body-image ... and that loss of a bodily ego is tantamount to a loss of being, or a loss in being' (*Habit* 301).[1] Here she is revisiting Freud's consistently misunderstood notion of the castration complex or penis envy, which I understand as simply the recognition that, for a child, it is the presence or absence of the penis that determines sex and that in a patriarchy being male is overprivileged and therefore enviable.[2] De Lauretis understands the female subject's recognition of her femaleness to result not in the wish for a penis (as Freud's theory has sometimes been crudely literalized) but as wish for wholeness, or sense of self. She explains: 'Thus the fantasmatic "lost object" of perverse [by which she means 'non-normatively heterosexual' (*Practice* xiii)] desire is neither the mother's body nor the paternal phallus; it is the subject's own lost body, which can be recovered in fantasy, in sexual practice, only in and with another woman' (*Habit* 301).

While De Lauretis's theory is understandably controversial, it resonates with Woolf's descriptions of both her aching sense of loss and dreary 'non-being' – relieved in fleeting moments of 'being' ('A Sketch of the Past' 70) – and her descriptions of the reparation she experienced in her fantasies of Sackville-West. Looking to Sackville-West to find 'what I am,' Woolf sought the recovery of self through the acceptance of loss. For De Lauretis, this is 'the psychic mechanism of disavowal [*Verleugnung*], which is at once the denial and the acceptance of castration' ('Habit Changes' 300). This position parallels what I have described in Sackville-West as having all and nothing: the female subject recognizes the Law of the Father (and thus itself as castrated) but does not care. In Lacanian theory this is Woman as 'not-all.' The Law is acknowledged, but the subject is not constrained by it. This is also the position occupied by the Biographer in *Orlando* in relation to the Law of biography: the Biographer knows the rules but disregards them without fear of reprisal. So the female subject, as theorized by De Lauretis (and demonstrated, I would argue, by Sackville-West), recognizes that she is castrated but, through sexual fantasies that arise through homoerotic practices, comes anyway – or rather, comes differently.

Lacan theorizes this particular type of coming as supplemental or the other (non-phallic) *jouissance*, which can be achieved through the feminine position. Darian Leader and Judy Groves explain that in supplemental *jouissance* 'the subject does not try to fill this lack [of the phallus] – which would be phallic *jouissance* – but to give it a new value as lack, *to produce jouissance through this absence*' (159; emphasis original). Lacan does not suggest that this position is unattainable within heterosexual desire, but for De Lauretis, it is lesbian sexuality that is restorative, and her theory depicts this acceptance and denial of loss much in the way Woolf describes her fantasy of Sackville-West: one woman completes the other.

When represented in language, which exists within a symbolic order structured by patriarchy, feminine desire copies the patterns of desire in patriarchy and thus ceases to be. When it is copied down, it vanishes. It can be represented as passive or masculine. It is the function of patriarchy to enforce the repression of feminine sexuality. Repressed desire emerges as a copy, a masquerade, of desire. A copy takes the place of desire. The attempt to resist patriarchal Law has failed. Desire has been censored. Orlando triumphs over the spirit of the age when, by marrying, she diverts attention from her constant desire for Sasha and is allowed to write what she wishes (243). She succeeds too well; her own desire is diverted into writing. She completes the manuscript, but at the sight of Sasha herself she turns away. Orlando has recreated desire and lost desire at the same time. Language takes the place of feminine desire. Once represented, desire itself is erased.

Woolf and Sackville-West sought to express feminine desire through disguised narratives, codes, hints, and images. They were not always successful in writing desire and having it too. Writing about the moments of 'being,' Woolf explains: 'It is only by putting it into words that I make it whole: this wholeness means that it has lost its power to hurt me; it gives me, perhaps because by doing so I take away the pain, a great delight to put the severed parts together. Perhaps this is the strongest pleasure known to me' ('A Sketch of the Past' 72). Her description of the reparation she finds in writing is a discovery of the wholeness that exists on the other side of pain. It is not a denial of pain or loss but the ability to be whole in spite of loss. She also reveals that her response to the loss of control inherent in the excruciatingly exquisite moment of 'being,' which is so powerful that it is painful, is to turn it into copy.

Fruit and kisses perform what words on paper can only speak of: desire. When desire is repressed, it is described instead of felt. *Orlando* is the book in which Woolf has the most fun, but it is also emotionally distant because she is both feeling desire and defending against it by intellectualizing emotional responses. More than turning desire into language, the disruption of the gendered subject creates a distraction from the desiring subject. Her intervention in the normative representation of Cartesian subjectivity prevents the emotional cathexis available between and with fictional characters.

Nigel Nicolson's description of *Orlando* as 'the longest and most charming love-letter in literature' (202) is often cited and generally accepted as a delightful description of the book.[3] But while Woolf was starting to write *Orlando*, Sackville-West was falling in love with Mary Campbell, who had recently settled nearby with her husband, the South African poet Roy Campbell. While Sackville-West's letters of this time indicate an attempt to placate the jealous Woolf, the intensity of their affair was coming to an end (Glendinning 175–80). In her first letter to Sackville-West about *Orlando*, Woolf wrote that the book would be all about Sackville-West, except for her heart: 'heart you have none, who go gallivanting down the lanes with Campbell' (9 Oct. 1927, 3:429). If *Orlando* is a love letter, it arrived too late.

While most critics attend to the loving aspects of *Orlando*, a few consider its other side, a side Woolf warned Sackville-West to beware of: 'If you've given yourself to Campbell, I'll have no more to do with you, and so it shall be written, plainly, for all the world to read in Orlando' (13 Oct. 1927, 3:431). Suzanne Raitt sees Woolf's revenge fulfilled in the comic nature of *Orlando*, which, she argues, illustrates Freud's theory that a joke is a judgment that silences the person at whom it is aimed. According to Raitt's perceptive reading, *Orlando* is an expression of Woolf's ambivalence towards Sackville-West, for whom Woolf felt both love and hostility: 'I believe that biography, notorious raiser of relatives' temperatures, is similarly hostile [as jokes are]; and that Woolf's choice of a "joke" form for her biography of the woman with whom she was so intimately and ambivalently involved, was more than a simple coincidence' (*Vita and Virginia* 30). The parallel function of biographies and jokes as acts of revenge is certainly consistent with *Orlando*'s persistent criticism of biographers, among whose ranks Woolf's friends and relatives, Sackville-West among them, figure so prominently.

Louise DeSalvo also sees *Orlando* as an attempt by Woolf to raise Sackville-West's class-consciousness: 'Whatever else *Orlando* may be, it is also a manual of instruction from Virginia Woolf to Vita Sackville-West about the dangers inherent in the way she had been thinking about inheritance, about her ancestry, about the relationship between the classes, about the idyllic nature of life in the country, about the fantasy that foreign cities temporarily can provide a woman with the freedom to be herself' ('Every Woman' 103). I would argue that Woolf's 'love-letter' was not simply an instruction manual in terms of such content; it went further, to instruct Sackville-West as a writer. Unlike DeSalvo, who concludes that Sackville-West got the point, I would suggest that Woolf's larger lesson on the nature of subjectivity went – at least initially – unnoticed.[4] Sackville-West wrote to Woolf after reading *Orlando*: 'you have invented a new form of Narcissism, – I confess, – I am in love with Orlando – this is a complication I had not foreseen. Virginia, my dearest, I can only thank you for pouring out such riches' (11 Oct. 1928, 289). Woolf responded to this letter with a telegram: 'Your biographer is infinitely relieved and happy' (289n). Here, Woolf clarifies the redefinition of their relationship: no longer lover, she takes on the role of copyist, recording the details of desire as Sackville-West's biographer.

Orlando was an immense relief to both of them: it was the end of their struggle to express the inexpressible. It was the end of desire: 'There's a dying hue over [our friendship],' Woolf wrote to Sackville-West, 'it shows the hectic dolphin colours of decay. Never do I leave you without thinking, its for the last time. And the truth is, we gain as much as we lose by this ... we gain in intensity what we lack in the sober comfortable virtues of a prolonged and safe and respectable and chaste and cold blooded friendship' (13 Oct. 1927, 3:429–30). Passion is exciting and exhausting. *Orlando* was the final *frisson*, the result of the intensity, as Woolf wrote, of the end of the affair. Jean Love says *Orlando* 'is best read, I think, as [Woolf's] ultimate comment on Vita and as her means of gaining perspective and detachment in order to continue their friendship on a different basis' (192).[5] Whether best read or also read in this way, I agree with Love's understanding of the role *Orlando* played for Woolf. But how can a novel transform a relationship? Why would Woolf need to do so?

A Piercing Cry

Dear Mrs. Woolf ... I regret that you have been in bed, though not with me.
Vita Sackville-West to Virginia Woolf (16 Aug. 1933, 380)

Their letters began slowly and grew longer and more frequent during the winter and spring of 1925, when Woolf moved back to Bloomsbury in search of more life and found it in more 'Vita.' Over that summer and fall Woolf was often ill. Letters replaced visits. Then, knowing Sackville-West was about to leave for Persia, Woolf spent the weekend with her at her home, Long Barn. They stayed up all night talking and touching. Afterwards, letters flew between them. Woolf wrote to no one else until Sackville-West left the country. When they were apart they talked about each other. Woolf wrote to Sackville-West that she and Clive Bell 'walk through the clods together talking, first one and then another, of Vita Vita Vita as the new moon rises and the lambs huddle on the downs' (22 Dec. 1925, 3:225). Bell asked Sackville-West point-blank if she had slept with his sister-in-law. She denied it, 'and did your answer differ from mine?' she wrote to Woolf, 'alas no' (17 Jan. 1926, 87).

On 20 January 1926 Sackville-West left for Persia; the journey took six weeks. She wrote her first letter to Woolf on the train to Dover, minutes after saying good-bye. 'I am reduced to a thing that wants Virginia,' she wrote the next day from Milan (21 Jan. 1926, 89). Because the mail arrived and departed from Teheran once every two weeks, their letters crossed and read as discontinuous. This was also the effect of the separation on their relationship. Woolf wrote eight letters to Sackville-West while she was away; they make up over half of the collected letters she wrote during this period. Their letters are vital, filled with longing and memories of their days and nights together. But they are also filled with the excitement of their current days, days they could not share, although Sackville-West repeats her entreaty to Woolf to join her on a trip somewhere instead of staying mired, as Sackville-West wrote, 'in your old misty Gloomsbury and your London squares' (29 Jan. 1926, 94).

Sackville-West was a good traveller. She became immersed in the people and places around her. This openness to new experience and fascination with detail is apparent in her extraordinary travel books, *Passenger to Teheran* and *Twelve Days*. She writes to Woolf of bathing on ship in water filled with phosphorus that poured out of the tap in a blue flame (8 Feb. 1926, 99). She writes on her body in glowing water in letters that shine and disappear. Glowing letters written on the body shimmer with longing. The letters she could mail only report: 'Now this letter is long if apparently un-loving,' she wrote from Teheran, 'but a lot of love gets spilt over them, like sand to dry the ink, of which no trace remains when the letter arrives, but which nevertheless was there, an important ingredient' (15 March 1926, 116). Love, like Persian sand, can only be imagined in Bloomsbury.

As Sackville-West wrote to Woolf in glowing letters showered with loving sand, Woolf was consumed with *To the Lighthouse*. She was writing faster than ever before: 'to tell you the truth, I have been very excited, writing. I have never written so fast' (26 Jan. 1926, 3:232). Within a month of Sackville-West's departure Woolf's letters have a more distant tone; she lets two weeks go by without writing. Both are becoming consumed with the parts of their lives they do not share, which they try unsuccessfully to imagine changing. Sackville-West invites Woolf into her world: 'it becomes clearer and more clear that I shall spend the next two years in tearing backwards and forwards across Europe and Asia, and it is my dream to take you with me,' she wrote (15 March 1926, 115).

Woolf's passion, on the other hand, was directed towards her novel. Referring to the 'Time Passes' section of *To the Lighthouse*, she asserted that she would rather be struggling with 'how to manage the passage of ten years, up in the Hebrides' than talking on the phone or having tea. Far from wishing to travel abroad, Woolf complained that even the daily life of London was too distracting. Only by locating Sackville-West within the novel could Woolf fantasize about their life together: 'I should like to be with you in the Hebrides at this moment,' she wrote, suggesting a fantasy leap into her novel instead of travel (2 March 1926, 3:244). Her fantasies made their way into the novel, which draws on their time together as a model for intimacy between women. As we have seen, her memory of Sackville-West, sitting on the floor with her head against Woolf's knees, is transformed into Lily Briscoe remembering her arms around Mrs Ramsay's knees as 'close as she could get' (78). In this way, Woolf's desire to be with Sackville-West in the Hebrides came true. Such fantasies were also, of course, a way of redirecting her desire for Sackville-West into writing, even as they signalled Sackville-West's importance in Woolf's life and work. The novel, not London, was where she now sought life and Vita. This may well explain why Woolf was writing so fluidly, setting a record, she notes to Sackville-West, of 40,000 words in the two months since Sackville-West's departure (16 March 1926, 3:249).

After Sackville-West returned, the letters once again begin to demonstrate the development of their intimacy. They are the letters of lovers arranging discreet meetings. 'Will you come on Wednesday? to lunch at 1? Leonard will be in London for the day,' wrote Woolf (19 Aug. 1926, 3:287). This was a time of arrangements and counter-arrangements, avoiding gossip, sneaking around, and hiding from Leonard Woolf.[6] They saw each other frequently during this time, and the letters reflect that intimacy, in part by lacking it: there was no need for letters. They served primarily to make arrangements to meet. What Woolf and Sackville-West had to say to each other they said face to face.

As Sackville-West prepared to depart once again for Persia, the wordless longing returns. Woolf writes, 'Why have you taught me this piercing cry? and then to go to Persia? and leave me?' (Christmas Day 1926 3:309). Before Sackville-West left, they spent two days together at Knole. On the day of departure, they spent the morning together, as they had the year before. After they parted, Sackville-West wrote: 'Beloved Virginia, one last goodbye before I go. I feel torn in a thousand pieces – it is *bloody* – I *can't tell you* how I hate leaving you. I don't know how I shall get on without you – in fact I don't feel I can – you have become so essential to me' (28 Jan. 1927, 163; emphasis original). In the postscript she added: 'Please, please. Put "honey" when you write –.'

Woolf did put 'honey' when she wrote. Once again the frequency of their letters was determined by Persian mail deliveries. Woolf wrote nine letters to Sackville-West, one more than during their previous separation. But instead of representing more than half of Woolf's collected letters, letters to Sackville-West make up less than a third during this three-month period. One reason was that Vanessa Bell was also away; Woolf wrote very nearly as many letters to her sister as to Sackville-West.

In the letters they exchanged during Sackville-West's second absence, both women tried to imagine not only each other – they have invented each other and they remember these inventions – but also what their future life together might be. For Sackville-West this was not difficult; the only trouble was in persuading Woolf to travel with her in the future. 'Where shall we go in October?' she wrote, 'Avignon? Italy? Or are you going to let me down over that?' (11 March 1927, 186).[7] Her letters are full of the excitement of her travels. She tried to imagine what it would be like to travel with Woolf: 'Are you the sort of traveller who constantly says "Oh look"?' (23 Feb. 1927, 177), she wrote in a letter in which she speculates on her plans for the following year. Long an advocate of Harold Nicolson's resignation from the Foreign Service, Sackville-West was realistic enough to imagine what it would be like to return to Teheran once again. If she did go, she wanted Woolf to come, too. She was also realistic enough to know that neither her own nor Woolf's marriage could be put in jeopardy by their relationship. Harold Nicolson did not mind the affair, but Leonard Woolf was another story. She wanted to telegraph her safe arrival to Woolf, but 'then I thought Leonard would open it and be annoyed' (23 Feb. 1927, 177). Despite the difficulties, Sackville-West may well have been content with continuing their relationship intermittently, even though she clearly wanted more contact with Woolf.

Woolf's letters are less optimistic about the possibility of a future together. It is harder to be left than to leave. They indicate anxiety over Sackville-West's absence and growing ambivalence about the dependability of their relationship. 'You wont go and leave poor Virginia again will you' (28 Feb. 1927, 3:337), she wrote, knowing full well that Sackville-West would always be about to leave – at least physically. Without the flexibility of Sackville-West's marriage, Woolf's primary obligations would always be to her husband and sister: there was no question of disrupting these relationships. Even if Nicolson gave up the Foreign Service (which he did in August 1929), Sackville-West would still be unobtainable. The thought of losing her was unbearable, and her absence must have demonstrated the pain that would necessarily be repeated in their future. Woolf would not leave Bloomsbury, and there was no room for Sackville-West there.

Woolf had planned to distract herself with reading while Sackville-West was away, as she had distracted herself with writing *To the Lighthouse* the year before. In the end, she was distracted more by other people (3:329–31). An argument between Clive Bell and his mistress, Mary Hutchinson, occupied a great deal of her time and energy. Her letters to Sackville-West detailed her busy work and social life, full of phone calls and having her hair cut: 'but let us get on to something interesting' she wrote, only to continue, 'Nothing occurs to me at the moment' (16 Feb. 1927, 3:331). She concluded another letter: 'Goodby dearest honey. Write to me please as much as you can. Yes yes yes I do like you. I am afraid to write the stronger word' (7 Feb. 1927, 3:328). Whether this reluctance signalled a fear of love or a fear of loss, Woolf seemed to be withdrawing. Even in her diary she was reticent: 'I must be fond of her, genuinely' (28 Feb. 1927, 3:129), was the most she would say.

Although Woolf's letters convey the intimacy of the time they had shared, moments of affection and references to their physical passion are quickly interrupted. Even references to her spaniel, Pinker, a present from Sackville-West, who is commonly used by Woolf to hint at erotic practice, turn unexpectedly, perhaps unconsciously, comic: 'Please Vita dear don't forget your humble creatures – Pinker and Virginia. Here we are sitting by the gas fire alone. Every morning she jumps on to my bed and kisses me, and I say thats Vita. But she has worms again' (16 Feb. 1927, 3:331). Then, two days later, Woolf wrote a letter of longing and insecurity: 'I assure you I'm conscious of you all day long, soaring above my head. And am I a bright bead, or a dull bead, in the plate? Or don't I exist?' (3:332).

Woolf's anxiety about their relationship would certainly have been enforced by the cultural repression of feminine sexuality, which was present even in Bloomsbury. Writing to Sackville-West about a discussion of 'love and sodomy and Bunny's [David Garnett's] last book, Vita and Eddy [Sackville-West], and Desmond [MacCarthy]'s fund ... with Lytton [Strachey], Clive [Bell], Morgan [E.M. Forster], Raymond [Mortimer], Mary [Hutchinson] etc.,' Woolf included an excerpt of the talk, which is somewhat unusual. Sackville-West knew Clive Bell, of course, but perhaps, since Vita was not admired in Bloomsbury, Woolf tended to avoid references to her group of friends. They were discussing the amount of time spent on food, sleep, love, and work. Lytton Strachey amended E.M. Forster's two hours on love to ten. Woolf described her own contribution: 'I say the whole day on love. I say its seeing things through a purple shade. But you've never been in love they say' (18 Feb. 1927, 3:332). Her friends' denial, which she reports as a group expression, of her feelings for Sackville-West might explain why she herself was 'unable to write the stronger word' (5 Feb. 1927, 3:328). With Sackville-West gone, there was no love for Woolf.

If Woolf seriously considered leaving the life she had made for herself, she did not record such thoughts in letters or diary. She had prior commitments that she apparently never thought of renegotiating. Sackville-West's proposal that they meet in Greece interfered with plans already made with Leonard Woolf and Vanessa Bell. Woolf wrote that it was impossible, but 'a divine thought' (28 Feb. 1927, 3:339). Indeed, Sackville-West was becoming more of a divine thought and less of a practical possibility. In outlining her plans for the summer, Woolf described several trips with various friends, concluding the letter: 'But there'll be one night with you at Long Barn. Snore – Snore – Snore' (18 Feb. 1927, 3:334).

If Sackville-West could be only a part of Woolf's life, the question remained: what part? Woolf answered that question in her next letter, in which she assigns particular roles to the people in her life: 'Oh and does it strike you that one's friendships are long conversations, perpetually broken off, but always about the same thing with the same person? With Lytton I talk about reading; with Clive about love; with Nessa about people; with Roger about art; with Morgan about writing; with Vita – well, what do I talk about with Vita? Sometimes we snore' (28 Feb. 1927, 3:337). Woolf's joke presumably turns on the literalization of 'sleeping together,' as Sackville-West described their erotic practice. In both letters this activity comes last in the list and is not integrated into the fabric of Woolf's plans or relationships. Both blamed Harold Nicolson's career for taking Sackville-West out of the country: 'Look here, Vita, you must wring Harolds neck, if the worst comes to the worst. You have my sanction. A dead diplomat in a dust heap' (28 Feb. 1927, 3:338). Nicolson did resign, but not before his next assignment, which was to Berlin. Woolf did agree to come to Germany to see Sackville-West, but Leonard Woolf accompanied her.

Sackville-West's letters, on the other hand, have the same intensity and self-conscious expressiveness as the year before: 'I want to be with you and not with anybody else – But you will get bored if I go on saying this, only it comes back and back till it drips off my pen' (29 Jan. 1927, 165). As she had been the year before, Sackville-West is affectionate, even as she is thrilled by the new experiences of her travels. This time she took an arduous twelve-day excursion on horseback across the Bakhtiari Mountains in Southern Persia, which she describes in *Twelve Days*. She exuberantly balanced her enthusiasm for her travels with her desire for Woolf: 'God, I do love you' she wrote while on this journey. 'You say I use no endearments. That strikes me as funny. When I wake in the Persian dawn, and say to myself "Virginia ... Virginia"' (30 March 1927, 190). Integrating her enjoyment of being in an unfamiliar place with her fantasies of Woolf, Sackville-West unites her pleasures.

Sackville-West's letters are consistent in their joy and longing, but Woolf's change. Not only does she express anxiety about her place in Sackville-West's life, but Sackville-West's place in hers also undergoes a serious adjustment. Her first letter after Sackville-West's departure ends: 'do you ever think of the basement and – and – a kiss from Pinker: one from me to the insect [Sackville-West]. I'll write weekly' (31 Jan. 1927, 3:321). Calling up their meetings in Woolf's writing room in the basement of Tavistock Square, which also housed the Hogarth Press, Woolf evokes the moments of their life together and passion for each other. This is a powerful moment of longing and hope for the continuation of their relationship.

Three weeks later Woolf reports that her longing for Sackville-West 'gets worse you'll be glad to hear, steadily worse.' She goes on to describe her wish for Sackville-West's presence: 'Todays the day when I should be trotting out to buy you your loaf, and watching for your white legs – not widow Cartwrights [who was employed at the Hogarth Press] – coming down the basement steps. Instead you're on the heights of Persia, riding an Arab mare I daresay to some deserted garden and picking yellow tulips' (3:332–3). The fantasy changes here slightly but significantly. Located in the present moment, Woolf wishes for Sackville-West's arrival and, when thwarted by the actual arrival of Mrs Cartwright, replaces her fantasy with a romantic image of Sackville-West elsewhere in the present moment. Rather than dreaming of their past together, Woolf has begun to imagine them separate: she is in the basement, and Sackville-West is a story she tells herself. Unlike the fantasy of their past intimacy, which turns into a fictional expression of that longing, the story of Sackville-West alone picking tulips has no place in it for Woolf or for desire.

In another two weeks the transformation is complete. Woolf's fantasies of Sackville-West no longer recall past intimacy, and the idea of her re-entering Woolf's life is inaccessible: 'I can't imagine you in the basement ... Still – oh yes – I am very fond of you, all the same – I lie in bed making up stories about you' (6 March 1927, 3:342). Not unlike her early proposal that they make one another up, now Woolf imagines Sackville-West almost as a character in a novel about whom stories can be invented. No longer insecure and needy, Woolf's tone in this letter is lively and engaged, full of details and eager for more: 'Do send me a heap of facts: you know how I love a fact: what you had for dinner: and any scrap of real talk for instance between you and Harold, upon which I can build pinnacles and pagodas, all unreal' (3:342). This request foreshadows Woolf's request for facts about Sackville-West with which to detail *Orlando*: 'Is it true you grind your teeth at night? Is it true you love giving pain? What and when was your moment of greatest disillusionment?' (13 Oct. 1927, 3:430).

What has occurred to explain this change? That the current reality and future prospect of separation from Sackville-West was too painful to continue to endure is something we can only speculate about. There is something significant that did occur: Woolf completed *To the Lighthouse*, a novel I believe her relationship with Sackville-West made possible. In the security of Sackville-West's love, Woolf was able to mourn her mother, whom she came to imagine in terms very much like those she uses to express her longing for Sackville-West ('A Sketch of the Past' 80–4). Woolf worked through her grief for her mother by writing *To the Lighthouse*, and I believe she did the same with Sackville-West when she wrote *Orlando*. For Woolf, the process of separation was a process of transformation in which she reinvented Sackville-West as Orlando. Woolf recorded the moment of conception in her diary as bound up with her thoughts of Sackville-West's continuing absence: 'Although annoyed that I have not heard from Vita by this post nor yet last week, annoyed sentimentally, and & partly from vanity – still I must record the conception last night between 12 & one of a new book' (14 March 1927, 3:131). In spite of – or perhaps because of – her 'annoyance' at not receiving a letter from Sackville-West, Woolf writes that she will nevertheless record the beginning of her new book, which occurred the night before. I would suggest that it began even earlier, as she began to transform her desire for Sackville-West into fiction.

Woolf also points to an earlier starting date for the beginning of *Orlando*, writing to Sackville-West on 8 March: 'Yes, I've thought of an entirely new book.' This pronouncement is made to conclude a description of the goal of writing that Woolf used again in *Orlando*: '[I] need write no more till the old fish, of whom I've told you – he's Gold, but has moulted several scales – his tails quite bald by the way, and he lost one eye in a fight with a Tench – rises to the top, and I net him' (8 March 1927, 3:344). Thus, 'the great fish who lives in the coral groves' (313) that ends *Orlando* leapt into Woolf's net as she wrote to Sackville-West. The powerful image of Sackville-West in the doorway of the fishmonger's shop in Sevenoaks, which Woolf says recurs again and again in her memory, is caught in Woolf's net and bound between hard covers.

To turn Woolf's inarticulate 'piercing cry' (*Letters* 3:309) of feminine desire into the words of fiction displaces desire, which cannot be expressed in the language of the symbolic order. When Sackville-West became Orlando, Woolf found a way to internalize the image of her lover so that she could never be lost again. In this way she mourned without succumbing to melancholia. The price was the loss of desire.

Desire and its repression is not a surprising theme to find in a book Virginia Woolf dedicated to her friend and secret lover, Vita Sackville-West. How better to express one's fantasies than in a fantastic book? Like the model of Orlando's substitution of writing for erotic practice,[8] however, the book itself can be seen to operate as a mechanism for the repression of desire. Sackville-West noted Woolf's tendency to redirect libido into intellectual contact; when she accuses Woolf of turning human relationships to copy (*Letters* 51), she implies that Woolf defends against intimacy by intellectual sublimation.

Ostensibly a confession of love to Vita Sackville-West, the great passion in *Orlando* is for words. It turns Sackville-West and the fantasies she arouses into copy. Letting 'other pens treat of sex and sexuality' (139), *Orlando* engages the problem of how to textually construct and represent subjectivity instead of sexual desire. Jean Love suggests that writing *Orlando* was a way for Woolf to get over her affair with Sackville-West: 'Whatever else it was, as a skillful fantasy and as a work of art, *Orlando*, I believe, was the principle instrument Virginia Woolf used to gain the distance she needed. Work on it had gradually changed the quality of her love, although, she continued to see Vita and never stopped caring for her as a friend' (218). Similarly, Suzanne Raitt suggests: 'The writing of *Orlando* injected a new energy and tension into their relationship, sustaining it and in a way *becoming* it. As Sackville-West's biographer, Woolf gained a new hold over her friend ... Beneath the desire to compliment and to flatter, so evident in *Orlando*, lay a more sinister impulse to punish and hurt' (*Vita and Virginia*, 18; emphasis original). Writing *Orlando*, according to Raitt, was a controlling act of aggressive appropriation in which Woolf 'attempted to take over Sackville-West's memory and identity' (143). On the other hand, Sherron Knopp reads *Orlando* as an extension of physical lovemaking, not a substitute for it (27).

If *Orlando* provided an arena in which Woolf could work through the traumatic loss of Sackville-West as a lover, the alternative focus of her passion was not a new lover to go gallivanting with but a return to writing. Focused on the theoretical problems raised by modernism, in the end the book is more concerned with the rules and problems of writing and the construction of identity than with wooing.

Even though the Hogarth Press, which Woolf and her husband owned, published Sackville-West's work[9] and Woolf made excuses for others' frequent harsh criticism of Sackville-West's writing, Woolf's own harsh literary judgments would seem to be a moderating influence on her passion for Sackville-West, just as the persistent commentary on textual experimentation dilutes the passionate potential of *Orlando*. Intellectualization allowed Woolf to avoid the erotic content of Sackville-West's work and the erotic practice of the friendship she offered.

While narrative self-reflexivity can be celebrated for making *Orlando* much more than a personal expression of desire, it is also important to note the ways in which formal concerns screen erotic impulses. Indeed, the text itself seems to modify the loving relationship it celebrates by relocating the energy of physical contact into literary intercourse. *Orlando* redirects libido from a bodily to a textual relationship. The narrow window Sackville-West opened, allowing Woolf to feel safe enough to lift the repression of her body, slammed shut with the withdrawal of the ripe fruit of Sackville-West's exclusive attention. Woolf turned to *Orlando*, where writing sublimated sexual desire for Woolf just as the

Biographer demonstrates it does for the main character. *Orlando* may be a biography of Sackville-West, but it also chronicles Woolf's own structures of desire.

Orlando makes fun of the idea that truth can be found in facts. Facts allow us to believe in the historical truth of biographies. The subject has been documented, accounted for, demystified. Imagination is avoided; it is the first gap in the armour that protects the illusion of the unified subject. The interior world is absent – no documentation exists to recreate it. Traditional biography thus represses the unconscious, smooths over the gaps of the intermittent ego, and substitutes constant facts for every desire. *Orlando* gestures towards homoerotic desire again and again, and while Woolf's self-censorship is overdetermined, it nevertheless allows her to avoid making this particular challenge to the factual biographical tradition overt. The challenge she does make doubly contains her displaced desire for Sackville-West: Orlando contains desire by replacing the object of desire and by limiting desire to language. The 'double discourse' (Caughie) that reveals and hides the sapphism Woolf said was only to be suggested is also a double container for Woolf's desire for Sackville-West. Redirecting her libido into the book that represents her lover, Woolf creates a narrative that resists and enacts traditionally feminine, passive desire. Like Orlando's, Woolf's constant desire is constantly repressed. *Orlando*'s celebration of imagination paves the way for the exposure of the intermittent ego, but it baulks at the desire its exposure threatens to reveal.

Her relationship with Sackville-West allowed Woolf to work through her relationships with her mother in *To the Lighthouse* and her biographer father in *Orlando*. Once she feels displaced – evidenced most explicitly in her jealousy over Mary Campbell but beginning, I would argue, even earlier – Woolf shuts down again. Desire turns to copy. Woolf writes to Sackville-West and receives a reply, but neither fully comprehends the letter she sends or the letter she opens. Neither fruit nor kisses, the letters are not full of desire. Yet there are moments, astonishing moments, when they try.

Another Love Letter: Lacan avec Woolf

There is a jouissance that is hers, that belongs to that 'she' that doesn't exist and doesn't signify anything. There is a jouissance that is hers about which she herself perhaps knows nothing if not that she experiences it – that much she knows. She knows it, of course, when it comes.

Lacan, *Feminine Sexuality* (74)

Boys can't dance because they don't have a dress. They can only watch girls dance and play.

Phillipa, age four (12 Sept. 1997)

Before they began exchanging love letters disguised as manuscripts, Woolf and Sackville-West exchanged letters disguised as love letters. When they truly longed for one another, they could not say so; when the longing stopped, the words began. When they were first separated, Sackville-West wrote: 'I am reduced to a thing that wants Virginia. I composed a beautiful letter to you in the sleepless nightmare hours of the night, and it has all gone: I just miss you, in a quite simple desperate human way. You, with all your undumb letters, would never write so elementary a phrase as that; perhaps you wouldn't even feel it. And yet I believe you'll be sensible of a little gap. But you'd clothe it in so exquisite a phrase that it would lose a little of its reality. Whereas with me it is quite stark: I miss you even more than I could have believed; and I was prepared to miss you a good deal. So this letter is just really a squeal of pain' (21 Jan. 1926, 89). Sackville-West's longing for Woolf merges into her anxiety about language. Woolf, she imagines, could find an exquisite phrase to close the gap between them, but in her own letter the gap is raw and blank. The letter marks a separation that, because it must be bridged, cannot be crossed. When there is no gap, there is no need for words to come between them. To say 'I miss you' is to create a gap that can do no more than point to the hope that their longing is mutual even if their words are not. Sackville-West's anxiety that Woolf will scorn her inability to speak of her longing evidences a struggle to put into words desire that is too elusive to be registered in the symbolic. Sackville-West's ability to traverse the fantasy led to her uncensored creation of fantasy in fiction (and thus her work is potentially more personal than enduring). In her letters, a form where revision and formal originality is not expected,[10] we see her trying to articulate the gap between feminine desire and the language's ability to allow its expression: she is reduced to a squeal of pain that wants Virginia.

Woolf also expressed the failure of language to communicate when confronted with her feelings for Sackville-West, finishing a letter: 'I can't form a word' (5 Jan. 1926, 3:226). When they could be together, their letters served them well to make dates and exchange information. But when they were apart, their letters show their struggle to force language to do the work they wished it to do. Wordily inarticulate, they wrote what they call 'dumb' letters, which are simultaneously stupid and silent. Forcing words towards the inexpressible, they share word games: Sackville-West writes of changing 'Adult' to 'Adulterer' on admission tickets to the zoo (13 Jan. 26, 85). Woolf writes in response: 'Oh and Vita won't be here next week to adulterate it [the world] – you know what I mean – Its a word I can't find at the moment' (15 Jan. 26, 3:229). In her last letter to Woolf before leaving for Persia for their first extended separation, Sackville-West writes: 'Someday I'll write and tell you all the things you mean to me in my mind. Shall I?' (17 Jan. 1926, 87). To do so would mean inventing a new language, a means of speaking beyond the symbolic. They began by inventing each other ('If you'll make me up, I'll make you,' Woolf wrote [23 Sept. 1925, 3:214]), but they would need letters of a different sort: an alphabet of sounds and gestures unrepresented in the words they could find.

In their early letters they practised recreating each other, imagining the other's days and conversations and activities. They built worlds for each other, which for Woolf culminated in *Orlando*. Woolf began this inventing when she writes to Sackville-West: 'I try to invent you for myself, but find I really have only 2 twigs and 3 straws to do it with. I can get the sensation of seeing you – hair, lips, colour, height, even, now and then, the eyes and hands, but I find you going off, to walk in the garden, to play tennis, to dig, to sit smoking and talking, and then I cant invent a thing you say –' (7 Sept. 1925, 3:204–5). Sackville-West responded with her version of Woolf, cataloguing Woolf's many accomplishments and activities and concluding: 'How is it done? I can only suppose that you don't fritter' (18 Sept. 1925, 68). It was how to fritter, perhaps, that Sackville-West taught Woolf.

They fulfilled their pact to make each other up, for a time. Their struggle to perform this act of invention was an attempt to create feminine sexuality. They were determined to eat the fruit, to speak of desire. They struggled to share their knowledge of what Lacan calls 'the other *jouissance*.'

Feminine desire, I have said, ends with speech. Language cannot represent that which is not configured by the symbolic, the world as we know it, which is mediated through language. This is a tautology, to be sure, but it is the logic of our conscious lives. There is another logic: the logic of the unconscious. It rules dreams and emerges in fiction. Feminine sexuality, as it is theorized by Lacan, is repressed as a threat to the patriarchal structure of the symbolic. When it emerges from the unconscious, it is necessarily unrecognizable, because the return of feminine sexuality from the repressed enters consciousness through the lens of patriarchy. The only categories available to feminine sexuality in the symbolic, therefore, are extreme and violent. This is the truth of feminine sexuality in patriarchy, since to patriarchy feminine sexuality is an extreme and threatening force. In patriarchy, sexuality and femininity are not reconcilable. A person who is feminine is sexually passive; a person who is sexually active is not feminine. Notice the way that gender becomes important to make sense of non-conforming women (and men): femininity is used to designate proper women. Sexually active women are wanton (the whore, the slut) and violent (the vampire, the dominatrix), and therefore unfeminine. They are located outside the domestic sphere. They are extreme. These stereotypes are countered by equally exaggerated images of women who are passive and desirable, and therefore feminine.

Lacan recognizes this structure in his theorization of the feminine position, or not-all, in *Feminine Sexuality*, especially in the chapter of that seminar entitled 'Une lettre d'amour' – a love letter or a letter from love, with a pun that suggests a connection between love and soul.[11] I have argued that Sackville-West received such a letter from love in the form of the hidden fruit given to her each day by her grandfather (see ch. 2). Through this gift, she had the *usufruit* of her desire. Incapable of recognizing feminine sexuality, patriarchal constructions transform feminine desire into an erotic version of psychotic hallucinations, since the repressed symptoms of feminine desire emerge in the symbolic out of context and outside meaning. Explanations of these eruptions of feminine desire are patriarchy's insane attempts to make sense of feminine sexuality when it emerges from the real.

If the feminine position is repressed, the possibility exists that it can emerge into the symbolic in the manner of a symptom, and the possibility exists that it will be recognized and thus emerge into consciousness. It seems to me that there is no place in the symbolic into which it could emerge – that its realization would threaten the very structure of the order that cannot recognize it. In this way it is foreclosed. We might think we know what it is, but that is an illusion. It is impossible to describe. When we speak of it, we are only reporting the story we make up to explain its power. As Lacan says, a woman 'knows it, of course, when it comes' (*Feminine Sexuality* 74). Sackville-West outed repressed desire. By accepting the Law and its consequences, she traversed the fantasy into the other *jouissance*. The advantage of the patriarchy lies in the very fact that it is so vulnerable. Based as it is on a failure to recognize the real, patriarchy allows us what the alternatives do not: room to play.[12] Recognizing the Law as external, as Sackville-West's privileged position allowed her to do, creates a space – a fold – within patriarchy in which to escape its crippling constraints. Seeing the assumption on which patriarchy rests creates an even larger space in which to desire. There is no space in which to speak of that desire, but she could feel it. She could write it in letters of glowing water and a squeal of pain, a little gap, or an envelope once filled with sand.

Feminine Sexuality: Playing in the Folds of the Patriarchy

I think of you: I have a million things, not so much to say, as to sink into you.
            Virginia Woolf to Vita Sackville-West (16 March 1926, 3:249)

'You are a miracle of discretion – one letter in another. I never thought of that. I'll answer when I see you – the invitation, I mean,' Woolf wrote to Sackville-West (19 Nov. 1926, 3:303). Woolf's allusion to it is the only trace of this forbidden letter. As soon as it was discovered and unfolded, it was gone – merely another letter received and answered.

The letter folded in the letter: that is feminine sexuality. Hidden, turned inward, multiple. The fold makes the interior continuous with the exterior. The letter, like feminine desire, is *extimité* (extimacy), Lacan's neologism combining exterior and intimacy (Bk 7, 139). It is excess. The purloined letter, the letter turned inside out, is phallic *jouissance*.[13] Exposed and easily stolen, it can hide in plain sight because it belongs to the symbolic. Like Wallace Stevens's jar, it organizes desire around itself. Sackville-West's hidden letter was out of sight, unrivalled, unread by the jealous husband, uncontrolled by the Law. It was sent without a stamp. It arrived without a validating postmark. It reached its destination without an address. It travelled free of charge, uncensored, hidden within the letter that is within the Law. Early in their friendship Sackville-West wrote to Woolf: 'I don't suppose this letter will ever reach you. It always seems to me quite incredible anyway that any letter should ever reach its destination' (49). Braced for rejection and censorship, they wrote anyway.

Hidden within the feminine writer is the ability to desire, to send the unstamped letter, which can be read only by a feminine reader. The Law can condone this sending, look the other way, even place the fruit in the drawer to be found, but it is a secret that must not be discovered in the presence of the Law. This other *jouissance* occurs only without the stamp of patriarchal approval. The price of the symbolic – that is to say, language – cannot be paid. This other *jouissance* occurs under cover of the authorized letter, to appease the Law. If it does not challenge the Law, it will be delivered.

The hidden letter arrives at its destination like all letters. Unaddressed, its origin and destination are beyond language. What is written on its folds is unimportant. It is written in phosphorescent water. It is written in Persian sand. It is fluid. It is untraceable. It moves around, carried within the sanctioned language. It is inside the false letter, sent as a decoy. Language is an envelope that enfolds the letter. Feminine desire is surrounded by the patriarchy, but the patriarchy cannot find it. The patriarchy cannot read it. The patriarchy cannot reply to it. It has no return address. It has no origin or destination within patriarchy. Nevertheless, it arrives. This is the *jouissance de la lettre* – a bad joke playing on the concept of the *jouissance de l'être*, which Nestor Braunstein calls 'the *jouissance* from before being, before being symbolized,' in other words, of the real. There is a trace of the letter, nothing more.

What of Virginia Woolf and Vita Sackville-West? They laughed as they folded and unfolded the letter, releasing the *jouissance de l'être* from its secret crevices. They laughed, and the juice from the secret fruit moistened their lips.

Copy Cats

Whereof one cannot speak. There one must remain silent.

Wittgenstein, *Tractatus*

In preparing for the publication of *To the Lighthouse*, the Hogarth Press made a dummy copy of the novel to see how it would look. Blank inside, but in all other respects identical to the real thing, the dumb volume was sent by Woolf to Sackville-West inscribed 'In my opinion the best novel I have ever written.' Instantly regretting this gesture, she wrote: 'Dear donkey West, Did you understand that when I wrote it was my best book I merely meant because all the pages were empty? A joke, a feeble joke' (9 May 1927, 3:372). Sackville-West responded: 'But of course I realised it was a joke; what *do* you take me for? a real donkey?' (10 May 1927, 195; emphasis original).

Sent under the cover of a legitimate book jacket, Woolf's blank book

might be her best work. What is not written might be the only place in
which to read her desire. The letters speak of this struggle. They demonstrate it best when describing seemingly mundane events of their
daily lives, which both women do with an eye for comic detail that
sometimes obscures the profoundly symbolic nature of the scenes they
describe. In a letter written just before their own physical intimacy
began, Sackville-West includes this description of identity confusion in
her pets: 'My spaniel has seven puppies. My cat has five kittens. The
spaniel steals the kittens, and, carrying them very carefully in her
mouth, puts them into the puppies' basket. She then goes out for a
stroll ... and the cat ... suckles the puppies. The spaniel ... suckles the
kittens ... The kittens will bark and the puppies will mew, – That's what
will happen. But at present it makes a charming family party, – such a
warm soft young heap' (8 Sept. 1925, 67). Sackville-West's letter describes the crossing of boundaries and its result in her fantasy of the
displacement of proper language: she imagines barking kittens and
mewing puppies. Despite claims of being unable to cope, what comes
across is the joy of this mixing of milk and fur: a snuggling pile of sleepy
animals.

The letter anticipates Sackville-West's and Woolf's own crossing of
the boundaries of friendship and convention, as well as heralding their
use of animals as a safe place in which to displace desire. After their
first night together, Sackville-West is transformed into a pet: 'My dear
Mrs Nicolson – ah hah!' Woolf's letter begins. It continues, 'I am sitting
up in bed: I am very very charming; and Vita is a dear old rough coated
sheep dog: or alternatively, hung with grapes, pink with pearls,
lustrous, candle lit, in the door of a Sevenoaks draper' (22 Dec. 1925,
3:224). Sackville-West takes up the transformation, calling herself
'Towser.' The use of animal stories and alter egos is a way to tease and
flirt, have mock quarrels, and speak of what cannot be spoken.

They tease about 'dumb letters' – letters that speak not of desire but
of the banal details of their lives apart. Woolf writes that hers 'is not a
dumb letter. Dogs letters are' (15 Jan. 1926, 3:230). Responding that she
had arranged to meet Woolf later that week, Sackville-West writes: 'So
you see that if my letters are dumb, my actions aren't' (17 Jan. 1926, 86).
Speaking louder than letters, actions facilitate desire. Letters are dumb,
silent, on the subject.

e letters between Woolf and Sackville-West different
ve letters that have been written and published? Is it
written between women? Is it only that they are
nability to speak? Is it only that they call themselves

dumb? Sackville-West is not a real donkey. The blank book is not Woolf's best work. The letters struggle to create a space in which feminine desire can exist. They themselves are written in the margins of desire. Sackville-West sent Woolf letters inside letters so that Woolf could show one to Leonard Woolf while keeping the other, the real letter, for herself – ripe fruit hidden in the envelope. But margins are defined by their empty space. The struggle to write in them cramps the hand. Words cannot be found.

When Woolf wrote in anticipation of Sackville-West's first return from Persia, the animal nicknames and alter egos they have played with sporadically in their letters emerge to express rather more than affection: 'Remember your dog Grizzle [an actual dog of the Woolfs] and your Virginia, waiting you; both rather mangy; but what of that? These shabby mongrels are always the most loving, warm hearted creatures. Grizzle and Virginia will rush down to meet you – they will lick you all over' (13 April 1926, 3:253). Typical of Victorian families, the Stephens used nicknames to tenderly tease one another. Woolf was 'the goat' and her sister Vanessa Bell was 'dolphin' (Lee 109–11).[14] It was unusual for Woolf to use her sister's pet name for someone else. It is indicative of Woolf's attachment to Sackville-West and of the way that Sackville-West participated, at times, in Woolf's family dynamics.

Similarly, Sackville-West commonly used pet names within her family, usually names that suggested her bilingual childhood and the playful nature of her intimate relationships: she and Harold, for example, were 'the mars,' or the children. Nature stories, also, were a common part of her letter-writing practice. Violet Trefusis describes their exchange when young women: 'I bombarded the poor girl with letters which became more exacting as hers tended to become more and more of the "yesterday-my-pet-rabbit-had-six-babies" type' (Glendinning 23). Describing the births of pets seems to have remained a staple of Sackville-West's letters.

Pet names functioned to permit the expression of affection, much as pets function within some households to allow for the redirection of emotional and physical contact that family members are too anxious or timid to otherwise exhibit towards one another. Towards the persona marked by a pet name, the Stephen family bestowed playful, affectionate attention. Woolf's use of pet names with Sackville-West did rather more than allow for unembarrassed attention. The shared fantasy, as in her story 'Lapin and Lapinova,' allowed her to imagine erotic practice in the guise of playful frolicking, which is acceptable to the patriarchy.

Sackville-West's references to animals consistently mingled stories about her pets with silly references to herself as Towser, generally to mark the extent to which she was in favour with Woolf: 'Towser's tail began to wag again,' she writes, upon being forgiven for giving too many presents (2 Jan. 1929, 302). Details about animals and nature dominated her poetry as well, especially *The Land*. Sackville-West had a reputation as a gardener, but she came from a long line of farmers, if it is permitted to thus describe the work of the aristocracy. Woolf parodies this when Orlando thinks: 'Peasants I like. I understand crops' (311–12). Sackville-West's letters remind us of her connection to country life. They have the charm of a Beatrix Potter story, where closely observed animal activity is given a mock-serious tone that is thoroughly amusing: 'Disaster last night: Pinker [the Woolf's spaniel whom Sackville-West was keeping], in sportive mood, sprang on to my writing table, upsetting the ink stand, which poured two floods of ink (one red and the other blue) down over the back of the sofa. Pippin was drenched in the blue ink, puppy in the red. Today Pippin looks like a bruise, puppy like an accident' (letter to Woolf, 11 Dec. 1926, 153). Exemplifying a common aspect of their letters (amusing anecdotes of the I-can't-believe-this-happened-to-me variety), this story served to amuse as well as to maintain their connection to each other's daily lives. In Sackville-West's letters in particular, such anecdotes seem to take on an allegorical function, which is another version of the hidden letter. Dogs covered with ink certainly suggest the converse: letters covered with dogs. Woolf and Sackville-West represented their desire via dogs even as they turned desire into ink. Inky dogs run through the letters. Love goes to the dogs, one might say – literally and figuratively – when sportive puppies take the place of fruit on the writing table.

What can be made of this series of references to an 'insect' beginning in a letter written while Sackville-West was back in England between trips to Teheran? Sackville-West introduced the insect into the correspondence, although it is clearly a reference they had used between them previously: 'I have introduced [Pinker] to the insect, but he is rather frightened of her because she puts her paw down on him, so he creeps away to his legitimate abode' (8 Dec. 1926, 152). Woolf concluded the first letter she wrote to Sackville-West after her departure for Teheran: 'do you ever think of the basement and – and – a kiss from Pinker: one from me to the insect' (31 Jan. 1927, 3:321). The blank spaces in the letters are telling, of course. But what of kisses to insects? Further, what of muffins? Woolf wrote: 'I invented a story about two little beasts with a passion for muffins (cousins of the insect they are)' (5 Feb. 1927,

3:326). From Teheran Sackville-West wrote: 'The insect is frightfully excited about meeting you in Greece. You wouldn't have the heart to disappoint it, – would you?' (19 Feb. 1927, 175); and: 'The insect cries sometimes, and I have to mop him up. I think he's a little scared by Persia altogether, – it's too big for him' (23 Feb. 1927, 179). In March Woolf wrote: 'I want Vita: I want Insect: I want currant bun; twilight – oh and night too if you insist, with the birds singing and the stars rising. How romantic the Sackvilles are to be sure!' (6 March 1927, 3:343). The editors of Woolf's letters suggest that 'insect' was a pet name for Sackville-West, but surely this is only a partial explanation. Or, rather, 'insect' was only a partial pet name: a name for one part of Sackville-West.

Woolf's fantasies were more fully developed and less connected to any real role play than Sackville-West's. Sackville-West usually referred to herself as Towser. But Woolf called her 'Donkey West' as well as fitting her to whatever image came to hand or mind. She herself had several alter egos, including, later on, Potto, a West African lemur or sloth (Lee 825 n15), which she first used with Leonard Woolf. 'Potto' apparently indicated Woolf's slothful, invalid state. Sharing a nickname developed at home with Sackville-West was consistent with their move away from passion to friendship. Sackville-West was invited as a legitimate guest into the family circle.

Woolf's development of extended animal fantasies became especially prevalent while the physical aspect of their relationship was cooling off: 'Yes you are an agile animal – no doubt about it, but as to your gambols being diverting ... I'm not so sure. Bad, wicked beast! ... You only be a careful dolphin in your gamboling, or you'll find Virginias soft crevices lined with hooks' (4 July 1927). This letter suggests possessive jealousy, but it is long past due. Sackville-West had moved on, and Woolf knew it. The game being played was more thoroughly make-believe than the creation of animal personas, but it was a pretence they kept up, fostered by the animal game. Although close enough to visit while in the country, they arranged to see (and to miss) one another in London. They wrote of how they wish to meet, but made no plans to do so. After Sackville-West gave Woolf a string of amber beads at Christmas 1928, Woolf wrote: 'That wretched Potto is all slung with yellow beads. He rolled himself round in them, and can't be dislodged – short of cutting off his front paws, which I know you wouldn't like. But may I say, once and for all, presents are not allowed: its written all over the cage. It spoils their tempers – They suffer for it in the long run – This once will be forgiven: but never again – The night you were snared, that winter, at Long Barn [18 Dec. 1925], you slipped out Lord Steyne's paper knife, and I had then to make the terms plain: with this knife you will gash our hearts I said and the same applies to beads' (29 Dec. 1928, 3:568).[15] The violent fantasy of Potto's severed paws suggests Woolf's insistence on disentangling herself from the passion of their relationship while maintaining the playfulness of their friendship. The letters allow them to keep alive the fantasy of their passion: remembering the 'night you were snared' and their pet names for each other holds open a door in the past and into alternative possibilities for the future. Nevertheless, Woolf's playfulness suggests pain: on their first night together, Sackville-West offered her a knife that 'will gash our hearts,' and the gift of beads threatens to wound once more. Most obviously, Sackville-West's gifts emphasized the difference in their class and economic positions; Woolf did not own seventeenth-century heirlooms, nor could she have afforded to reciprocate. She had other concerns, as well. The animal jokes, like the joke copy of *To the Lighthouse*, hide anxiety over passion, success, desire and loss.

During their separations, in the midst of their greatest intimacy, they remembered each other standing in doorways. Sackville-West wrote as she travelled to Teheran for the first time that the shaking of the train kept her from pretending she had not yet left: 'and I did leave Virginia standing on her doorstep in the misty London evening' (20 Jan. 1926, 88). This image comes back again and again. It is doubled when she leaves for Teheran a second time: 'and what do I think of? of Virginia in her blue overall, leaning against the doorpost of Tavistock Square and waving ... That's what I think of' (2 Feb. 1927, 169). Similarly, Woolf recalls Sackville-West 'hung with grapes, pink with pearls, lustrous, candle lit, in the door of a Sevenoaks draper' (22 Dec. 1925, 3:224).[16] A reference to the day they first touched each other, this image of Sackville-West occurs first in Woolf's diary: 'I like her and being with her, & the splendour – she shines in the grocers shop in Sevenoaks with a candle lit radiance, stalking on legs like beech trees, pink glowing, grape clustered, pearl hung' (21 Dec. 1926, 3:52). These images persist in Woolf's fantasy of Sackville-West, who on that day opened a new door for Woolf. The parallel images of Woolf and Sackville-West standing in doorways signals more than a memory of a beloved woman. These memories suggest women on the threshold of a new world. Poised for either arrival or departure, they stand in the doorway, silent, waiting. In patriarchy, femininity is inscribed as passive and gender is

Kamp. heavy-weight

cra— interpretation

conflated, as Valerie Traub argues, with sex and with object choice. This normative elision of multiplicity enforces a structure in which women feel desire only because they are desired. Women are sexual objects; the objects of desire. Woolf and Sackville-West illustrate an alternative to this structure. They attempt to represent desire, not to be desirable. Remembering each other perpetually standing in doorways, they refuse, for a moment, the forced choice: neither entering the symbolic nor leaving it to regress into psychosis, they remain at the threshold of the real, where sense dissolves into non-sense.[17] The structure of feminine desire in the patriarchy is demonstrated in the letters, in *Orlando*, in the Woolf/Sackville-West relationship as a 'now you see it, now you don't' affair.[18]

What is the difference between Woolf and Sackville-West's relationship and other Bloomsbury love affairs? Between them, the inhibition was lessened. Feminine sexuality could not be represented, but its absence could be noticed. The squeal of pain and the piercing cry tore a hole in the symbolic. Just like the hole in Orlando's papers discovered after the revolution, the hole they created was 'big enough to put your finger through' (*Orlando* 119).

Woolf and Sackville-West employed a number of devices to resist the forced choice. But they could not stand in the threshold forever, except in their inventions of each other. '"Come in or go out, Cam,"' says Mrs Ramsay to her daughter (*To the Lighthouse* 86). But Mrs Ramsay remains seated in the open window, and it is there that Lily Briscoe sees her again when she has her vision (299). Woolf and Sackville-West did eventually come in and go out. But when she died, a picture of Woolf was on Sackville-West's writing table and four of Woolf's letters were hidden there in a secret drawer.[19]

On the day that Woolf died Leonard Woolf wrote to break the news to only one person: Vita Sackville-West.[20]

Playing in Margins of the Copy

We have left the borders and fields of the fatherland.

insignia on Vita Sackville-West's seal

Orlando was the culmination of Woolf's and Sackville-West's games of invention, but it was also their undoing. In *Orlando*, Sackville-West became copy. Woolf's desire for her was redirected into a desire to create her in words. Woolf wrote of this process to Sackville-West even before she began the book: 'Orlando will be a little book, with pictures and a map or two. I make it up in bed at night, as I walk the streets, everywhere. I want to see you in the lamplight, in your emeralds. In fact, I have never more wanted to see you than I do now – just to sit and look at you, and get you to talk, and then rapidly and secretly, correct certain doubtful points ... Please tell me beforehand when you will come, and for how long: unless the dolphin has died meanwhile and its colours are those of death and decomposition' (14 Oct. 1927, 3:430–1). Woolf's desire for Sackville-West turned into a wish to observe her in order to correct the manuscript. No longer lying in bed frittering, Woolf now put her energy to a less secret purpose. In recreating Sackville-West as Orlando, Woolf made public and speakable that which could not be said. The gap between them was filled with words.

Orlando is a love letter and revenge and a refusal to choose between the two. As Orlando herself realizes, 'Nothing is any longer one thing' (305). Woolf's novel, like Derrida's postulate of language (Of Grammatology), is both and/or and or/and. The slash separates and connects; it represents the Law of the Father (/), which informs of the possibility of transgression even as it forbids transgression. Orlando's slash anticipates Lacan's in barring the feminine position as well as marking the space of its absence. Or/andO! It is an exclamation at the discovery of alternatives.

In Three Guineas Woolf calls for a Society of Outsiders to resist the constraints of patriarchy. The members of the society would refuse social recognition – no degrees or markers of success could be accepted. The members of the society would refuse to participate in any activity that supported violence, even refusing to tend those wounded in war. The members of the society would exist in the margins of patriarchy. They would play on the edge of the Law. They would read letters received from the real. They would leave, as Sackville-West's seal attests, 'the borders and fields of the fatherland.'

Or they could eat the ripe fruit hidden from view. They could refuse to turn the peaches and cherries into copy. Their writing tables could drip with sticky juice. They could publish without revising. They could have instant success with no chance at a lasting reputation – unless their secret fruit could be discovered hidden under their oh-so-conventional covers.

Or they could exist in the real, unknown to themselves except in the moment of jouissance – a moment without words that they know when it comes.

Woolf's Society of Outsiders, Sackville-West's secret fruit, Lacan's feminine position all recognize the same thing. But they did not exchange letters about their discoveries. They published their secrets, keeping them hidden.

Even Lacan's 'Love Letter' cannot speak of itself, if that is what it sets out to do. But when the exchange of letters focuses on the letters themselves – even on their arrival or failure to arrive – what is omitted is that which is unwritten: the anticipation of the receiver. The receiver waits for a letter that may or may not have been sent. 'Oh damn, Vita –,' Woolf writes, 'no letter at all ... You seem utterly disappeared, at the moment ... You seem gone, gone, for ever' (29 March 1927, 3:353). The receiver waits for a letter that may or may not have been written. The receiver does not know whether to wait. The receiver may not wait. The letter may arrive unexpectedly. The letter may not arrive at all. How is the receiver to know? The receiver can know only that which has been received. The foreclosed letter, the letter never sent, never written, cannot be opened. The writer remembers the receiver standing in the doorway.

What is repressed in Lacan's 'Love Letter' is the affective response to the letter. Emotion, repressed as an effect of the foreclosure of feminine sexuality, is translated into theory – the most valued language of the patriarchy. Try as he might – and he tries mightily – Lacan's letter is mere copy. Perhaps it is for this reason that he turns to the graphs and to set theory. Does this escape the limits of language? Graphs further repress affective response – at least at first. Later they can glow like sandy phosphorescence.

Like *Orlando*, Lacan is difficult. Like Orlando, Lacan turns away from desire. But that is because we all turn away. Patriarchy's love letter has wide margins, but they are blank. What we feel, what we desire, how we play (*jouer*) in those margins cannot be recorded. Even if we receive the letter, all we can do in response is to copy it down. Because we all must live here now, we all are copy cats.

What is different about the letters between Woolf and Sackville-West? Are they interesting to us because they are lively letters written by two consummate letter writers? Certainly. But they are more than that. Are they fascinating because they help us to understand the structure of a forbidden relationship before the problematic, indefinable term 'lesbian' was even available for use and misuse? Without a doubt. But, again, they are even more than that. They help us to see, despite their clever words, where language breaks down into the barking of kittens and the mewing of dogs. Desire, however we might define it now, however it might be used to describe their relationship, is redefined by Woolf and Sackville-West as feminine desire. As such, it is failed by language. Yet as long as they write, they do not fail each other. Their letters invent each other; their letters reinvent desire. They stand waiting in a doorway.

8 Subverted Subjects

Embracing Lack

Everything, in fact, was something else.

Woolf, *Orlando* (143)

Orlando realizes, while making metaphors about nature, that 'Every-thing, in fact, was something else' (143). This somewhat literal under-standing of the fluid nature of figures of speech has its practical side for Orlando, who has just turned, inexplicably, from a man into a woman. Orlando awakens one morning to find that he, in fact, is something else. When she recognizes this same process of transformation abounding in descriptions of nature, her own change of sex assumes a larger context. No longer simply a bewildering incident, Orlando's sex change be-comes another moment of glorious instability that both demands and resists interpretation.

These moments of holding open a space that cannot, need not, be filled are necessary moments for the emergence of feminine sexual desire. A much quoted axiom of Lacan is that The Woman does not exist.[1] While lacking in subtlety, the most accessible gloss on this notori-ous notion is offered by Catherine Clément: 'Wave after wave of femi-nists have been saying the same thing for a century, and they were saying the same thing when Lacan made the point in his own way. When women rise up against the myth of women that men have foisted upon them in our cultures, they too are denying the existence of the eternal Woman' (62). Celebrating the absence of The Woman, then, is one way of resisting patriarchal repression of women.

Patriarchy's insistence on stability and decidability – its repression of lack and female sexuality – cannot be easily fought. Its regulations are internalized in what Freud called the superego. A struggle against external restrictions (whether legislated or social) would be easier if the superego were recognized as a structure of internal domination that undermines an individual's conscious efforts to free herself or himself from political and psychological oppression. By this formulation, the superego is equivalent to ideology. In Freud's words, the superego is the source of 'the critical agency' ('Group Psychology'), a mechanism by which the Law of the Fathers is recognized and questioned as well as enforced. In his reading of Freud, Lacan argues that Freud's formulation of the tripartite structure – ego, superego, and id – was the result of his repression of the unconscious, which, in Lacan's view, cannot be organized so neatly. Freud's repression similarly obliterates the critical function of the superego that recognizes the Law as constructed, a recognition illustrated in the work of Woolf and Sackville-West.

If The Woman does not exist, then she is not subject to the repressions of patriarchy. Feminine desire is unregulated, albeit unrecognized. Woolf and Sackville-West communicated their desire for one another in code, simultaneously marking and escaping the censorship of representation. Even after sexology and psychoanalysis introduced categories and descriptions of sexuality into the common language, Woolf and Sackville-West consciously refused to identify with a group defined by sexuality or sexual practice. Emma Donoghue argues that women do not need to have a vocabulary in order to experience passion (8). Woolf and Sackville-West did not need one in order to express it. As Lacan posits, feminine desire is outside the symbolic order; this can be taken as repressive or, as Woolf and Sackville-West exemplify, it can be liberating.

My attention to the psychological aspect of repression is not intended to diminish the pain of physical suffering and abuse or to dismiss political activism. On the contrary, I believe that lasting social change can be brought about only if we change the unconscious structures that enforce obedience to patriarchal Law. Both literature and psychoanalysis provide access to the unconscious and therefore offer the potential to create real and lasting social change. By reading literature, biography, and psychoanalysis reciprocally, I hope to have brought the insights of each to bear on the others. Like the case study, biography is an arena for the representation and analysis of subjectivity. Biography was an important genre for Woolf, not only because of the way that biography functioned as a common form among members of the Bloomsbury

Rayu all be nord
for reading

Group, but also because it was her father's métier. It is not surprising to find that Woolf's struggle to create an alternative to dominating patriarchal authority would occur in *Orlando: A Biography*. I suggest that *Orlando* posits an alternative to Freud's ultimate understanding of the superego as enforcer of patriarchal Law.

Thinking about *Orlando* and the way its narrative voice offers alternatives to structural constraints led me to reinvestigate Freud's construction of the superego as initially containing a critical agency or self-consciousness. Woolf's Biographer in *Orlando* embodies this abstract concept, suggesting that a more flexible relationship to authority is possible and is a way to escape the Oedipal stalemate of openly fighting the father (and thus taking his place), submitting to patriarchal Law (and perpetually struggling in hysterical silence), or regressing into the pre-Oedipal fantasy of maternal merger (which is actualized as psychosis). *Orlando*'s Biographer's comfort with recognizing the existence of the Law and indifference to complying with it poses a possibility on the other side of the Oedipal resolution that Freud's theory does not reach.

I see *Orlando*'s Biographer as the rare emergence of the feminine position, which is (usually) repressed into unconsciousness.[2] The feminine position is so abstract that proposing such a concrete example of it seems both miraculous and heretical. Nevertheless, the Biographer functions, I believe, from that position. *Orlando* calls up resistance because identity depends on the belief that the ego is constant and that lack can be filled. It is upon these beliefs that patriarchy (and thus much of the feminist fight against patriarchy) is sustained. *Orlando* does not directly attack patriarchy. While critical, it contains no overt plan for a takeover or the destruction of the world as we know it. Instead, *Orlando*, like the feminine position, reveals patriarchy as constructed and empty of intrinsic power. The Law has power only in the ways we grant it power. This is a difficult message. It does not offer the satisfaction of political action as feminists have typically conceived it. Outwardly, it changes nothing. At the end of an analytic session, the analysand rises up from the couch physically unchanged; at the end of *Orlando*, the reader looks up from the book physically unchanged. But everything has changed: 'Everything, in fact [is] something else' (*Orlando* 143).

I believe that to resist the notion that women are inherently sexually repressed, passive, hysterical, or simply asexual is crucial, even central, to the work of feminism. Just as early feminist critics such as Mary Ellmann, Sandra Gilbert and Susan Gubar, and Kate Millet rejected the polarizing of women into the categories of virgin or whore, so too must current feminist scholars frustrate attempts to skirt this dichotomy by simply ignoring female sexuality altogether.

Throughout their love affair and friendship, Woolf and Sackville-West wrote: they wrote to each other, they wrote for each other, and they wrote for publication. There are instances, as in the case of *Orlando*, when these three gestures coincide. *Orlando* is a very personal book. An extended in-joke between Woolf and Sackville-West, it is the work of an obsessed lover packaged for public consumption. But *Orlando*'s declarations are not simply about love; they are also about writing – particularly the writing of biography.

Orlando is the most widely noted instance of the Woolf/Sackville-West textual exchange, and, apart from their letters, it is the most overt example of the way they extended their relationship into the literature they produced under each other's influence. Written during the end of their affair, Woolf and Sackville-West wrote to each other about the book, playfully referring to its date of publication, 11 Oct. 1928, as the end of their relationship: 'If October 11th is to see the end of our romance, it would be as well to make the most of the short time that remains to us,' Sackville-West wrote (9 Aug. 1928, 276). Yet *Orlando*'s publication did not end their romance: it marked its change in emphasis from physical to textual expression.

The life and work of Sackville-West influenced Woolf's playful biography, and after publication *Orlando* influenced Sackville-West's work. *Orlando* occurred within the multiple context of a relationship that ran persistently on three tracks: personal contact, private correspondence, and literary publications. The strategy of subtle disobedience Woolf employs in *Orlando* can be seen in Sackville-West's earlier biography of Aphra Behn. Behn, Orlando, Sackville-West, Woolf. There are several points of similarity among these four women. Four writers, four cross-dressers,[3] two lovers. All defiant, triumphant women who spoke their minds.

What Woolf and Sackville-West wrote under each other's influence, most successfully in their letters, attempts to represent women who cherish other women, as they themselves cherished each other. They tried again and again to represent and to embrace lack insofar as Woman is that which is absent from patriarchy. While they may not have succeeded, they did, for a time, escape the social pressure against attempting such an embrace. They embraced each other.

They embraced each other as women and as writers. They influenced each other in life and work. During the period of greatest mutual influence, the time in which their relationship was turning into 'copy,' they collaborated in integrating form and content to create biographies that present a radical critique of the unified subject. Woolf and Sackville-West embraced lack and indeterminacy in biographies that challenge the biographical form and the very structure of subjectivity.

A Mobile Biography

... it sprung upon me how I could revolutionise biography in a night: and so if agreeable to you I would like to toss this up in the air and see what happens.

Virginia Woolf, proposing *Orlando* to Vita Sackville-West
(9 Oct. 1927, *Letters* 3:427–9)

Woolf scholars have been much agitated over the representation of Virginia Woolf in Stephen Daldry's film version of Michael Cunningham's brilliant novel *The Hours*.[4] While Cunningham's intertextual tour de force is a homage to Woolf, the sensibility of the film seems unaware of the complexities of Woolf's work and life. Regardless of the film's merits, Woolf scholars are understandably anxious about the projection of Woolf on screen. While many have rejoiced over the increased attention the film has brought to Woolf and her work, objections have been raised to the pathologizing of Woolf as a tortured genius out of touch with reality who seems to be sexually attracted to her sister, who appears to be more of a socialite than a successful painter. My own informal survey confirmed that the film misleads viewers into thinking Woolf's suicide occurred at the completion of *Mrs. Dalloway* rather than sixteen years later, when Woolf was nearly sixty. The film's reductive presentation of her life represses the unknown and overdetermined causes of her final decision even as it romanticizes it. While it is not surprising that a film made for popular consumption would participate in the comforting repression of subjectivity into a unified identity, it is particularly distressing to see Woolf, who fought diligently against such dumbing down of representations of women, become the victim in this way.

By way of resistance, then, and in an attempt to put into practice the lessons of the partnership between Woolf and Sackville-West that produced *Aphra Behn*, *Orlando*, and *A Room of One's Own*, what follows is a subverted biography of Woolf, which abandons chronology and puts into play the irreconcilable facets of her life. Ideally, this interactive biography would escape the restrictions of the page as a mobile, so that the terms could undulate in space and time as well as conflict in unstoppable oscillation.

Step 1: Photocopy the following pages of words, all of which describe Virginia Woolf. Consider using various colours of paper in the copier.

Step 2: Tear or cut the words apart from one another. Do not think about this step for long, but be guided by your own responses as you create shapes that are regular, organic, abstract, or some combination. I have found that squares and amoeba-like shapes give the final product variety. Discard, combine, mutilate, or add words as you like. If you wish, you can attach the bits of paper to other objects. Your choice will affect the longevity of the project. For example, it is a creative way to use CDs you cannot overwrite and no longer need, and the shiny prism effect is particularly nice on a sunny day. This version will last quite a long time, depending on your choice in step 4. If you attach the bits of paper to, say, pieces of fruit, the effect is striking but short lived.

Step 3: Optional: decorate the slips of paper with paint, glitter, or any medium that appeals to you. A range of highlighters works well, especially if you are doing the project in your office.

Step 4: Attach the bits of paper to strings. Tape or glue would be traditional choices, but I have found that paper clips, although frustrating, produce a nice snow-flurry effect over the course of time. You might want to vary the length of the string you use, and be sure to consider string alternatives. I highly recommend tape from old cassettes.

Step 5: Attach the strings to something that you can hang. This structure can be as simple or as elaborate as you like. Clothes hangers work well, as do exposed pipes and the slats of Venetian blinds.

Step 6: Enjoy the spinning instability that is the life of Virginia Woolf as you have created it, knowing that you have made her up.

A Virginia Woolf Mobile

ANTI-SEMITIC

AUNT

BIOGRAPHER

BLOOMSBURY GROUP MEMBER

BOOK REVIEWER

CHILDLESS

DAUGHTER

DIARIST

DEPRESSIVE

DOG OWNER

EMPLOYER

ENGLISH

ESSAYIST

FAMOUS

FEMINIST

FRIGID

HOMEOWNER

HOSTESS

INCEST SURVIVOR

ICON

INSECURE

JOURNALIST

LESBIAN

LETTER WRITER

LIBERAL

LONDONER

LOVER

MARRIED

MIDDLE CLASS

MODERNIST

MEMOIRIST

NOVELIST

ORPHAN

PATRON

PRIVILEGED

POLITICAL ACTIVIST

PRANKSTER

PUBLIC SPEAKER

PUBLISHER

SAPPHIST

SATIRIST

SELF-EDUCATED

SEXUALLY ABUSED

SHORT-STORY WRITER

SISTER

SMOKER

SNOB

SOCIALIST

STEPSISTER

SUICIDE

VITA SACKVILLE-WEST'S LOVER

WHITE

WRITER

WOMAN

Appendix A: A Chronology of Virginia Woolf and Vita Sackville-West's Relationship

1922	Woolf's novel *Jacob's Room* was published.
	Sackville-West published her story collection *The Heir* and also *Knole and the Sackvilles*.
14 Dec.	Woolf and Sackville-West met at a dinner party given by Woolf's brother-in-law, Clive Bell. Later that month the Woolfs dined with Sackville-West and Harold Nicolson at the Nicolson's London house in Ebury Street.
1923	Sackville-West's novel *Grey Wethers* was published, as was *The Diary of the Lady Anne Clifford*, which was edited by Sackville-West. Interest in this diary was created by references to it in *Knole and the Sackvilles*. Sackville-West began to write book reviews for the *Nation*, where Leonard Woolf had become literary editor.
11 Jan.	Sackville-West and Harold Nicolson dined with the Woolfs at Hogarth House, their home in Richmond.
15 March	At Woolf's invitation, Sackville-West and Harold Nicolson dined with Vanessa Bell and Duncan Grant at Gordon Square, Bloomsbury. The Woolfs, Clive Bell, and Lytton Strachey also were guests. Woolf's invitation included a suggestion that they look at Julia Margaret Cameron's photographs (*Letters* 3:18–19).
26 March	Sackville-West invited Woolf to join PEN.
15 April	Woolf declined the invitation.
1924	Woolf's essay 'Mr. Bennett and Mrs. Brown' was published, and she was writing *Mrs. Dalloway* and the essays

	for *The Common Reader*. The Hogarth Press published Freud's *Collected Papers*. Sackville-West's novel *Challenge* was published in the United States.
Jan.	Woolf dined with Sackville-West, Siegfried Sassoon, and Lord Berners
13 March	The Woolfs moved from Richmond to Tavistock Square in Bloomsbury. Sackville-West offered to lend them her car to help with the move, but neither of the Woolfs could drive (*Letters* 3:93).
19 March	Sackville-West visited Woolf (alone) in Bloomsbury. Sackville-West wrote to Harold Nicolson that afterwards her 'head [was] swimming with Virginia' (*Letters* 3:94n3).
5 July	Sackville-West took Woolf, Geoffrey Scot (with whom Sackville-West was having an affair), and Dorothy Wellesley (who was in love with Sackville-West) to Knole and then, after lunching with Lord Sackville, to Long Barn, where they were joined by Harold Nicolson.
6 July	Woolf requested an intimate letter (*Letters* 3:117).
16 July	Sackville-West wrote an intimate letter in which she charged Woolf with looking upon human relationships as copy and promised her *Seducers in Ecuador*.
13 Sept.	Sackville-West stayed overnight at Rodmell for the first time. Both Leonard and Virginia Woolf were present. On this visit, Sackville-West delivered *Seducers in Ecuador*, which was dedicated to Woolf. Sackville-West subsequently published her fiction with the Hogarth Press until Woolf's death, after which Leonard Woolf rejected her work.
1925	During the winter and spring, Woolf and Sackville-West met more and more often; Woolf was ill with headaches in summer and fall, during which time their letters became more frequent and longer, more substantive (especially in their discussions of literature), and occasionally flirtatious.
Nov.	Harold Nicolson went to Teheran; Sackville-West agreed to join him in January.
7 Nov.	Madge Vaughan (the original of Sally Seton) died.
17–19 Dec.	Woolf spent three nights at Long Barn with Sackville-West. This was the start of the physical aspect of their relationship, which continued at least until fall 1927. Sackville-West confessed in a letter to Harold Nicolson: 'I *have* gone

to bed with her (twice), but that's all. Now you know all about it, and I hope I haven't shocked you' (17 Aug. 1926, 158).

1926

Jan. Sackville-West, along with Dorothy Wellesley, travelled to Teheran, where Harold Nicolson was posted with the Foreign Office. Sackville-West returned in May.

Spring Woolf published *Mrs. Dalloway* and *The Common Reader* and began planning *To the Lighthouse*. Sackville-West worked on her long poem *The Land*.

June Sackville-West spent two nights with Woolf at Monk's House. On the first night Leonard was present; on the second night he returned to London. ('I did sleep with her at Rodmell' Sackville-West wrote to Nicolson [150].)

Summer Sackville-West wrote about her trip to Persia in *Passenger to Teheran*. Woolf and Sackville-West went out together in London to the theatre and ballet, to dinner and parties.

26 July Sackville-West gave the Woolfs a dog called Pinker.

30 Sept. Sackville-West's long poem *The Land* was published and received highly positive critical attention.

1927

Jan. Sackville-West returned to Teheran.

14 March Woolf wrote in her diary that she had conceived a new book, 'The Jessamy Brides,' which would become *Orlando*.

May Sackville-West returned. Woolf sent Sackville-West a dummy copy of *To the Lighthouse*, followed by a real copy. Sackville-West met Mary Campbell.

18 May Woolf lectured at Oxford; Sackville-West accompanied her.

16 June Sackville-West was awarded the Hawthornden Prize for *The Land*; Woolf attended the presentation.

28–9 June The Woolfs, Nicolsons, and others travelled to Yorkshire to watch the eclipse of the sun at dawn.

Summer Sackville-West wrote *Aphra Behn*, which was published that fall, and *Twelve Days*, which described her trip across the mountains of southern Persia on horseback. Woolf began to plan *The Waves*.

Oct. Sackville-West and Campbell began an affair. Woolf decided to write *Orlando* about Sackville-West. She wrote to

Sackville-West: 'But listen: suppose Orlando turns out to be about Vita; and it's all about you and the lusts of your flesh and the lure of your mind (heart you have none, who go gallivanting down the lanes with Campbell – suppose there's the kind of shimmer of reality which sometimes attaches to my people?' (9 Oct. 1927, 3:429).

1928

Sept.   Sackville-West's travel book *Twelve Days* was published. Woolf and Sackville-West went to France for a week.

11 Oct.   *Orlando* was published.

26 Oct.   Woolf gave the lectures that would be published as *A Room of One's Own*. Sackville-West attended as her guest.

9 Nov.   Woolf attended the Radclyffe Hall obscenity trial; Sir Chartres Biron ruled her evidence inadmissible, since she was an expert on art, not obscenity.

16 Nov.   *The Well of Loneliness* was ruled an obscene libel.

14 Dec.   Radclyffe Hall's appeal was rejected; *The Well of Loneliness* was ordered to be destroyed.

1929   *The King's Daughter*, Sackville-West's book of love poems to women, was published by the Hogarth Press; she also published a critical study, *Andrew Marvell*. Woolf's *A Room of One's Own* was published. Sackville-West became involved with Hilda Matheson, a producer at the BBC. Sackville-West and Harold Nicolson gave a series of radio talks on marriage, which Matheson produced.

1931   Sackville-West's novel *All Passion Spent* was published, and Woolf's novel *The Waves* was published.

1936   Sackville-West's biography *Saint Joan of Arc* was published; Woolf was critical of its emphasis on facts.

1940   Woolf published both *Flush*, a parody of biography inspired by the cocker spaniel Pinker, and the real biography *Roger Fry*.

1941   Woolf died.

1943   Sackville-West published *The Eagle and the Dove: A Study of Contrasts, St. Teresa of Avila*, and *St Thérèse of Lisieux*.

1964   Sackville-West died.

1973   Nigel Nicolson's *Portrait of a Marriage* was published.

1975–80   Woolf's *Letters* was published.

1977–84   Woolf's *Diaries* was published.

1985   *The Letters of Vita Sackville-West to Virginia Woolf*, edited by Louise DeSalvo and Mitchell Leaska, was published.

Appendix B: A Chronology of Virginia Woolf's and Vita Sackville-West's Publications, 1922–9

	Sackville-West	Woolf
1922	*The Heir: A Love Story* *Knole and the Sackvilles*	*Jacob's Room*
1923	*Grey Wethers: A Romantic Novel* *The Diary of the Lady Anne Clifford* (ed.)	
1924	*Challenge* (published in New York) *Seducers in Ecuador*	'Mr. Bennett and Mrs. Brown'
1925		*The Common Reader* *Mrs. Dalloway*
1926	*The Land* (winner of the Hawthornden Prize for Poetry) *Passenger to Teheran*	
1927	*Aphra Behn: The Incomparable Astrea*	*To the Lighthouse*
1928	*Twelve Days: An Account of a Journey across the Bakhitari Mountains in South-Western Persia*	*Orlando: A Biography*
1929	*The King's Daughter* (poems) *Andrew Marvell*	*A Room of One's Own*

Appendix C: A Selected Chronological Bibliography of Virginia Woolf and Sexuality, 1972–99

1972

Bell, Quentin. *Virginia Woolf: A Biography*. 2 vols. New York: Harcourt. 1972.

1973

Heilbrun, Carolyn. *Toward a Recognition of Androgyny*. New York: Knopf, 1973.

Nicolson, Nigel. *Portrait of a Marriage*. New York: Atheneum, 1973.

1975

Rubin, Gayle. 'The Traffic in Women: Notes toward a Political Economy of Sex.' Ed. Rayna Reiter. *Toward an Anthropology of Women*. New York: Monthly Review P, 1975.

Smith-Rosenberg, Carroll. 'The Female World of Love and Ritual: Relations between Women in Nineteenth-Century America.' *Signs: The Journal of Women in Culture and Society* 1 (1975): 1–29.

Woolf, Virginia. *The Letters of Virginia Woolf*. Ed. Nigel Nicolson and Joanne Trautmann. Vol. 1: *1888–1912*. New York: Harcourt, 1975.

1976

Woolf, Virginia. *The Letters of Virginia Woolf*. Ed. Nigel Nicolson and Joanne Trautmann. Vol. 2: *1912–1922*. New York: Harcourt, 1976.

– *Moments of Being: Unpublished Autobiographical Writings*. Ed. and intro. Jeanne Schulkind. New York: Harcourt, 1976.

1977

Weeks, Jeffrey. *Coming Out: Homosexual Politics in Britain from the Nineteenth Century to the Present*. London: Quartet, 1977.

Woolf, Virginia. *The Diary of Virginia Woolf*. Ed. Anne Olivier Bell. Vol. 1: *1915–1919*. New York: Harcourt, 1977.
– *The Letters of Virginia Woolf*. Ed. Nigel Nicolson and Joanne Trautmann. Vol. 3: *1923–1928*. New York: Harcourt, 1978.

1978

Auerbach, Nina. *Communities of Women: An Idea in Fiction*. Cambridge: Harvard UP, 1978.
Faderman, Lillian. 'The Morbidification of Love between Women by 19th-Century Sexologists.' *Journal of Homosexuality* 4.1 (1978): 73–90.
Foucault, Michel. *The History of Sexuality*. Vol. 1: *An Introduction*. Trans. Robert Hurley. New York: Pantheon, 1978.
Woolf, Virginia. *The Diary of Virginia Woolf*. Ed. Anne Olivier Bell with Andrew McNeillie. Vol. 2: *1920–1924*. New York: Harcourt, 1978.
– *The Letters of Virginia Woolf*. Ed. Nigel Nicolson and Joanne Trautmann. Vol. 4: *1929–1934*. New York: Harcourt, 1978.

1979

Cook, Blanche Wiesen. '"Women Alone Stir My Imagination": Lesbianism and the Cultural Tradition.' *Signs: The Journal of Women in Culture & Society* 4 (1979): 718–39.
Marks, Elaine. 'Lesbian Intertextuality.' *Homosexualities and French Literature: Cultural Contexts / Critical Texts*. Ed. George Stambolian and Elaine Marks. Ithaca: Cornell UP, 1979.
Woolf, Virginia. *The Letters of Virginia Woolf*. Ed. Nigel Nicolson and Joanne Trautmann. Vol. 5: *1932–1935*. New York: Harcourt, 1979.

1980

Rich, Adrienne. 'Compulsory Heterosexuality.' *Women: Sex and Sexuality*. Ed. Catherine Stimpson and Ethel Spector Person. Chicago: U of Chicago P, 1980.
Woolf, Virginia. *The Diary of Virginia Woolf*. Ed. Anne Olivier Bell with Andrew McNeillie. Vol. 3: *1925–1930*. New York: Harcourt, 1980.
– *The Letters of Virginia Woolf*. Ed. Nigel Nicolson and Joanne Trautmann. Vol. 6: *1936–1941*. New York: Harcourt, 1980.

1981

Faderman, Lillian. *Surpassing the Love of Men: Romantic Friendship and Love between Women from the Renaissance to the Present*. New York: Morrow, 1981.

Licata, Salvatore J., and Robert P. Peterson, eds. *Historical Perspectives on Homosexuality*. Binghamton, NY: Haworth, 1981.

Marcus, Jane, ed. *New Feminist Essays on Virginia Woolf*. Lincoln: U of Nebraska P, 1981.

Stimpson, Catharine R. 'Zero Degree Deviancy: The Lesbian Novel in English.' *Critical Inquiry* 8.2 (1981): 363–80.

Zimmerman, Bonnie. 'What Has Never Been: An Overview of Lesbian Criticism.' *Feminism Studies* 7.3 (1981): 451–75.

1982

DeSalvo, Louise. 'Lighting the Cave: The Relationship between Vita Sackville-West and Virginia Woolf.' *Signs: The Journal of Women in Culture and Society* 8 (1982): 195–214.

Woolf, Virginia. *The Diary of Virginia Woolf*. Ed. Anne Olivier Bell with Andrew McNeillie. Vol. 4: *1931–1935*. New York: Harcourt, 1982.

1983

Glendinning, Victoria. *Vita: A Biography of Vita Sackville-West*. New York: Knopf, 1983.

Irigaray, Luce. *Speculum of the Other Woman*. Trans. Gillian Gill. Ithaca: Cornell UP, 1983.

Zimmerman, Bonnie. 'Is "Chloe Liked Olivia" a Lesbian Plot?' *Women's Studies International Forum* 6.2 (1983): 169–75.

1984

Newton, Esther. 'The Mythic Mannish Lesbian: Radclyffe Hall and the New Woman.' *Signs: Journal of Women in Culture and Society* 9.4 (1984): 557–75.

Woolf, Virginia. *The Diary of Virginia Woolf*. Ed. Anne Olivier Bell with Andrew McNeillie. Vol. 5: *1936–1941*. New York: Harcourt, 1984.

1985

Irigaray, Luce. *This Sex Which Is Not One*. Trans. Catherine Porter with Carolyn Burke. Ithaca: Cornell UP, 1985.

Sackville-West, Vita. *The Letters of Vita Sackville-West to Virginia Woolf*. Ed. Louise DeSalvo and Mitchell Leaska. New York: Morrow, 1985.

Sedgwick, Eve Kosofsky. *Between Men: English Literature and Male Homosocial Desire*. New York: Columbia UP, 1985.

1987
Whitlock, Gillian. '"Everything Is Out of Place": Radclyffe Hall and the Lesbian Literary Tradition.' *Feminist Studies* 13.3 (1987): 555–82.

1988
Greenberg, David. *The Construction of Homosexuality*. Chicago: U of Chicago P, 1988.
Hoagland, Sarah. *Lesbian Ethics: Toward New Value*. Institute of Lesbian Studies, 1988.
Knopp, Sherron E. '"If I Saw You Would You Kiss Me?": Sapphism and the Subversiveness of Virginia Woolf's *Orlando*.' *PMLA* 103.1 (1988): 24–34.

1989
Caughie, Pamela L. 'Virginia Woolf's Double Discourse.' *Discontented Discourses: Feminism/Textual Intervention/Psychoanalysis*. Ed. Marleen S. Barr and Richard Feldstein. Urbana: U of Illinois P, 1989. 41–53.
DeSalvo, Louise. *Virginia Woolf: The Impact of Childhood Sexual Abuse on Her Life and Work*. Boston: Beacon, 1989.
Duberman, Martin Bauml, Martha Vicinus, and George Chauncy, Jr, eds. *Hidden From History: Reclaiming the Gay and Lesbian Past*. New York: NAL, 1989.
Roof, Judith. 'The Match in the Crocus: Representations of Lesbian Sexuality.' *Discontented Discourses: Feminism/Textual Intervention/ Psychoanalysis*. Ed. Marleen S. Barr and Richard Feldstein. Urbana: Illinois UP, 1989.
Rosenman, Ellen Bayuk. 'Sexual Identities and *A Room of One's Own*: "Secret Economies" in Virginia Woolf's Feminist Discourse.' *Signs: Journal of Women in Culture and Society* 14 (1989): 634–50.

1990
Butler, Judith. *Gender Trouble: Feminism and the Subversion of Identity*. New York: Routledge, 1990.
Jay, Karla, and Joanne Glasgow, eds. *Lesbian Texts and Contexts (Feminist Crosscurrents)*. New York: New York UP, 1990.
Segdwick, Eve Kosofsky. *The Epistemology of the Closet*. Berkeley: U of California P, 1990.

1991
Hobby, Elaine, and Chris White, eds. *What Lesbians Do in Books*. London: Women's P, 1991.

1992

Dynes, Wayne R., and Stephen Donaldson, eds. *Homosexual Themes in Literary Studies*. New York: Garland, 1992.

Marcus, Jane, *Virginia Woolf and the Languages of Patriarchy*. Bloomington: Indiana UP, 1987.

Meese, Elizabeth. 'When Virginia Looked at Vita, What Did She See; or Lesbian: Feminist: Woman – What's the Differ(e/a)nce?' *Feminist Studies* 18.1 (1992): 99–117.

1993

Butler, Judith. *Bodies That Matter: On the Discursive Limits of 'Sex.'* New York: Routledge, 1993.

Castle, Terry. *The Apparitional Lesbian: Female Homosexuality and Modern Culture*. New York: Columbia UP, 1993.

Raitt, Suzanne. *Vita and Virginia: The Work and Friendship of V. Sackville-West and Virginia Woolf*. Oxford: Clarendon P. 1993.

1996

Lee, Hermione. *Virginia Woolf*. London: Chatto, 1996.

1997

Barrett, Eileen, and Patricia Cramer, eds. *Virginia Woolf: Lesbian Readings*. New York: New York UP, 1997.

1998

Kaivola, Karen. 'Virginia Woolf, Vita Sackville-West, and the Question of Sexual Identity.' *Woolf Studies Annual* 4 (1998): 17–40.

1999

Silver, Brenda. *Virginia Woolf Icon*. Chicago: U of Chicago P, 1999.

Notes

Chapter 1: Desiring Women

1 Bell was well aware that Woolf was attracted to women prior to this conversation. Indeed, Bell teased her sister about it in a letter responding to Woolf's (brief) engagement to Lytton Strachey: 'with your cultivation of Sapphism ... and Lytton's of Sodomism ... you will be a fine couple worthy of each other when you both come out' (94). Eileen Barrett's liberal list of Woolf's love interests includes Violet Dickinson, Ottoline Morrell, Octavia Wilberforce, and Ethel Smyth, in addition to Sackville-West (4–6).

2 Queen Victoria's comment was allegedly made in response to the question of whether or not to make lesbianism as well as male homosexuality illegal in the Labouchère Amendment (i.e., sec. 2) of the Criminal Law Amendment Act of 1885. It is more likely that the wording of the amendment was made deliberately vague in order to avoid giving people ideas.

3 Martha Vicinus calls for further study of the period before and after the First World War: 'The public discourse on sexuality had clearly altered by the 1920s, but we have yet to unravel the complex historical elements that brought about these changes' (228). Many critics have answered this call. Building on and revising the important early work of critics such as Vicinus, Lillian Faderman, Carroll Smith-Rosenberg, and Jeffrey Weeks, work in cultural criticism, gender studies, and lesbian and gay studies has begun to give us a much fuller picture of the discourses on sexuality in Britain throughout history. See, for example, Doan, Donoghue, Lisa Moore, and Traub. My discussion of Sackville-West's journal, letters, poetry, and fiction shows how that transformation occurred for her. Bloomsbury's open closet is another example. Although publications of group members stop at iconoclasm, their private lives and conversations were carefully

provocative. When Foucault refers to Queen Victoria as 'the imperial prude' (3), he shows himself heir not only to Lytton Strachey's public project of historical debunking but also to the private attitude of mocking defiance members of the Bloomsbury Group used among themselves.

4 Woolf typically capitalizes all forms of 'Sapphic.' I will employ current usage, which distinguishes between Sapphic as a reference to the poet Sappho and sapphic as a reference to lesbianism. Following the editors of Woolf's and Sackville-West's letters, I will not regularize their spelling and punctuation in quotations even though doing so results in inconsistencies between my usage and theirs.

5 Four letters from Woolf to Sackville-West, discovered by researcher Patty Brandhorst in a hidden drawer of Sackville-West's writing table at Sissinghurst, have convinced some Woolf scholars that Woolf and Sackville-West continued to engage in sexual intimacy longer than was previously assumed. Although they are flirtatious, I do not find the letters conclusive. The most suggestive, dated 24 August 1932, ends: 'And when am I going to see you? Because you know you love now several people, women I mean, physically I mean, better, oftener, more carnally than me' (Banks 2).

6 Vanessa Bell's husband, Clive, had a mistress before and throughout most of their marriage, and her own companion, Duncan Grant, who had previously been involved with her brother Adrian Stephen, was primarily gay.

7 As her biographer, Gretchen Gerzina, describes her, Carrington typifies the conflicts experienced by many women coming of age in early twentieth-century England: 'As a product of the late Victorian period, she shared with a great many young women a personal dilemma. Her adolescent rebellions had been against the restrictions of religion and social convention, as interpreted by her mother, yet to a large extent these prejudices lasted throughout her life. Although she had fought against sexual repression, she herself remained sexually "repressed" for years' (73).

8 This is a point undisputed by Woolf's many biographers. Quentin Bell writes that Woolf 'shr[a]nk from the crudities of sex, a disposition which resulted from some profound and perhaps congenital inhibition ... she regarded sex, not so much with horror, as with incomprehension' (2:5–6). Phyllis Rose comments: 'What pleasure Leonard got from this sexless union ... we can only imagine' (86–7).

9 An outsider to Bloomsbury, Sackville-West was an aristocrat, whose grandmother was a Gypsy dancer. This exotic history raises important questions about national and racial identity in her work that are beyond the scope of this study. Both topics have been addressed extensively by

Woolf scholars. See Jane Garrity, *Step-Daughters of England*; Patricia Laurence, *Lily Briscoe's Chinese Eyes*; and Jane Marcus, *Hearts of Darkness*. Gretchen Holbrook Gerzina, in her keynote speech at the 2004 Virginia Woolf Conference, 'Bushmen and Blackface: Bloomsbury and Race,' argued that 'race often provided a cultural and artistic touchstone' (n.p.) for members of the Bloomsbury Group.

10 Especially influential are Louise DeSalvo, 'Lighting the Cave' and Jane Marcus, *Virginia Woolf and the Languages of Patriarchy*.

11 Others are understandably less forgiving of Quentin Bell's handling of Woolf's sexuality than I am. Patricia Cramer writes: 'It is worthwhile to emphasize Woolf's lifelong battle with external censorship because so many readers, influenced by Quentin Bell's biography and by stereotypes about what constitutes the sexual, miss the articulations of lesbian desire that permeate the novels. External censorship – not personal inhibition – is the primary cause for Woolf's circumspect treatment of lesbian themes in her writing' (Barrett and Cramer 120).

12 This sort of structure, while admittedly inherent in language itself, seems markedly pronounced around women's sexuality, especially same-sex desire between women. See, for example, Valerie Traub, 'The Ambiguities of "Lesbian" Viewing Pleasure' as well as Barrett and Cramer.

13 Louise DeSalvo, Suzanne Raitt, Sherron Knopp, and Jane Marcus all have endeavoured to place their work in the context of Woolf and Sackville-West's relationship, asking us to take Sackville-West's writing seriously and to see the innovative content in her use of traditional forms.

14 Judith Butler's essay 'Desire' is an excellent introduction to the problem of desire and its role in the formation of the sexed subject.

15 See, for example, Barrett and Cramer (41–5), Lilienfeld on animal imagery in Woolf's letters to Violet Dickinson (121–2), Cramer on flowers (117–27), and Hankins on the letter V (180–202) (all in Barrett and Cramer). Also, Karen Kaivola argues that Woolf's and Sackville-West's 'lives and works challeng[e] dominant 20th-century understandings of sexual identity, inviting an understanding of sexuality that is more accurately figured by temporal metaphors of process, change, and becoming' ('Virginia Woolf, Vita Sackville-West' 20).

16 Although in this book Raitt focuses on the work of Sackville-West, her introduction and first chapter have been highly influential for subsequent work on Woolf and Sackville-West, including my own.

17 Several critics have written about the biographies Woolf wrote, especially *Roger Fry* (see Broughton, Gillespie, Hirsh, and Johnston). Fewer have considered the biographical issues of *Orlando* (see Cooley). Raitt includes a

chapter on Sackville-West's later religious biographies in *Vita and Virginia* (117–45). My argument is that Woolf and Sackville-West had a reciprocal and profound influence on one another's writing that emerges most clearly in the biographies they wrote.

18 Among the eighteen books published during her lifetime, Woolf wrote two more biographies long after their affair had waned: the parody *Flush* and the more traditional *Roger Fry*. Sackville-West's 1936 biography, *Saint Joan of Arc*, represents the divided subject Woolf and Sackville-West theorized. See my article 'Crossing-dressing for (Imaginary) Battle' for a discussion of the biography that resulted from Woolf and Sackville-West's engagement with desire and subjectivity.

19 'Sapphic' would have been the term most current in England during the 1920s and was the word Woolf used to describe Sackville-West. 'Lesbian' (defined as a woman who is sexually attracted to other women) was used in medical texts (including a translation of Krafft-Ebing's *Psychopathia Sexualis*) in the 1890s, but it was not a term used (at least in writing) by Woolf or Sackville-West. The *Oxford English Dictionary* (*OED*) gives 1890 as the earliest use of 'lesbian' as an adjective and 1925 for the first use as a noun. Emma Donoghue challenges the *OED*, pointing to William King's use of the phrase 'Lesbian Loves' in 1732 and description of a group of women as 'Tribades or Lesbians' in 1736 (3). As convincing as Donoghue's argument is, 'lesbian' still does not seem to be a common term for Woolf and Sackville-West. 'Homosexual' generally would have been understood to refer to a male. 'Bisexual' was used in the nineteenth century primarily in botanical research and does not appear to have been in common usage in written texts to refer to people sexually attracted to both men and women until the 1950s (*OED*). However, A.A. Brill uses 'bisexually' is his 1913 English translation of Freud's *The Interpretation of Dreams*, which Leonard Woolf read in 1914. Brill's usage suggests a possible transition for the word: 'It is true that the tendency of dreams and of the unconscious phantasy, to employ the sexual symbols *bisexually*, reveals an archaic trait, for in childhood the difference in the genitals is unknown, and the same genitals are attributed to both sexes' (246; emphasis added). James Strachey also uses 'bisexuality' in this sentence in his 1953 translation of *The Interpretation of Dreams* for *The Standard Edition of the Complete Psychological Works of Sigmund Freud* for the Hogarth Press (5:359). During the late nineteenth and early twentieth centuries, sexology was rapidly introducing a new vocabulary, ranging from Edward Carpenter's 'intermediate sex' to Havelock Ellis's 'female sexual invert.' This language filtered down from medical and legal sources to English intellectuals, including mem-

bers of the Bloomsbury Group, during the early twentieth century. The acceptance of such terms was expedited by the publication of Radclyffe Hall's *The Well of Loneliness* and the trial that followed. See Laura Doan, *Fashioning Sapphism*, for a thorough history of the development of what we would now call lesbian culture during the first decades of the twentieth century, including an extended discussion of *The Well of Loneliness* as well as the dissemination of sexual knowledge and terminology via sexology (128–44). According to Doan, 'Prior to 1928 [the date of publication of *The Well of Loneliness*], and for some years after, the terms "lesbian," "homosexual," "sexual invert," or "Sapphist" often overlapped with one another and ... did not generally connote a specific sexual behaviour, identity, or appearance' (xx).

20 That said, there is also a growing backlash, in which Woolf's sexuality is once again in danger of being repressed by the position that there is no more to say on the subject and thus it should be dropped from the critical conversation.

21 See Marcus (*Languages* 173–4) for an interpretation of the significance of this creature from the Isle of Man.

22 See Slavoj Žižek for a thorough explication of Lacan's distinction between identity and subjectivity (173–8).

23 In developing his notion of the Law (which he sometimes capitalizes), Lacan was influenced by Claude Levi-Strauss. Dylan Evans notes this and elaborates: 'The law is the set of universal principles which make social existence possible, the structures that govern all forms of social exchange, whether gift-giving, kinship relations or the formation of pacts. Since the most basic form of exchange is communication itself, the law is fundamentally a linguistic entity – it is the law of the signifier' (98).

24 See Lacan's theorization of Woman as non-existent in *Feminine Sexuality* and also Mitchell's 'Introduction – I' (1–26) and Rose's 'Introduction – II' (27–57) to *Feminine Sexuality*. In addition to Freud and Lacan, I have been influenced by Chodorow, Cixous, Clément, Irigaray, and Kristeva, all of whom integrate feminism into psychoanalytic structures. Regarding my use of the term 'dominant assumptions,' it is well to heed Eve Kosofsky Sedgwick's early but still important critique of Foucault that the dominant culture is not a well-organized and monolithic entity, but rather is any number of structures that are positioned to take advantage of a given situation (*Between Men* 87). The effects of this accident of privileging in the case at hand include the silencing, if not the repression, of women's expressed desire – particularly when that desire is for other women.

25 Charles Bernheimer developed this connection in his graduate seminar on

Woolf and French feminism (State University of New York at Buffalo, Fall 1982). Other Woolf critics who have made productive connections between Woolf and psychoanalysis are Elizabeth Abel (Woolf, Freud, and Klein), Lisa Coleman (Woolf and Cixous), and Makiko Minow-Pinkney (Woolf and Kristeva).

26 For Lacan, the central conflict for an individual is the negotiation with the Other, begun in the mirror stage (six to eighteen months). Lacan thus remaps the Oedipus complex, thereby rectifying Freud's failure to imagine a female version. (The so-called 'Electra Complex,' used by Jung in *Versucheiner Darstellung der psychoanalytischen Theorie* (1913) was dismissed by Freud in *Female Sexuality* (21:229) as misleading.) During the mirror stage the young child individuates from the primary caregiver (usually imagined to be the mother) and through the course of the process acquires language, develops the unconscious, and suffers an irreparable sense of loss that is imagined as separation from the Other. Desire also emerges as the yearning to reunite with the Other. If one accepts the existence of the unconscious, then it follows that the subject is constructed on the illusion of stability, since one cannot, by definition, have control over or even direct access to the unconscious. Desire straddles the conscious and the unconscious, emerging from the unconscious into consciousness where it is misidentified (*Écrits* 312–13).

27 Throughout this book I make frequent references to letters as well as diary and journal entries. All of these sources have been published. Woolf's letters to Sackville-West are included in her collected letters (*The Letters of Virginia Woolf*). Sackville-West's letters to Woolf have been published as *The Letters of Vita Sackville-West to Virginia Woolf*. A selection of Sackville-West's letters to her husband have been published as *Vita and Harold: The Letters of Vita Sackville-West and Harold Nicolson*. Much of Woolf's diaries has been published (*The Diaries of Virginia Woolf*). Sackville-West's diaries and journals have not been collected; however, her son Nigel Nicolson published the journal she wrote between 23 July and 22 October 1920 as part of his biography of his parents, *Portrait of a Marriage*. In this journal, Sackville-West tells the story of her relationships with women, particularly Violet Trefusis, and considers the development of her own gender identity and sexuality.

Chapter 2: Forbidden Knowledge: Vita Sackville-West's Secret Fruit

1 Woolf was attracted to women before and after her relationship with Sackville-West, but there is less evidence that these relationships involved erotic practice.

2 According to *The Oxford English Dictionary*, 'sapphism' was included as an
   entry in *Billings National Medical Dictionary* in 1890. Illustrating sexology's
   transition from medical to popular discourse, 'sapphist' was an entry in
   the supplement to the 1902 edition of *Webster's Dictionary*.

3 Havelock Ellis equates sapphism with cunnilingus in his description of
   the erotic practice of female 'inverts': 'The passion finds expression in
   sleeping together, kissing and close embraces, with more or less sexual
   excitement, the orgasm sometimes occurring when one lies on the other's
   body; the extreme gratification is *cunnilingus (in lambendo lingua genitalia
   alterius)*, sometimes called sapphism' (98). Ellis's narrow definition of
   sapphism appears to be unique. There is no suggestion that Woolf,
   Sackville-West, or their contemporaries shared his understanding of
   sapphism as a specific erotic practice. The Bloomsbury Group appeared
   to use 'bugger' more generally to refer to a gay man, but buggery was
   commonly understood to mean anal intercourse between men.

4 In 'Innocent Femina Sensualis in Unconscious Conflict,' Peter Cominos
   cites, for example: Samuel Smiles, *Self-Help* (1859); Thomas Clifford Allbut,
   ed., *A System of Medicine*, 8 vols (1896–1899); E.M. Sewell, *Principles of
   Education, Drawn From Nature and Revelation, and Applied to Female Education in the Upper Classes*, 2 vols (1865); W.J. Dawson, *Young Woman* (1892);
   Josephine Butler, *The Education and Employment of Women* (1869); M.D.
   Mulock, *A Woman's Thoughts About Women* (1858); Furneaux Jordan,
   *Character as Seen in the Body and Parentage; with a Chapter on Education,
   Careers, Morals and Progress* (1890). Cominos argues that the Victorian models for the gentleman, Homo Economicus and Homo Sensualis, were
   developed for the lady, Femina Domestica and Femina Sensualis, with
   crippling effects: '[Women] were alleged to have no physical desire to
   control so long as their innate "island of innocence" [a core of chastity left
   untouched by original sin] was kept pure by the proper surveillance of
   mothers and chaperons and by the sense of shame which every manifestation of their own erotic desire aroused. Theoretically and ideally, gentlemen were to be masters of themselves, responsible and self-controlled;
   ladies had nothing to master or to be responsible for and were to be controlled or 'protected' by others. Thus, in the Victorian battle of the sexes,
   women were disarmed of the weapon of their sexuality. Gentlemen imposed unilateral disarmament upon them which they simultaneously
   denied doing through the theory of feminine sexual anaesthesia' (163).

5 Repressing knowledge of the female body realizes the goal of the theory of
   innate innocence: without genitals women have no sexual desire, nothing
   to masturbate, no ability to commit adultery. Women would pose no threat
   to patriarchal control of reproduction and thus (through inheritance) prop-

erty. By being hyper-castrated, women would cease to be reminders of potential castration and thus reduce male anxiety. The theory is over-determined in its usefulness in controlling feminine sexuality, which is a necessary condition of patriarchy. That such a theory would become codified during a time when a woman was the supreme monarch is no surprise, since women's leadership creates cultural anxiety that calls for reparation of exactly this sort. Recent work on early modern sexuality exposes a similar repression of feminine sexuality during the reign of Elizabeth I; see, especially, Traub, 'The (In)significance of "Lesbian" Desire in Early Modern England.'

6 Simone de Beauvoir makes this point more generally in *The Second Sex*, where she gives a brief history of reproductive hypotheses and discoveries ('The Data of Biology' 3–41): 'The use of the microscope enabled von Baer in 1827 to discover the mammalian egg, contained inside the Graafian follicle. Before long it was possible to study the cleavage of the egg – that is, the early stage of development through cell division – and in 1835 sarcode, later called protoplasm, was discovered and the true nature of the cell began to be realized. In 1879 the penetration of the spermatozoon into the starfish egg was observed, and thereupon the equivalence of the nuclei of the two gametes, egg and sperm, was established. The details of their union within the fertilized egg were first worked out in 1883 by a Belgian zoologist, van Beneden' (9).

7 Recognition of the connection between repressed sexual desire and a loss of control of the body enabled Freud's treatment of hysteria. While obviously a product of a patriarchal society, Freud's work with women not only led to the talking cure, which is the basis for psychoanalysis, but also posed a direct challenge to the doctrine of feminine innocence.

8 Leonard Woolf reviewed A.A. Brill's English translation of *The Psychopathology of Everyday Life* for the *New Weekly*. He called the book 'far easier and more popular' than *The Interpretation of Dreams*, the only other Freud volume available in translation, which he read in preparation for the review. To the question of whether or not Freud's conclusions are 'too far-fetched,' Leonard Woolf responds: 'But this may be said categorically and confidently, that there can be no doubt that there is a substantial amount of truth in the main thesis of Freud's book, and that truth is of great value' (190). Freud's work was subsequently translated by James and Alix Strachey – brother and sister-in-law of Lytton Strachey – and published by the Hogarth Press beginning in 1924. Additional connections between the Bloomsbury Group and psychoanalysis were made through Virginia Woolf's brother and sister-in-law, Adrian and Karin Stephen, both of

whom were practising analysts. See Elizabeth Abel, *Virginia Woolf and the Fictions of Psychoanalysis* (particularly 13–20) on Virginia Woolf's contact with psychoanalysis.

9 In 1915 British feminist Frances Wilder wrote to Carpenter, after reading his book, to thank him for explaining to her what she was: 'I have recently read with much interest your book ... & it has lately dawned on me that I myself belong to that class & I write to ask if there is any way of getting in touch with others of the same temperament.' The letter is reprinted by Ruth F. Claus in 'Confronting Homosexuality' and discussed by Smith-Rosenberg (*Hidden From History* 273), Newton (286), and Faderman (*Odd Girls* 58).

10 Information about Sackville-West's family background can be found in her books *Pepita* and *Knole and the Sackvilles* and especially in Victoria Glendinning's biography *Vita*, where it is elaborated in greater detail than I have given here.

11 While not a part of the Left Bank scene described so well by Shari Benstock in *Women of the Left Bank*, Sackville-West was well aware of the alternative culture Paris offered. It was to France that she eloped with Violet Trefusis and to France that she later travelled with Woolf.

12 Glendinning suggests that Sackville-West's 'open marriage' to diplomat Harold Nicolson was not pioneering but Edwardian (18).

13 The occasion for this declaration was the prospect, which did not materialize, of being joined on vacation by Violet Trefusis, Sackville-West's former lover.

14 Nigel Nicolson published Sackville-West's journal of her relationships with Grosvenor and Trefusis as part of his biography of his parents, *Portrait of a Marriage*. All quotations from *Portrait of a Marriage* are from this journal.

15 This circumscribed understanding of sex is echoed in Toni McNaron's metaphor of her own 'tightly fitted heterosexist blinders' ('Lesbian Reading' 11) that supported compulsory heterosexuality in the mid-twentieth century.

16 Smith-Rosenberg cites Samuel Gregory, *Facts and Important Information for Young Women on the Subject of Masturbation* (Boston: George Gregory, 1857); and Gross and Co., *Hygieana: A Non-Medical Analysis of the Complaints Incidental to Females* (London: G. Booth, 1829). For an expanded discussion of this material see Smith-Rosenberg, *Disorderly Conduct* (266). Recent historical and cultural scholars have been critical of the groundbreaking work of Smith-Rosenburg and Lillian Faderman. Lisa Moore, for example, criticizes them for viewing sexuality as a subcategory of gender (10).

While the perspectives of Smith-Rosenburg and Faderman pre-date theoretical developments in cultural studies, gender studies, and queer theory, their work, particularly the primary sources to which they call attention, is nevertheless valuable. See Traub (*Renaissance* 357) for a particularly balanced discussion of this debate.

17 The desire to censor female homosexuality was accompanied by the development of a more precise vocabulary. One of the catalysts in this process was the 1928 obscenity trial of Radclyffe Hall's *The Well of Loneliness.*

18 The Labouchère Amendment, section 11 of the 1885 Criminal Law Amendment Act, made all acts of 'gross indecency' between two men punishable by up to two years imprisonment 'with or without hard labour.' Buggery, which had been punishable by death until 1861, was still punishable by imprisonment for ten years to life (Weeks, *Coming Out* 14).

19 Carpenter's paper was later published as the title piece of a collection of his essays on homosexuality in 1908.

20 Begun as a collaboration, the book was entirely revised by Ellis after Symonds's death in 1893. At the request of Symonds's family, his name was removed after the first English edition. For the complex publishing history of this book, including its confiscation as evidence in the Bedborough trial, see Grosskurth (173–204). Resistance to publication was strong. One publisher refused the manuscript because 'he feared that it could not be confined to specialists and might contaminate the wider public' (180). Soon after its publication it was confiscated and subsequently released only in America, where it appeared as the second of Ellis's six-volume *Studies in the Psychology of Sex.*

21 See Faderman, 'Why Some Lesbians Accepted the Congenital Invert Theory' (*Odd Girls* 57–61), Newton, and Weeks (*Coming Out*).

22 See Foucault's *History of Sexuality* (especially 53–7) for a discussion of the absence of any scientific basis in sexology, which he describes as establishing 'an entire pornography of the morbid' (54). Lillian Faderman's 'The Morbidification of Love' reveals the internal inconsistencies in Ellis's work and argues that his conclusions are unsupported and even contradicted by his evidence. In turn, Laura Doan criticizes Faderman's view of sexology for being reductive (128). See Rosario and Bland and Doan for various reassessments of sexology.

23 See Valerie Traub, *Desire and Anxiety*, particularly chapter 4, for an examination of 'the disturbance of gender by its non-correspondence to sexuality' (12).

24 Jeffrey Weeks makes this point in *Coming Out*. Faderman earlier argued

('Morbidification' and *Surpassing the Love of Men*) that the sexologists functioned to damage women's ability to contract and maintain romantic friendships by labelling them deviant. Doan criticizes Faderman for painting sexology with too broad a brush (128). Vicinus reprises this early conflict over the impact of sexology (212–13). In *Odd Girls and Twilight Lovers*, Faderman expresses a more balanced view: for some women sexology was enabling and for others it was limiting. Foucault makes this point about the dual function of discourse to both limit and enable, using the example of sodomy: 'There is no question that the appearance in nineteenth century psychiatry, jurisprudence, and literature of a whole series of discourses on the species and subspecies of homosexuality, inversion, pederasty, and the "psychic hermaphrodism" made possible a strong advance of social controls into this area of "perversity"; but it also made possible the formation of a "reverse" discourse: homosexuality began to speak in its own behalf, to demand that its legitimacy or "naturality" be acknowledged, often in the same vocabulary, using the same categories by which it was medically disqualified' (101). Faderman's connection between the development of a lesbian subculture and women's growing economic independence cannot be stressed enough.

25 On *The Well of Loneliness*, see the work of Laura Doan, Jonathan Dollimore, Leigh Gilmore, Ester Newton, Adam Parkes, Katrina Rolley, Gillian Whitlock, and, of course, Catharine R. Stimpson's now classic 'Zero Degree Deviancy.'

26 See Jane Marcus, 'Sapphistry: Narration as Lesbian Seduction in *A Room of One's Own*' in *Virginia Woolf* on Virginia Woolf's (non)involvement in the trial and response to Hall.

27 This could be translated: 'One is sometimes proud of oneself in comparison with others.' Thanks to Tamara Root and Don Rice, who discussed all the translations in this chapter with me and offered invaluable advice.

28 Raitt argues that Sackville-West's 'serially gendered personality ... combines the beliefs of late nineteenth century homosexual activists, such as Karl Heinrich Ulrichs, with the findings of contemporary psychiatric practice' ('Sex, Love' 162n9). My reading of Sackville-West and her journal differs significantly from Raitt's, who sees Sackville-West's shame at her callous treatment of those she loves as shame over her lesbian desire. While I agree that Sackville-West felt guilty for the suffering she caused Harold Nicolson in the three years during which she was uncertain about whether she would remain in the marriage, I do not see evidence that she felt guilty for her sexual attraction to women or even for the affair per se.

29 On cross-dressing see Garber.

30 Sackville-West and Trefusis were in Paris and Monte Carlo from the end of November 1918 until late March 1919 and again from October to December 1919. Sackville-West does not date her first appearance as Julian, but it was prior to November 1918. According to Nigel Nicolson's preface to the 1974 edition, *Challenge* was written between May 1918 and November 1919: 'Much of the novel had been written in Monte Carlo at the height of the affair ... *Challenge* was her declaration of defiance, an apologia for her conduct. She wished to publish it as a memorial to what she had endured, as her statement of what love could and should be' (8).

31 Love between cousins is a theme of sorts in Sackville-West's work. Her first novel, *Heritage,* centres on two cousins who are the only two members of the family to show evidence (by their dark hair and passionate natures) of their Spanish ancestry. They marry with disastrous results. That novel was dedicated to Sackville-West's mother, who, it will be remembered, had a Spanish mother and suffered an unhappy marriage to her cousin.

32 For the 1924 New York edition the dedication was changed to a Turkish love poem:

Dedication
ACABA EMBEO SIN TRIO, MEN CHAUJANI;
LIRENAS, BERJARAS TIRI OCHI BUSNE,
CHANGERI, TA ARMENSALLE

33 Until the 1974 edition with Nicolson's explanatory introduction appeared, the real reason for the novel's withdrawal was not widely known. When it was finally issued in New York, there was speculation as to why it had been suppressed. It was assumed that the story was based on a real English family. Sara Ruth Watson's volume on Sackville-West explains: 'it was withdrawn from publication in England because descendants of the ancient Davenant family objected to the characters in the novel of that name ... What, exactly, the Davenants could find objectionable is difficult to comprehend' (91). Such responses confirm Violet Trefusis's view that publication of the novel would not have contributed further to the scandal surrounding the affair, since it would add nothing to what people already knew and would be lost on those who knew nothing. See Nigel Nicolson's introduction to the 1974 edition and Glendinning (130) for details of the decision to suppress the novel.

34 Furious that Sackville-West would not set a date for her return to England from Cannes, Nicolson wrote: 'when you fall into V.'s [Violet Trefusis's] hands your will becomes like a jelly-fish addicted to cocaine' (8 Feb. 1921, 113). Usually tolerant, there are moments when Nicolson's impatience shows.

Sexology is a theory of the emotions

35 Sackville-West was bilingual in English and French, the latter being her mother's first language. She commonly uses French phrases and double entendres within and across languages – particularly in her letters. My thanks to Jack Marmorstein for pointing out this one, as well as others.

36 This notion of dual personality would have been available to Sackville-West in a general way. Her development of it in terms of national character (the Spanish Gypsy / British aristocrat duality explored in *Heritage*) and, especially, sexuality warrants further investigation. My thanks are due to Stephen Kellert for his valuable recommendations on this topic, which include pointing out the relevance of Ian Hacking's work to my reading of Sackville-West's theory of gender identity.

37 Multiple-personality disorder became an official diagnosis of the American Psychiatric Association in 1980 (Hacking 8).

38 See, in Bland and Doan, Suzanne Raitt's persuasive argument that sexology is a theory of emotions rather than biology.

39 Clearly, Sackville-West's theory derives from experience mapped onto those parts of contemporary sexology that fit, but her conclusions – lived even more than articulated – are remarkably similar to Butler's more elaborately theorized arguments in *Gender Trouble* and *Bodies That Matter*.

40 In a Lacanian model, Sackville-West suggests the feminine position (the not-all), a position not entirely inscribed by the symbolic. This is distinct from the abject, which Judith Butler claims is in a position to challenge the Law much in the way I argue Sackville-West challenges it: 'The abject designates here precisely those "unliveable" and "uninhabitable" zones of social life which are nevertheless densely populated by those who do not enjoy the status of the subject, but whose living under the sign of the "unliveable" is required to circumscribe the domain of the subject ... The task will be to consider this threat and disruption not as a permanent contestation of social norms condemned to the pathos of perpetual failure, but rather as a critical resource in the struggle to rearticulate the very terms of symbolic legitimacy and intelligibility' (*Bodies That Matter* 3). Sackville-West is not a subject in the symbolic, because she does not recognize the Law, but she is not in the position of the abject, as Butler defines it, since she is not aware of her position outside the 'domain of the subject' and does not negatively define possible subject positions. I see Sackville-West doing work that is more radical and potentially more enabling than the abject could accomplish, since she reveals that which the symbolic cannot conceive (as opposed to that which it cannot contain): feminine sexuality.

41 I am grateful to Susie Steinbach for leading me to evidence supporting this generalization. See Patricia Hollis and Mary Shanley. Oscar Wilde's *An*

a big claim — buried in the note but not hidden

Ideal Husband gives a literary example of a woman whose class status exempts her from gender restrictions.

42 Lisa St Aubin de Teran makes this claim in her introduction to the Virago edition of the text. As Sackville-West does in *Knole and the Sackvilles* (4), St Aubin de Teran gives four acres as the size of the house; Glendinning says the complex of structures covers more than six acres. For a description and comparison to the house in Sackville-West's novel *The Edwardians* see Glendinning (9–11). The most detailed account of Knole can be found in *Knole and the Sackvilles*.

43 St Aubin De Teran writes: 'perhaps much of her subsequent sexual ambiguity stemmed from that twist of fate. Even as a child, she must have known that she was really expected to have been a boy' (v). This is a frequently expressed point of view.

44 The actual dedication reads: 'To B.M.' Sackville-West referred to her mother, Lady Sackville, by the initials that stood for Bonne Mama. After reading a draft of *The Heir*, Sackville-West's mother advised: 'take out the old housekeeper and make her an old butler, and there will be no woman in the Book' (Glendinning 117). Sackville-West followed this recommendation.

45 Although it is tangential to my argument, I cannot ignore the name of the house in this story: 'Blackboys.' An understanding of the racial implications of this choice would require an investigation into images of race and imperialism throughout Sackville-West's work.

46 Sackville-West uses much the same language to describe the house in *Knole and the Sackvilles*, which was published in the same year as *The Heir*: 'One looks down upon the house from a certain corner in the garden ... the house lies below one in the hollow, lovely in its colour and its serenity. It has all the quality of peace and permanence; of mellow age; of stateliness and tradition. It is gentle and venerable ... It has the deep inward gaiety of some very old woman who has always been beautiful, who has had many lovers and seen many generations come and go, smiled wisely over their sorrows and their joys, and learnt an imperishable secret of tolerance and humour' (2). As the dedication of *The Heir* suggests, the description of the houses evokes Lady Sackville and suggests maternal more than erotic qualities. While she does not discuss *The Heir*, Raitt sees Sackville-West's later country house novels as politically conservative and her vision of nature as Romantic: 'Sackville-West's writing, and in particular her poetry, like that of Sylvia Townsend Warner and Radclyffe Hall, reimagined the natural world as a space in which sexuality could be renegotiated and enjoyed in seclusion and safety ... Images of a lost paradise also accommo-

dated their fantasies of a pastoral social stability that the multiple crises of
the early twentieth century had apparently destroyed' (*Vita and Virginia*
12–13). In this, Raitt echoes DeSalvo's reading of the end of story as 'ultimately conservative,' wherein Chase 'falls in love with the landholding
tradition' ('Every Woman' 100).

47 See Irigaray, *This Sex Which Is Not One*, on *écriture féminine*. Unlike Irigaray,
Sackville-West does not conflate erotic spaces with a lesbian subject.
Valerie Traub criticizes Irigaray: 'Irigaray's conflation of body part(s) and
erotic identity maintains the psychomorphology of the clitoris by positing
body part(s) as a sufficient sign of desire, and desire as adequately expressed through the rubric of (constructed) identity' ('Psychomorphology
of the Clitoris' 102). This, in Traub's analysis, serves to reify phallocen-
trism, in terms of which both the clitoris and the lesbian are constituted.
Sackville-West's dismissal of available sexual identities is duplicated in
the erotics of private space developed in *The Heir*. For a more developed
theorization of the relationship between houses and the female body see
Gaston Bachelard and Gillian Rose.

48 Valerie Traub usefully invokes the Derridian notion of the supplement to
argue that the dildo and enlarged clitoris enjoyed by early modern women
were 'both additive and substitutive: as a material addition to the women's
body and as a replacement of the man's body *by* the woman's, it not only
displaces male prerogatives, but exposes 'man' as a simulacrum, and
gender as a construction built on the faulty ground of exclusive, binary
difference' ('(In)significance' 155; emphasis original). The penetrating
abilities of women deconstruct gender and reveal the defining male
attribute as impotent to maintain masculine authority. For women, then,
cross-dressing functions as supplement. Marjorie Garber makes a related
point in Lacanian terms. She argues that cross-dressing disrupts binary
gender difference to introduce a third term that functions like Lacan's
symbolic order, in which meaning is understood to be linguistically
constructed (12–13).

49 I am grateful to Jack Marmorstein for the fruitful association of Vita's
Drawer and *jouissance*. 'Usufruct' is a legal term, originating in Roman
law. The word derives from the Latin *usus* (use) and *fructus* (enjoyment).
The correspondence between the French '*usufruit*' and the English 'fruit' is
not without significance. In 'De la Jouissance,' Lacan says: 'L'usufruit veut
dire qu'on peut jouir de ses moyens, mais qu'il ne faut pas les gas-piller.
Quand on a l'usufruit d'un héritage, on peut en jouir à condition de ne pas
trop en user' (*Le Séminaire livre XX* 10). Which can be translated: 'Usufruct
means that one can enjoy the means, but must not waste it. When one has

the usufruct of an inheritance, one can enjoy it on the condition that one does not consume too much of it.' See also Fink (*Lacanian Subject* 96–7) on usufruct and surplus value. *Le Séminaire livre XX: Encore*, in which Lacan distinguishes between phallic *jouissance* and the *jouissance* that is not phallic (i.e., accessed from the feminine position), is foundational to the argument I am proposing. Thanks to Peter Canning and Tamara Root for discussing the translation of Lacan's text with me.

50 'Working through,' in psychoanalytic terms, occurs when one is able to re-experience, at an emotional level, a traumatic event that has been repressed. While this process is typically described as the result of a successful analysis, I suggest here, and elsewhere, that the writings of Woolf and Sackville-West accomplished the work of analysis. By 'working through,' as I posit she does, the trauma of the loss of Knole, Sackville-West appears to use Knole to enable a fantasy of access to the maternal body. Inheritance laws are another version of the father's interdiction. As the father intervenes in the infant's merger with the mother, the male child is encouraged to identify with the father's position and defer desire, easily becoming subject to the Law, which is internalized as the superego. The female child, who is not allowed an easy identification with the father, has more difficulty in separating from the mother (Chodorow 125–40). But if this separation can be sufficiently accomplished, she can more easily gain access to desire as a result of her recognition of the external authority of the Law. Instead of ambivalent identification with the father, which brings on punishment from the superego, she can *jouer* through the Other. *Knole and the Sackvilles* traces this process, arriving at the point of supplemental *jouissance* through the story of the hidden fruit. For an elaborated discussion of the working through and literature see LaCapra and Caruth.

Chapter 3: Making Use of the Fruit: Vita Sackville-West's Influence on Virginia Woolf

1 I rely here on the distinction between incorporation and introjection made by Maria Torok, who describes incorporation as a fantasy that maintains the status quo, whereas introjection is a process ('working through') in which the subject is transformed by the integration of new, painful material (e.g., the loss of the mother): 'If accepted and worked through, the loss would require major readjustment. But the fantasy of incorporation merely simulates profound psychic transformation ... we fantasize swallowing (or having swallowed) that which has been lost, as if it were some kind of thing ... The magical 'cure' by incorporation exempts the subject

from the painful process of [psychic] reorganization' (126–7). *To the Light-house* invites discussion of how Woolf's complex feelings for her mother are played out through multiple narratives. Elizabeth Abel argues that in this novel 'Woolf anticipates and interrogates Lacan's reading of the Oedipal structure as a gateway to the symbolic register,' with Lily enacting a Kleinian model: 'Lily's sustained and recuperative matricentric story offers a powerful alternative to James's and Cam's Oedipal fictions' (47). Marcus emphasizes Woolf's influence on Sackville-West: 'But Woolf's relationship with Vita Sackville-West is the only one in which she was willing and able to play mother to another woman's mind and to give the intellectual nourishment she had so often taken from her own mental "mothers"' (*Virginia Woolf* 107). Juhasz, reading the novel from the perspective of relational psychoanalysis, emphasizes Lily's relationship with Mrs Ramsay as a mother/daughter relationship: 'if Lily possesses lesbian desire for Mrs. Ramsay, that desire is clearly connected with daughterly desire' (70). Juhasz argues that *To the Lighthouse* does not allow Woolf to successfully mourn her mother, since Woolf writes about her again in 'A Sketch of the Past' (66); whereas my sense is that writing about a person in one's memoir is very different from being haunted by that person, as Woolf says she was by her mother until she wrote *To the Lighthouse*. I also differ from Juhasz in my unwillingness to necessarily link lesbian desire with what Juhasz calls 'daughterly desire' (70). While I certainly agree that the complex and changing manifestations of desire have unconscious origins that derive from imaginary (for Lacan) or pre-Oedipal (for Freud) roots and are thus linked to fantasies of the primary caregiver, I am unwilling to generalize beyond this point. My argument in this chapter is that Woolf was unable to mourn her lost mother in large part because she had not yet introjected her at the point of separation (entry into the symbolic) in early childhood. The mutual mothering she experienced in her relationship with Sackville-West allowed her to feel safe enough – (mothered enough and also adult (i.e., individuated) enough – to face the psychic pain and disruption of the mourning process.

2 Woolf also describes such meetings in her diary of this time; see, for example, the entry for 23 November 1926 (3:117).

3 The allusion is to Shakespeare's *Cymbeline*, in which Posthumus Leonatus says to Cymbeline: 'Hang there like fruit, my soul, / Til the tree die' (5.5.262–3).

4 In his biography of Woolf, Bell writes: 'I would ... suggest that she [Woolf] regarded sex, not so much with horror, as with incomprehension; there was, both in her personality and in her art, a disconcertingly aetherial

quality' (2:6). My reading of Woolf's biography is not at variance with standard interpretations (see Quentin Bell; DeSalvo *Virginia Woolf*; Lee; Broughton; and Phyllis Rose). My narrative differs substantially from Bell's only in ascribing to Gerald, not George, primary responsibility for Woolf's subsequent symptoms. I am here interested more in the pattern of her associations than in the allocation of blame, of which there is more than enough to go around. Also, I am not attempting to diagnose Woolf's mental condition as other critics have been tempted to do (e.g., Caramagno; DeSalvo *Virginia Woolf*; Trombley); I do think it is important, however, to attend to the consistencies between Woolf's self-described symptoms and those of other victims of incest. See Hacking for a history of the symptoms and diagnoses resulting from sexual abuse in the late nineteenth and twentieth centuries.

5   In a clinical context this might be called a 'positive mother transference.' Such transference between a patient and an analyst could initiate the process of working through.

6   The note to this entry speculates that Clive Bell had communicated Sackville-West's opinion of Woolf to her, implying that he took a lively interest in the developing relationship between Woolf and Sackville-West (2:187n1).

7   This passage suggests one reason that Woolf found Proust, whose work she had read fourteen years earlier (in 1925; see *Diary* 3:7, 37), so affecting. It is also suggestive of the scene in *To the Lighthouse* in which Mrs Ramsay comforts the sleepless Cam. After covering the objectionable boar's skull with her shawl: 'she came back to Cam and laid her head almost flat on the pillow beside Cam's and said how lovely it looked now; how the fairies would love it; it was like a bird's nest; it was like a beautiful mountain such as she had seen abroad, with valleys and flowers and bells ringing and birds singing and little goats and antelopes and ...' (172).

8   See Chodorow for a fully developed theory of the incomplete separation of identity between mothers and daughters, which Woolf's work strongly evokes.

9   As Chris Buttram Trombold demonstrates, Woolf was keenly aware of the physicality of others, which she often connects to internal characteristics. This is not the case with Sackville-West, whose mind and body Woolf often describes as at odds; for example, 'as a body hers is perfection ... but as usual, that fatal simplicity or rigidity of mind which makes it seem all a little unshaded, & empty. More mind, my God –' (*Diary* 2:306–7).

10   Sackville-West's mother echoes Trefusis's emphasis on Sackville-West's skin and eyes in the description she wrote of her daughter at age thirty,

the year she met Woolf: 'Her complexion is beautiful; so are her eyes, with their double curtain of long eyelashes ... She has such dignity and repose' (Glendinning 123).

11 See Glendinning for a review of the responses to the novel from the press as well as from Sackville-West's non-Bloomsbury friends (141–2). It is particularly interesting to note that *Seducers* was reviewed by the *New York Post*'s 'Literary Review' on the same page as Woolf's *Mrs. Dalloway*. Sackville-West got top billing and a more favourable review.

12 See Joan Riviere's classic essay on this topic, 'Womanliness as Masquerade.'

13 See Woolf's diary entry of 5 July 1924 for a description of this trip (2:306–7).

14 Woolf told the story to members of the Bloomsbury Group as well as to Janet Case, childhood friend Elena Rathbone Richmond, Ottoline Morrell, and family members (Lee 154–6).

Chapter 4: *Orlando*: A Biography of Desire

1 *Knole and the Sackvilles* was so popular that it led to a sequel in the form of the diary of Lady Anne Clifford, one of the major figures in the story of Knole, which Sackville-West edited and published in 1923. In 1947 she wrote the guidebook to Knole for the National Trust, which took over the property in 1943. James Naremore suggests that Sackville-West's *Knole and the Sackvilles* exemplifies the trend of the current biographies Woolf describes as part of her essay 'The New Biography,' in which the author has an equal (not idealizing) relationship to the subject (206).

2 This was not the first time Woolf had gone to Knole: the first was in July 1924. On that visit, Woolf was more impressed with Sackville-West's appearance than the house (*Diary* 2:306–7). On the second occasion, Harold Nicolson was in Persia; Sackville-West left at the end of January to visit him, as she had done the previous year.

3 Violet Trefusis was the original of Sasha. While writing *Orlando*, Woolf wrote to Sackville-West: 'Tomorrow I begin the chapter which describes Violet and you meeting on the ice. The whole thing has to be gone into thoroughly. I am swarming with ideas. Do give me some inkling what sort of quarrels you had. Also, for what particular quality did she first choose you?' (13 Oct. 1927, 3:430).

4 See Susan Squier for an explication of the term 'Jessamy Bride' (128). Jones discusses the Ladies of Llangollen, another of Woolf's early associations for the book.

5 In particular, Edel praises Woolf's representation of time: 'Orlando's central and gentlest mockery is of time and of history: its insistent theme is that human time does not accord with clock time and that our mechanical way of measuring the hours makes no allowance for the richness of life embodied in a given moment, which can hold within it the experience of decades' (139–40). In Edel's view, the work's status as fiction is responsible for its failure to have had a greater influence on biography. More recently, Ira Nadel discusses Orlando as a commentary on biography (140–50).

6 See Doan (1–30) and Parkes (144–77) for full accounts of the trial. Doan's work is particularly important in contextualizing the trial in terms of the more general critical reception of the novel. Parkes considers the trial's effect on Orlando, celebrating, as I do, the instability of the narrative but seeing it as an aid in escaping censorship: 'Where Orlando succeeds in carrying out Woolf's intention to suggest sapphism, it does so by vacillating, by casting doubt, by intimating that it may be nothing but a joke, so that any obscenity may pass unnoted like the unobserved female observer' (177).

7 'Happy the mother who bears, happier still the biographer who records the life of such a one [as Orlando]! Never need she vex herself, nor he invoke the help of novelist or poet' (15; emphasis added). The Biographer later claims for himself an absence of gender altogether: 'let us, who enjoy the immunity of all biographers and historians from any sex whatever, pass it over' (220). In her essays about biography, Woolf also refers to biographers with the, presumably, universal masculine pronoun (e.g., 'The Art of Biography' 255). Woolf is careful to create a female narrator in A Room of One's Own, which immediately followed Orlando. For the proposes of this study, I will use masculine pronouns to refer to the Biographer in accordance with the book's references to biographers. The notion that only male biographers upheld the traditions of biography is erroneous but, I believe, deliberate. The masculine pronoun is also useful in that it distinguishes the Biographer from Woolf. For similar reasons of clarity, I capitalize 'Biographer' when referring to the intrusive narrator of Orlando.

8 Gillian Beer also sees desire as constant in Orlando, although she sees constant desire as part of the stability of the self: 'Can we give or take a few genitalia and remain ourselves, our desires not altered, our will hampered maybe, but the same? In Orlando the central self endures the vicissitudes of translation – through time, through gender, through changing language – not itself much changed. Primary alliances (to "The Oak Tree," to Sasha) are unmoved. The form of desire is peremptorily inscribed

at the start' ('Body' 98). For Beer, the constancy of desire is evidence of the unchanging self.

9 Even his interest in the initially ambiguously gendered Sasha is held in check pending a confirmation that she is female. One might be tempted to count the erection Orlando gets when the cross-dressed Archduchess Harriet fits a golden shin case to Orlando's leg (116), but Orlando does not know that Harriet will become Harry, and I am not sure that we should assume any more stability of sex for this character than we can for Orlando.

10 See Minow-Pinkney's interesting reading of Orlando's alternation of men's and women's clothes as a Hegelian synthesis that exemplifies the Kristevean dialectic of oscillating masculine and feminine identifications (130–1).

11 This detail evokes (as does Orlando's cross-dressing) Sackville-West's affair with Violet Trefusis between 1918 and 1921. While writing *Orlando*, Woolf wrote in her diary: 'the balance between truth & fantasy must be careful. It is based on Vita, Violet Trefusis, Lord Lascelles, Knole, &c.' (3:162). It also echoes the plot of a Restoration comedy of the sort Aphra Behn was famous for writing. Behn herself had fled England for the Low Countries, where she operated as a spy for Charles II.

12 Joan Riviere's 'Womanliness as Masquerade,' which argues that femininity is always a performance, appeared the year after *Orlando* was published. Jaime Hovey notes that Riviere's psychoanalytic essay 'contains a narrative whose plot bears a striking resemblance to that of *Orlando*' (396). Hovey reads Woolf's narrator as ambiguous not only about gender and sexuality but also about national and racial identity.

13 The allusions of this section to *Wuthering Heights* and *Jane Eyre* have been much noted in the criticism.

14 Minow-Pinkney's reading parallels my own; our conclusions, however, differ: 'What convinces Orlando of her womanliness is a feeling of maternal protectiveness incited by the odd vision of Shelmardine as a "boy ... sucking peppermints" [252] during his passionate struggle against the waves. Here Woolf seems to be betraying some intractable personal limitation, a kind of feminist "bad conscience," about what real womanhood is' (137). Madeline Moore calls Orlando's marriage 'the Platonic ideal of marriage' and 'a marriage based on respect, friendship, distance and asexuality' (*Short Season* 109).

15 Many critics suggest that this was the strategy Woolf and Sackville-West employed during their affair to avoid social suspicion. However,

Sackville-West's lesbianism was well known in her own social circle. Woolf had heard about it even before they met. While marriage may have provided a setting for the larger world, who knew and accepted Sackville-West in her role as wife (e.g., on radio shows with Harold Nicolson discussing the secrets of their happy marriage; 17 June 1929; partially reprinted in the *Listener*, 26 June 1929), it is hard to know how much she suffered from the social ostracism she surely experienced in some circles. See Raitt (*Vita and Virginia* 92–3) and Glendinning.

16 See McNaron for a reading of Woolf's narrative techniques as parallel to her omission of lesbianism. McNaron explores Clarissa Dalloway through a lesbian-feminist 'lens to illustrate the effect Woolf's decision to cap her lesbian energy and impulses had on her ability to portray women as integrated and whole' ('"The Albanians"' 135).

Chapter 5: Genre Instability and *Orlando*: Biography as a Feminist Practice

1 While critics refer to *Orlando* variously and even interchangeably as both a satire and a parody, I consider it a satire, since, as I argue, its comic exaggeration has a larger political agenda. As in previous chapters, I use the capitalized 'Biographer' to refer to *Orlando*'s narrator.

2 See Nadel on Craik as well as on Stephen's influential career as a biographer (30–61).

3 Writing biography and memoir was endemic among members of the Bloomsbury Group, particularly after the commencement of the Memoir Club in 1920, in which they convened to read their own memoirs to each other. Strachey, the only trained historian in the group, produced the only biographies that achieved critical attention, including *Eminent Victorians* (1918), *Queen Victoria* (1921), *Elizabeth and Essex* (1928), and *Portraits in Miniature* (1931). Molly MacCarthy wrote *A Nineteenth-Century Childhood* (1924). Desmond MacCarthy wrote *Portraits* (1931). J.M. Keynes wrote *Essays in Biography* (1933). David Garnett wrote a biography of Pocahontas in 1933. Roger Fry wrote single-artist studies of Giovanni Bellini (1988), Cezanne (1927), and Matisse (1930). E.M. Forester wrote *Goldsworthy Lowes Dickinson* (1934) and *Marianne Thornton: A Domestic Biography* (1956). Clive Bell wrote *Old Friends: Personal Recollections* (1956). Vanessa Bell, Carrington, Roger Fry, and Duncan Grant painted dozens of portraits. Leonard Woolf is a notable omission from this collective production; he was a member of the Memoir Club, however, and published his five-volume memoir between 1960 and 1969. See S.P. Rosenbaum's *The Bloomsbury Group* for essays by members of the group about the group as well as

biographical sketches and portraits of each other. See Hoberman for a
discussion of Woolf's engagement with biography (133–45). Never members of the Bloomsbury Group, Sackville-West and her husband, Harold
Nicolson, achieved considerable popular success as biographers. Virginia
Woolf reviewed Nicolson's biography *Some People* in her essay 'The New
Biography.'

4 *Orlando* is a particularly rich text for discussions of race and nation. See
Jaime Hovey's '"Kissing a Negress in the Dark,"' which argues that
'*Orlando*'s exploration of queer white female sexuality can ... be seen as
firmly anchored in the national and racial concerns of 1920s England, as
paradoxically and ambivalently concerned both with establishing a place
for the sexually polymorphous white woman within her class and nation
and with contesting the ideological parameters of national inclusion' (394).

5 See also Nadel and William Epstein on the rhetoric of biography and
experimental biographies. There were several experimental biographers
among Woolf's and Sackville-West's contemporaries, for example, A.J.
Symons (*Quest for Corvo*) and Sackville-West's one-time lover Geoffrey
Scott (*The Portrait of Zélide*). One might also include George Bernard Shaw
(*Saint Joan*) and Gertrude Stein (*The Autobiography of Alice B. Toklas*) in this
number. Nevertheless, following Nagourney, I would agree that the structure of the genre of biography resists experimentation, just as most of us
resist recognizing the lack of unity of the subject.

6 While some scholars contend that the unified subject is a straw man in
post-structuralist analyses, in my experience even people who accept that
there is an unconscious rarely integrate this acceptance into the ways in
which they imagine others. I contend that biographers such as Leon Edel,
who freely employ psychoanalysis, do so to advance interpretive theories
with little effect on the representation of the subject. See Elizabeth Young-
Bruehl on an alternative biographical practice. See Nagourney for an
excellent discussion of the unified subject in biography.

7 See J.J. Wilson's wonderful 'Why Is *Orlando* Difficult?' for another reading
of *Orlando*'s challenge to genre. I realize that I differ sharply from the critical tradition in describing *Orlando* as a biography. I was encouraged to
consider it as a serious biography in conversation with scholar and noted
biographer the late James E.B. Breslin.

8 Quentin Bell describes another instance of self-analysis in response to
Leslie Stephen's death. Describing the Stephen children's reaction to their
father's death, Bell reports: 'They all felt some affection and some guilt.
Vanessa, who, more than any of them, was relieved – glad even – to be
orphaned, dreamed after her father's death that she had committed a

Oedipal awareness
(if not formal murder)

× murder and although she had never heard of Freud, realized the connection and promptly stopped such dreaming' (84).

9 There is universal agreement that *Orlando* is a parody or satire, although
critics differ in their interpretations of how it is performed. John Graham
sees Woolf's parody of biography as an attack on masculine thinking in
general: 'From the stereotyped flourishes of the preface to the learned
uselessness of its scholarly index, *Orlando* parodies this type [i.e., tradi-
tional] of biography. But the ridicule goes farther than that. The absurdities of the biographer are the absurdities of the whole approach to things
which she considered typically masculine: the pompous self-importance;
the childish faith in facts, dates, documents and 'evidence'; the reduction
of truth to the logical conclusions deducible from such evidence; and the
reluctance to deal with such nebulous aspects of life as passion, dream,
and imagination' (107).

While I agree with Graham's description of what *Orlando* parodies, my
reading of the Biographer differs. I see the Biographer as performing the
attack, not as the subject of it. Minow-Pinkney eloquently describes *Orlando* as a feminist attack on the patriarchy: 'the aesthetic strength of the
book is not in making history vivid but rather in rupturing history itself
by the laughter of an outsider, of a woman excluded from the historical'
(142). In her contextualizing of *Orlando* within the tradition of biography,
Raitt argues that Woolf's project is analogous to the *DNB*: 'The construction of the dictionary was, like the writing of *Orlando*, a piecing together of
national culture' (*Vita and Virginia* 20). Squier also makes the point that in
Orlando Woolf 'confronted the influence of both literal and literary fathers
to reshape the novel, and so to create a place for herself in the English
novelistic tradition which was their legacy to her' (122). Although Squier
notes that *Orlando*'s subtitle evokes Woolf's father's biographical work,
Squier is more concerned with 'acknowledging [Woolf's] debt to Defoe ...
subverting his influence and challenging the genre of the realistic novel
which he initiated' (122) than with her engagement in the biographical
tradition. Many critics discuss the parodies of literature in *Orlando*.
DiBattista argues that Woolf employs these parodies 'in order to test,
acquire, and defend her own literary power and prestige' (115). See also
Fox, DiBattista (126), Lee (142–3), Naremore (209), and Schlack.

10 While comparatively under-theorized, biography's static reputation is not
entirely deserved. See Nadel for a fascinating discussion of eighteenth-
century (and earlier) biographical experiments (183–5). Such exploration
all but ceased during the nineteenth century. Nadel comments: 'in the age

of evidence, the nineteenth century, biography appeared less adaptable to experimental forms' (185).

11 *Orlando* dramatizes Lacan's theorization of the ego as intermittent by literalizing the subversion of the subject. According to Lacan, it is ego, not desire, that is inconstant: 'It should be noted that a clue may be found in the clear alienation that leaves to the subject the favour of stumbling upon the question of [his] essence, in that he cannot fail to recognize that what he desires presents itself to him as what he does not want, the form assumed by the negation in which the *méconnaissance* [misrecognition] of which he himself is unaware is inserted in a very strange way – a *méconnaissance* by which he transfers the permanence of his desire to an ego that is nevertheless intermittent, and, inversely, protects himself from his desire by attributing to it [desire] these very intermittences' (*Écrits* 312–13). We protect ourselves, according to Lacan, from becoming aware of our disunified subjectivity by ascribing the inconstancy of the ego to desire. Orlando's sex change gives shape to the instability of ego, while her unchanged sexual attraction to women concretely illustrates constant desire.

12 On Strachey's ironic tone see Hutch. An example of Strachey's ironic tone can be found in his description of the young Florence Nightingale in *Eminent Victorians*: 'why,' asks the narrator, 'as a child in the nursery, when her sister had shown a healthy pleasure in tearing her dolls to pieces, had *she* shown an almost morbid one in sewing them up again?' (112).

13 Excellent articles have appeared to challenge the notion that *Orlando* is not a book to take seriously. See Knopp, Little, and especially Meese. I am particularly sympathetic to Nadel's discussion of *Orlando* as a commentary on biography.

14 See DiBattista, Guiguet, and Rosenthal. While Rosenthal does say that Woolf is self-conscious (130), he tends to take the book as seriously as other critics believe the Biographer does: '*Orlando*'s method, of course, is to rely on historical documents whenever possible, though sometimes Woolf admits, when sources are destroyed as in the case of the records dealing with Orlando's tenure as ambassador to Turkey, other measures must be employed' (129).

15 See Beer, Gilbert, Graham, and Schlack. Beer sees the Biographer not as self-conscious but as thwarted: 'The joke is on the ungendered biographer who seeks to plumb the depths of personality but finds the pen skimming on the surface' ('Body' 101). Schlack also believes that the Biographer takes himself seriously: 'The ludicrous inadequacy of this prim biographer,

armed with pedantic facts, fussy details, and pompous asides, becomes more evident as the narrative progresses, but he maintains his scholarly exactitude to the very end, where readers are presented with an Index as irrelevant as it is incomplete' (80). For Gilbert the biographer has no critical awareness: 'Woolf wittily parodies the intrusive and often absurd speculations of the scholar who presumes to know the "truth" about "life" and "self" of his subject' ('Orlando' 206). In this view, the Biographer believes himself to be following the traditions of the genre, and it is by his obvious failure (evident to those of us who know what a real biography should be) that he is indicted. Biography itself is not necessarily implicated in this reading; it is this particular Biographer who is inadequate. Graham sees this work of parody as that of Woolf, not the Biographer, whom he takes as one more object of her criticism: 'The parody of the biographer is most emphatic in those passages where he pauses solemnly to explain the obvious, to record with meticulous precision a trivial detail, to shake his head over the shocking state of the documents, to lament the paucity of facts, or to confess his dismay at having to deal with matters which decorum would suppress but which the dedicated scholar must record ... The biographer is a bore' (107).

16 See Gilbert, Graham, and Madeline Moore (who will be discussed in the text) as well as Wilson, Naremore, and Hafley. Wilson, who calls the Biographer 'Woolf in sheep's clothing' (176) simply states: 'Woolf has provided us with a false father-figure, the kindly, inadequate biographer who lets the reader in on all his little problems' (176). Naremore describes the Biographer as 'an often unreliable narrator' (190), who is easily confused. Although Naremore describes *Orlando* as 'largely devoted to conflicts between the biographer and the artist – conflicts from which the artist always emerges victorious' (202), he still conflates the narrator and author, even though he says that the narrator does not get the joke (212): '*Orlando*'s biographer is probably best described as a mask, a pose which Mrs. Woolf can assume or drop at will' (212). Naremore concludes by going a step further and connecting author, narrator, and character: 'Mrs. Woolf's characters always tend to merge with the narrator and become slightly disembodied ... it is hard to determine whether character or novelist is speaking' (216). Hafley, on the other hand, emphasizes the distinction between Woolf and the biographer: 'Like *Jacob's Room*, *Orlando* has two narrators; but here the device is used purely for its ironic value; there is never any doubt that the prim and coy man who is writing Orlando's biography is himself a comment upon himself – a comment made by the central intelligence who, through most of the novel, backs away from the biographer so that he

becomes part of the total perspective' (95). As I understand it, Hafley sees 'the central intelligence' of the novel operating as a second narrator, whose irony turns the Biographer into yet another subject to be criticized.

17 Among the myriad literary references that crowd *Orlando* are those to Laurence Sterne's *Tristram Shandy*. *Orlando*'s Biographer has much in common with the autobiographical narrator of this dazzling novel. See Schlack for a thorough survey of the literary allusions in *Orlando*.

18 I will develop this point more thoroughly in chapter 7, where I argue that Freud's development of the concept of the superego allows space for positing an alternative to the authoritarian, masculine superego that develops from internalizing the Law of the Father at the conclusion of negotiating the Oedipus complex in the traditional way. *Orlando*'s narrator demonstrates the way such an alternative, which I have called the feminine superego, would function.

The superego as it is developed in the woman is, according to Freud, weak. It is derived from outside social pressures instead of becoming fully internalized through identification with parental, often paternal, authority. I have argued that even when identification creates the internalization of authority, the ambivalent nature of identification requires the repression of the application of the critical agency to the representation of Law in order to escape the self-conscious aspect of the superego, an aspect that would allow the subject to be aware of censorship instead of experiencing it as unquestionable. The feminine superego, as I have conceived it, differs from Freud's (masculine) superego in that such repression is lessened. The feminine superego represents the Law of the Father self-consciously, structuring for the subject a more flexible relationship to both external and internalized authority.

The qualities one would expect to find in such a superego would be the representation of laws (by which, as throughout, I refer to cultural expectations rather than emanations of the legal system, although there are connections between the two) without the injunction of obedience to the Law. Censorship would be represented instead of enforced. Reduced fear of the Law would support the subject's sense of humour, allowing him or her to laugh at the Law and, because the subject would feel less defensive, at him or herself. Finally, such a superego would criticize the ego if it rigidly followed the Law or attempted to claim authority itself.

19 Below I will deal explicitly with the first two enabling assumptions. For a discussion of how Orlando defies the notion of character (which includes, by implication, growth) see Squier. As I read the novel, the character Orlando does grow and develop over time in accordance with the psycho-

analytic model of maturation. In *Orlando*, however, history is not equated with progress but is cyclical. The writer and literary critic Nick Greene appears unaltered at the end of the book (although Orlando's attitude towards him has changed). A more thorough analysis of *Orlando* as a challenge to the notion of historic progress is outside the scope of the current study. See Edel for a discussion of time in *Orlando* and how it influenced his biographical practice.

20 This phrase strongly suggests Ford Madox Ford's *The Good Soldier* (1927), which is narrated by a character who is deceived in precisely the way the Biographer suggests the 'good biographer' is. While Ford's novel is narrated from a position within this self-deception, *Orlando*'s Biographer makes it clear that he is fully aware of the blinders traditional biographers wear and that he has removed them.

(BUT)

21 See Raitt (*Vita and Virginia* 29) Naremore (196). Naremore places *Orlando* in the context of the *DNB*, Strachey, Sackville-West's *Knole and the Sackvilles* and *Some People*, also discussing, as does Raitt, Woolf's review of *Some People* in 'The New Biography.' Naremore concludes by quoting Woolf's intention to revolutionize biography in a night and commenting: 'Of course [Woolf] did not even write a biography, much less revolutionize the form, and it is difficult to say just how seriously she went about this task' (202).

silly guy

22 Woolf wrote to Sackville-West about the critical reception of *Orlando*: 'Enthusiasm in the Birmingham Post [Mail]. Knole is discovered. They hint at you' (12 Oct. 1928, 3:544). The points of similarity between Sackville-West and Orlando are too many to enumerate. Aside from Orlando and Sackville-West themselves, the most obvious resemblance is between Orlando's estate and Knole. Another is between Orlando's trial and one involving Sackville-West's mother. Pepita, the woman Orlando is said to have married, was the name of Sackville-West's grandmother, who was the subject of her biography *Pepita*. Many of the details Woolf used in *Orlando* come from *Knole and the Sackvilles* and *Pepita*. Critics who, in discussing *Orlando*, focus on the relationship between Woolf and Sackville-West offer a myriad of references. See particularly Baldanza, Green, and Kellerman.

23 Like Schlack, in her reading of the discussion of genius, Wilson sees no conflict or irony in this passage; instead, she takes it as a call for a 'non-lazy, ideal kind of reader, those who do their part' (176).

Chapter 6: Making up Women: Revolutions in Biography

1 See also Sidonie Smith, *Subjectivity, Identity and the Body* for a discussion of Woolf's problematizing of 'I' in *A Room of One's Own*. The issues of iden-

tity in autobiography that Smith is thus led to engage are central to biography as well.

2 The subjects of the other volumes listed in the series are Mrs Annie Bezant; Blanca Coppell; Elizabeth Churlish, Duchess of Kingston; Lady Hester Stanhope; Sarah Churchill, Duchess of Marlborough; La Duchesse Due Maine; Leticia Bonaparte; Mary Shelley; Rachel; Christina of Sweden; Jane Welsh Carlyle; Charlotte Corday; and Elizabeth Barrett Browning. Critical analysis of *Aphra Behn* is scarce. The Twayne series book on Sackville-West gives *Aphra Behn* a paragraph (Watson 55), and Michael Stevens says: 'In summing up what has been said about V S-W as a biographer, her two early works in the genre, *Aphra Behn* and *Andrew Marvell*, have not been taken into account; by reason of their briefness and their slighter nature, they are more to be reckoned as sketches than as biographies proper' (97).

3 *A Room of One's Own* was not Woolf's first publication on this topic. In *Our Women* (1920), Arnold Bennett claimed that women were intellectually inferior to men and that education would not alter their condition. Bennett's position was supported by Desmond MacCarthy in his review of Bennett in the *New Statesman*. Woolf's response was a letter to the editor (2 Oct. 1920) in which she argues that women have become more intellectually powerful as the result of education. To support her argument she compares, among other pairs of women, Aphra Behn with Charlotte Brontë, concluding that 'the advance in intellectual power seems to me not only sensible but immense' (Appendix 3: 'The Intellectual Status of Women,' *Diary* 2:339–42). As we shall see, Woolf omits her assertion of Behn's lower intelligence in *A Room of One's Own*.

4 On 23 June Sackville-West wrote to Woolf that she had not yet started the book, which was due at the publishers by 15 August (211), but on 25 July she wrote that she had finished the biographical section: 'I have killed her off today, which means I have done 3/4 of my book' (216). In a letter to Woolf dated 16 August Sackville-West says that she has 'finished with Mrs Behn' (222). On 7 August Woolf suggested that she review the biography, but there is no evidence that she did so (3:408, 411n).

5 See Goreau, Reconstructuring Aphra; Hunter, *Rereading Aphra Behn*; and Janet Todd, *Secret Life of Aphra Behn*. The introduction to Behn in *The Longman Anthology of British Literature* (1999) claims that Behn 'dominates cultural-studies discourse as both a topic and a set of texts' (Damrosch 2130). However, I have yet to encounter an undergraduate who has heard of Behn.

6 Goreau elaborates: 'The very act of publishing her writing would have been sufficient to destroy a lady's reputation in the seventeenth century;

exposing oneself in print was a violation of feminine propriety. But Aphra offended the modesty of her sex still further by writing as her fellow playwrights did – bawdy' (14). Both Todd and Goreau chronicle the history of Behn's disappearance and recovery at various times. Her works were reprinted in an expensive limited edition in 1871, and in 1905 Ernest Baker published some of her novels. Neither of these publications promoted Behn enthusiastically, nor did they seem to have had much effect on Behn's popularity. Goreau quotes the comment from Baker's preface that Behn's works 'have now been many years out of print ... nor is this much to be regretted' (Goreau 16). Neither Todd nor Goreau comments on Sackville-West's biography (although Goreau uses a quotation from it as an epigraph to her second chapter (6)) or the six-volume edition of Behn's works edited by Montague Summers, which was published in 1915. Sackville-West relied on Summers's edition and (heavily) on his introductory biography of Behn. Todd criticizes Woolf for failing to appreciate Behn's literary excellence (3).

7 Poems such as Behn's 'To the Fair Clarinda, Who Made Love to Me, Imagined More than Woman' (1688) have led to considerable speculation. Janet Todd argues that Behn's poems present a carefully created persona rather than autobiography. See also new historical critic Catherine Gallagher on Behn's self-fashioning and Derek Hughes's critique of Gallagher.

8 Celia Marshik explores this connection between writing and prostitution in Woolf, arguing that 'Woolf's novels indicate that she saw more than a metaphorical connection between publication and prostitution' (853).

9 Sackville-West is scrupulous in citing her sources, the major one being Montague Summers's introduction to an edition of Behn's works. Sackville-West thanks Summers in her foreword 'for his kindness in answering various enquiries and for the loan of books' (9). She explains her detailed response to Dr Bernbaum by saying 'if I have gone at some length into the destructive arguments advanced by Dr Bernbaum, it is because Father Summers in his Memoir has allotted only a brief footnote to Dr Bernbaum's two pamphlets, and also because I have had the advantage of studying several articles in a Dutch magazine, which have appeared since Father Summers' Memoir was written' (9).

10 Woolf's mother, Julia Stephen, wrote the entry for her aunt, photographer Julia Margaret Cameron, of whom Woolf had written an earlier portrait. It is extremely interesting that Woolf did not explore the canon of women writers included in the volumes of the *DNB* compiled after her father retired from editorship. While Stephen did considerably enlarge the scope

of subjects worthy of biographies, the number of women included was still quite small. Even in the most recent issue of the *DNB* only 4 per cent of the entries are of women (Fenwick 1). The space devoted to entries on women in the first issue also compares unfavourably with that accorded men. Jane Austen, for example, received two pages and the Brontës received seven, while Defoe was given thirteen pages, Swift twenty-three pages, Dickens twelve pages, and Thackeray sixteen pages (5).

11 Stephen's more extensive criticism of Charlotte Brontë can be found in his essay on her in *Hours in a Library* (3:1–30).

12 In this Stephen anticipates his own distress at the disruption to his life caused by the marriage of his stepdaughter Stella. See Bell 1:47–53.

13 In this way Woolf unites women across time, just as Jane Marcus argues she unites them across economic differences: 'The rhetorical strategies of *A Room of One's Own* construct an erotic relationship between the woman writer, her audience present in the text, and the woman reader. Seduction serves the political purpose of uniting women across class' (*Languages* 186).

14 The 1918 Qualification of Women Act granted limited suffrage to women over thirty who were householders, wives of householders, paid an annual rent of over £5 a year, or who had graduated from a British university. The Equal Franchise Act gave the vote to all women over twenty-one. This would have been an important change for the young women Woolf was addressing who could anticipate voting for the first time as a result of the new law.

15 For discussions of androgyny in *Orlando* see DiBattista, DuPlessis, Meese, Minow-Pinkney, and Trautmann. The most influential early studies of androgyny in Woolf are by Bazin and Showalter. Rachel Bowlby's reading of *A Room of One's Own* in *Virginia Woolf* presents a critique of Bazin's and Showalter's formulations of Woolf's concept of androgyny. Bowlby's analysis of Woolf's own text leads to suspicions that Woolf's androgyny is not viable for feminism. Bowlby concludes her discussion of Woolf's comment on the need for all writers to be androgynous by raising serious objections to Woolf's conception: 'Ironically, then, the passage reinforces the existing differences in the very act of asserting their irrelevance' and 'we have returned to another version of the patriarchal structure' (194).

16 When erotic practice is considered, the discussion usually takes the form of narrating the details of Woolf's affair with Sackville-West. Since these details have not been preserved (Woolf and Sackville-West had no need to write to each other about them and apparently no desire to communicate them to any one else) the discussion is thrown into the safe and pleasur-

able uncertainty that leads to perpetual and inconclusive speculation. The habit of discussing gender as if it were an equivalent substitute for sexuality and erotic practice is particularly troubling in discussions that purport to be redressing this sort of critical censorship. An extreme case can be found in Jane Marcus's reading of *A Room of One's Own* (*Languages* ch. 8); she argues that women conspiring together against patriarchal censorship are lesbians. While this may at first be an appealing notion, the construction of a homogeneous audience occurs at the expense of sexuality and erotic practice.

17 See Marcus for an excellent contextualized reading of *A Room of One's Own*, in which she argues that, with these references, 'The conspiracy [Woolf] sets up with her audience is of women in league together against authority' (*Languages* 166). See Doan for details about the creation of the case against Hall, in which she argues that whatever outrage was felt against *The Well of Loneliness* was not representative but was limited to a small group stimulated by a single review (ch. 1).

18 Lee (502–3), Glendinning (179). The driving lessons were held during the summer of 1927. Woolf stopped driving, possibly because she had hit a cyclist (*Letters* 3:400).

Chapter 7: Love Letters and Feminine Sexuality

1 De Lauretis describes her theory as 'an eccentric reading of Freud, through Laplanche and the Lacanian and feminist revisions, for the purpose of articulating a formal model of perverse [i.e., 'non-normatively heterosexual'] desire' (*Practice of Love* xiii). The position I propose is distinct from that of De Lauretis': I suggest that the feminine position is available to all subjects, not only a lesbian or even female subject, via the weakening of the superego. In his model of development, Freud posits a weaker superego for women, which I take to be an enormous advantage ('Some Psychical Consequences of the Anatomical Distinction between the Sexes' 19:248–58). See Clayton for a useful placement of De Lauretis's earlier work in the context of 'an otherwise diverse group of literary theorists who have begun to explore the role of desire in narrative' (35).

2 See Freud (ibid.) as well as 'The Dissolution of the Oedipal Complex' (19:173–9), Mitchell (95–104), and Chodorow (111–29).

3 The quotation is given pride of place on the Harcourt Brace trade edition of the book, where it is located over Woolf's name on the cover. It is a rare discussion of *Orlando* that does not repeat Nicolson's comment. For a discussion of the quotation see Meese.

4 Sackville-West's biography of Joan of Arc engages the problem of how identity is represented in biography (see my essay 'Cross-Dressing for (Imaginary) Battle'). Sackville-West may not have theorized this issue or even consciously attempted to consider it, but it dominates that biography in ways connecting it directly to Orlando and Sackville-West's biography of Aphra Behn. Sackville-West's under-theorized understanding of the complexity of identity formation is also apparent in her journal record of her affair with Violet Trefusis. DeSalvo argues that Sackville-West demonstrates her understanding of Woolf's social criticism in *All Passion Spent*, in which Lady Slane gives up her aristocratic social position to live in a modest house in Hampstead and actually befriends her non-aristocratic landlord and contractor ('Lighting the Cave'). While the move from ostentatious luxury to simple comfort may be indicative of a willingness to embrace downward mobility, the novel seems to me to be concerned more with feminist than class issues. Lady Slane's move is made in order to free herself from the sexist oppression she experienced in her marriage, not from the burden of property. In the end, it is her social position that allows her to live independently. If Sackville-West can be said to have learned anything from Woolf, it is likely that it was to develop and express a feminist position more openly in her work. Lady Slane's position that it is not worth sacrificing your life for money is powerful, but it is not located in a larger political context.

5 Love interprets Orlando as a work written out of jealousy: '*Orlando* was not all admiration and love ... It was satire after all, and in keeping with that genre, it also contained some rather nasty fun at Vita's expense ... among hostile interpretations of some of Vita's supposed wishes, the most unpleasant joke was the author's refusal to grant one of Vita's most persistent desires: to be a writer of the first rank' (214). The evidence Love offers for this reading doesn't really work, although I agree with her conclusion. Love claims that Orlando never finishes her poem, but this is not the case: 'Orlando pushed away her chair, stretched her arms, dropped her pen, came to the window, and exclaimed, "Done!"' (271).

6 Harold Nicolson was in Persia during this time and wrote to Woolf to say that he was not jealous. Woolf reported this letter to Sackville-West (4 Jan. 1927, 3:316).

7 Woolf and Sackville-West did go to France in September 1927. Sackville-West had proposed this itinerary: 'sun and cafes all day, and ? all night' (30 March 1927, 190).

8 The substitution of writing for sexual desire is made explicit in the scene in which Orlando completes her manuscript while the bored Biographer wanders among the birds and bees in search of amusement (266–71).

9 Despite Woolf's criticism, Sackville-West was a popular writer – far more
   popular and acclaimed than Woolf was during her lifetime. Beginning
   with her 1924 novel, *Seducers in Ecuador*, the Hogarth Press published
   fourteen of Sackville-West's books, the last being *Country Notes in Wartime*
   in 1940. Virginia Woolf sold her half of the Press to John Lehmann in April
   1938, prior to the publication of Sackville-West's long poem 'Solitude' in
   October. While the list of titles Sackville-West published with the Hogarth
   Press includes novels, poems, translations, and essays, Hogarth published
   neither of the serious biographies she wrote during that time. Gerald
   Howe brought out *Aphra Behn* in 1927, and Cobden Sanderson published
   Saint Joan of Arc in 1936. Sackville-West's relationship with the Hogarth
   Press was discontinued after Woolf's death.

10 It is in her letters and travel writing that I think Sackville-West is most
    engaging and creative as a writer. She composed a letter to Woolf, for ex-
    ample, in a stunning alphabet that catalogues her response to Egypt; it
    begins with 'Amon, Americans, alabaster' and ends with 'vultures, Vir-
    ginia; water-bullocks, warts; Xerxes, Xenophon; yaout; zest, (my own)'
    (29 Jan. 1926, 93).

11 If we take the right side of Lacan's graph of desire (*Le Séminaire livre XX*
    73) to be the real (the *objet a*, that little piece of the real, is located on the
    right side of the graph), we could say that Lacan recognizes the foreclo-
    sure of feminine sexuality by the barred La, which Bruce Fink translates as
    'Woman' (Lacan *Feminine Sexuality* 78), but I would call 'the feminine,'
    since it is gender, not sex, that is at stake here. The barred La, the not-all, is
    unknown to the divided subject (the barred S) on the left of the graph. As
    Lacan says, there is no sexual relation in the symbolic. Just as, in Lacan's
    formulation, the Name of the Father does not exist for the psychotic, the
    feminine subject does not exist for subjects in the symbolic order. The mas-
    culine subject exists in the symbolic; the feminine subject does not. The
    feminine position emerges from the real and is understood only within
    the fantasy of the two becoming one or as that which makes man whole
    again (e.g., the mother or the chaste beloved). This is, of course, Plato's
    fantasy of the androgyne. The effects of the right side of the graph are
    unintelligible to the left side. The *objet a* causes desire, which is inevitably
    misinterpreted.

12 See MacCannell on the advantages of patriarchy over the alternatives.

13 This reference is to Lacan's seminar on Edgar Allen Poe's 'The Purloined
    Letter' (Muller and Richardson 28–54).

14 Julia Stephen apparently referred to her elder daughter, Stella, as 'The Old
    Cow' (Lee 110). It is also interesting to note that during their courtship,

Woolf's father compared himself to his collie Troy, indicating that he would be as devoted to his future wife as his dog was to himself. Lee comments that this promise was made 'somewhat misleadingly.'

15 Sackville-West's reply continues the game: 'I was beginning to wonder if you were cross with poor Towser, – whether the amber beads had been so many cannon balls fired against your heart, or what, – and then this morning I got a nice loving solicitous letter – and Towser's tail began to wag again' (2 Jan. 1929, 302).

16 In a reference to this vision in a letter to Sackville-West on Christmas Day 1926 Woolf writes that the door was to the Sevenoaks fishmonger's (3:309). Sevenoaks is the town in which Knole is located.

17 On the forced choice see Lacan's 'The Agency of the Letter in the Unconscious,' which contains the diagram of the two doors, one marked 'Ladies' and the other 'Gentlemen,' and the joke of the two children at the train station (Écrits 151–2). Whether or not we find this amusing, it is true that in most instances we must pick a door (we are forced to make a choice). There are, of course, exceptions ...

18 Valerie Traub also describes this structure in her analysis of the film Black Widow in 'The Ambiguities of "Lesbian" Viewing Pleasure.'

19 These letters were recently discovered by Patty Brandhorst, who was cataloguing Sackville-West's manuscripts (Banks 2–3).

20 Woolf's sister, Vanessa Bell, happened to drive over on that afternoon and so learned the news in person. Woolf's brother, Adrian Stephen first discovered it through the newspapers. It was only Sackville-West that Leonard Woolf tried to contact before the news got out.

Chapter 8: Subverted Subjects

1 This statement is most thoroughly explicated by Lacan in Le Séminaire livre XX: Encore and is subsequently discussed by Mitchell and Rose, Clément, and Barnard and Fink, among many others.

2 According to Lacan, the feminine is positioned in relation to the phallic function while simultaneously exposing the lack in the Other that subverts the phallic function. Orlando's Biographer (like the analyst) makes a cut in the discourse that disrupts identification with the objet a (the object cause of desire), pushing the reader into the position of the analysand, who can hear the unconscious speak through the symptom and thus recognize the initial lack that produces gender difference (Le Séminaire livre XX).

3 It stretches the point, I realize, to describe Woolf as a cross-dresser, since the only known incident of this practice occurred as part of the Dread-

nought Hoax, which, as Gerzina has noted, was cross-racial as well as cross-gender ('Bushmen'). See Adrian Stephen's account of the prank for details.

4 Much of this agitation has been expressed at conferences and in conversation – so much so, in fact, that the Virginia Woolf session at the 2004 Modern Language Association Convention, chaired by Mark Hussey, was entitled 'Apart from *The Hours*: Virginia Woolf's Continuing Presence on the Intellectual Scene,' in an attempt to broaden scholarly attention. See Byrd and Newman.

Works Cited

Abel, Elizabeth. *Virginia Woolf and the Fictions of Psychoanalysis*. Chicago: U of Chicago P, 1989.

Apter, T.E. *Virginia Woolf: A Study of Her Novels*. London: Macmillan, 1979.

Austen, Jane. *Mansfield Park*. 1814. New York: Knopf, 1992.

Bachelard, Gaston. *The Poetics of Space*. 1958. Trans. Maria Jolas. Boston: Beacon, 1994.

Baldanza, Frank. '*Orlando* and the Sackvilles.' *PMLA* 70.1 (1955):274–9.

Banfield, Ann. *The Phantom Table: Woolf, Fry, Russell and the Epistemology of Modernism*. Cambridge: Cambridge UP, 2000.

Banks, Joanne Trautmann. 'Four Hidden Letters.' Spec. issue of *Virginia Woolf Miscellany* 43 (Summer 1994): 1–3.

Barnard, Suzanne, and Bruce Fink, eds. *Reading Seminar XX: Lacan's Major Work on Love, Knowledge, and Feminine Sexuality*. Albany: State U of New York P, 2002.

Barrett, Eileen, and Patricia Cramer, eds. *Virginia Woolf: Lesbian Readings*. New York: New York UP, 1997.

Bazin, Nancy Topping. *Virginia Woolf and the Androgynous Vision*. New Brunswick: Rutgers UP, 1977.

Beauvoir, Simone de. *The Second Sex*. 1952. Trans. and ed. H.M. Parshley. New York: Random, 1974.

Beer, Gillian. 'The Body of the People in Virginia Woolf.' *Women Reading Women's Writing*. Ed. Sue Roe. Brighton: Harvester, 1987. 85–114.

– *Virginia Woolf: The Common Ground*. Ann Arbor: U of Michigan P, 1997.

Behn, Aphra. *The Works of Aphra Behn*. 1915. Ed. Montague Summers. 6 vols. New York: Blom, 1967.

Bell, Quentin. *Virginia Woolf: A Biography*. 2 vols. New York: Harcourt, 1972.

Bell, Vanessa. *Selected Letters of Vanessa Bell*. Ed. Regina Marler. New York: Pantheon, 1993.

Benstock, Shari. *Women of the Left Bank: Paris, 1900–1940*. Austin: U of Texas P, 1986.

Birrell, Francis. Series description. *Aphra Behn: The Incomparable Astrea*. By Vita Sackville-West. London: Howe, 1927. 95.

Bland, Lucy. 'Trial by Sexology? Maud Allan, *Salome* and the "Cult of the Clitoris" Case.' *Sexology in Culture: Labeling Bodies and Desires*. Ed. Lucy Bland and Laura Doan. Chicago: U of Chicago P, 1994. 183–98.

Bland, Lucy, and Laura Doan, eds. *Sexology in Culture: Labeling Bodies and Desires*. Chicago: U of Chicago P, 1994.

Bogan, Louise. 'Virginia Woolf: The Skirting of Passion.' *New Republic* 29 (May 1950): 18–19.

Bowlby, Rachel. 'The Crowded Dance of Life.' *Virginia Woolf: Introductions to the Major Works*. Ed. Julia Briggs. London: Virago, 1994. 279–303.

– 'The Trained Mind: *A Room of One's Own.' Virginia Woolf: A Collection of Critical Essays*. Ed. Margaret Homans. Englewood Cliffs, NJ: Prentice-Hall, 1993. 174–95.

– *Virginia Woolf: Feminist Destinations*. Oxford: Blackwell, 1988.

– 'A Woman's Essays.' *Virginia Woolf: Introductions to the Major Works*. Ed. Julia Briggs. London: Virago, 1994. 249–77.

Braunstein, Nestor. Lecture. Philadelphia Lacan Soc. Conf. University of Pennsylvania. 26 Sept. 1997.

Briggs, Julia. 'The Story So Far ...: An Introduction to the Introductions.' *Virginia Woolf: Introductions to the Major Works*. Ed. Julia Briggs. London: Virago, 1994. vii–xxxiii.

Broughton, Panthea Reid. '"Virginia Is Anal": Speculations on Virginia Woolf's Writing *Roger Fry* and Reading Sigmund Freud.' *Journal of Modern Literature* 14.1 (1987): 151–7.

Bussy, Dorothy Strachey. *Olivia*. London: Hogarth, 1949.

Butler, Judith. *Bodies That Matter: On the Discursive Limits of 'Sex.'* New York: Routledge, 1993.

– 'Desire.' *Critical Terms for Literary Study*. Ed. Frank Lentricchia and Thomas McLaughlin. 2nd ed. Chicago: U of Chicago P, 1995. 369–86.

– *Gender Trouble: Feminism and the Subversion of Identity*. New York: Routledge, 1990.

Byrd, Carolyn. 'An Examination of Two Wives and Mothers in *The Hours*.' *Virginia Woolf Miscellany* 64 (Fall-Winter 2003): 5–8.

Caramagno, Thomas C. *The Flight of the Mind: Virginia Woolf's Art and Manic-Depressive Illness*. Berkeley: U of California P, 1992.

Carlyle, Thomas. *Critical and Miscellaneous Essays in Five Volumes. The Work of Thomas Carlyle in Thirty Volumes*. New York: Scribner's, 1899.

Carpenter, Edward. 'The Intermediate Sex.' *Love's Coming-of-Age: A Series of Papers on the Relations of the Sexes*. London: Swan, 1906. 114–34.

– *Love's Coming-of-Age: A Series of Papers on the Relations of the Sexes*. London: Swan, 1906.

Caruth, Cathy. *Unclaimed Experiences: Trauma, Narrative, and History*. Baltimore: Johns Hopkins UP, 1996.

Castle, Terry. *The Apparitional Lesbian: Female Homosexuality and Modern Culture*. New York: Columbia UP, 1993.

Caughie, Pamela L. 'Virginia Woolf's Double Discourse.' *Discontented Discourses: Feminism/Textual Intervention/Psychoanalysis*. Ed. Marleen S. Barr and Richard Feldstein. Urbana: U of Illinois P, 1989. 41–53.

– *Virginia Woolf & Postmodernism: Literature in Quest and Question of Itself*. Urbana: U of Illinois P, 1991.

Chasseguet-Smirgel, Janine, ed. *Female Sexuality*. Ann Arbor: U of Michigan P, 1970.

Chauncey, George, Jr. 'From Sexual Inversion to Homosexuality: Medicine and the Changing Conceptualization of Female Deviance.' *Salmagundi* 58/59 (Fall 1982/Winter 1983): 114–46.

ChicKnits: Guest Male Knitter. Ed. Bonnie Marie Burns. 2000–2. Curious Graphics, Chicago. July 2002 <http://www.chicknits.com/russell.shtml>.

Chodorow, Nancy. *The Reproduction of Mothering*. Berkeley: U of California P, 1978.

Cixous, Hélène, and Catherine Clément. *Newly Born Woman*. Trans. Betsy Wing. Minneapolis: U of Minnesota P, 1988.

Claus, Ruth F. 'Confronting Homosexuality: A Letter from Frances Wilder.' *Signs: The Journal of Women in Culture and Society* 2.4 (1977): 928–33.

Clayton, Jay. 'Narrative and Theories of Desire.' *Critical Inquiry* 16.1 (1989): 33–53.

Clément, Catherine. *The Lives and Legends of Jacques Lacan*. Trans. Arthur Goldhammer. New York: Columbia UP, 1983.

Coleman, Lisa. 'Rereading Woolf and Writing.' 14th Ann. Int. Conf. on Virginia Woolf. Senate House, London. 25 June 2004.

Cominos, Peter T. 'Innocent Femina Sensualis in Unconscious Conflict.' *Suffer and Be Still: Women in the Victorian Age*. Ed. Martha Vicinus. Bloomington: Indiana UP, 1972.

Cook, Blanche Wiesen. '"Women Alone Stir My Imagination": Lesbianism and the Cultural Tradition.' *Signs: Journal of Women in Culture and Society* 4 (1979): 718–39.

Cooley, Elizabeth. 'Revolutionizing Biography: *Orlando*, *Roger Fry*, and the Tradition.' *South Atlantic Review* 55.2 (90): 71–83.

Copjec, Joan, ed. *Supposing the Subject*. New York: Verso, 1994.

Cramer, Patricia. 'Introduction to Part II.' *Virginia Woolf: Lesbian Readings*. Ed. Eileen Barrett and Patricia Cramer. New York: New York UP. 117–127.

Dalgarno, Emily. *Virginia Woolf and the Visible World*. Cambridge: Cambridge UP, 2001.

Damrosch, David, gen. ed. *The Longman Anthology of British Literature*. Vol. 1. New York: Longman, 1999. 2129–93.

De Lauretis, Teresa. 'Habit Changes.' *differences: A Journal of Feminist Cultural Studies* 6.2–3 (1994): 296–314.

– *The Practice of Love: Lesbian Sexuality and Perverse Desire*. Bloomington: Indiana UP, 1994.

DeSavlo, Louise. 'Every Woman is an Island: Vita Sackville-West, the Image of the City, and the Pastoral Idyll.' *Women Writers and the City: Essays on Feminist Literary Criticism*. Ed. Susan Merrill Squier. Knoxville: U of Tennessee P, 1984. 97–113.

– 'Lighting the Cave: The Relationship between Vita Sackville-West and Virginia Woolf.' *Signs: The Journal of Women in Culture and Society* 8 (1982): 195–214.

– *Virginia Woolf: The Impact of Childhood Sexual Abuse on Her Life and Work*. Boston: Beacon, 1989.

DiBaṭṭista, Maria. *Virginia Woolf's Major Novels: The Fables of Anon*. New Haven: Yale UP, 1980.

Doan, Laura. *Fashioning Sapphism: The Origins of a Modern English Lesbian Culture*. New York: Columbia UP, 2001.

Doan, Laura, and Jay Prosser, eds. *Palatable Poison: Critical Perspectives on* The Well of Loneliness. New York: Columbia UP, 2001.

Dollimore, Jonathan. 'The Dominant and the Deviant: A Violent Dialectic.' *Homosexual Themes in Literary Studies*. Ed. Wayne R. Dynes and Stephen Donaldson. New York: Garland, 1992. 87–101.

Donoghue, Emma. *Passions Between Women: British Lesbian Culture 1668–1801*. London: Scarlet, 1993.

DuPlessis, Rachel Blau. '"Amor Vin–": Modifications of Romance in Woolf.' *Virginia Woolf: A Collection of Critical Essays*. Ed. Margaret Homans. Englewood Cliffs, NJ: Prentice, 1993. 115–35.

Edel, Leon. *Literary Biography*. Toronto: U of Toronto P, 1957.

Ellis, Havelock, and John Addington Symonds. *Sexual Inversion*. 1897. New York: Arno, 1975.

Ellmann, Mary. *Thinking about Women*. New York: Harcourt, 1968.

Epstein, Julia, and Kristina Straub, eds. *Body Guards: The Cultural Politics of Gender Ambiguity*. New York: Routledge, 1991.

Epstein, William H., ed. *Contesting the Subject: Essays in the Postmodern Theory and Practice of Biography and Biographical Criticism*. West Lafayette: Purdue UP, 1991.

Evans, Dylan. *An Introductory Dictionary of Lacanian Psychoanalysis*. New York: Routledge, 1996.

Faderman, Lillian. 'The Morbidification of Love between Women by 19th-Century Sexologists.' *Journal of Homosexuality* 4.1 (1978): 73–90.

– *Odd Girls and Twilight Lovers: A History of Lesbian Life in Twentieth-Century America*. New York: Columbia UP, 1991.

– *Surpassing the Love of Men: Romantic Friendship and Love between Women from the Renaissance to the Present*. New York: Morrow, 1981.

Felman, Shoshana. *Jacques Lacan and the Adventure of Insight: Psychoanalysis in Contemporary Culture*. Cambridge: Harvard UP, 1987.

Fenwick, Gillian. *Women and the Dictionary of National Biography: A Guide to DNB Volumes 1885–1985 and Missing Persons*. Aldershot, Eng.: Scholar, 1994.

Fetterley, Judith. *The Resisting Reader: A Feminist Approach to American Fiction*. Bloomington: Indiana UP, 1981.

Fink, Bruce. *The Lacanian Subject: Between Language and Jouissance*. Princeton: Princeton UP, 1996.

– Preface. *Reading Seminar XI: Lacan's Four Fundamental Concepts of Psychoanalysis*. Ed. Richard Feldstein, Bruce Fink, and Marie Jaanus. Albany: State U of New York P, 1995. ix–xv.

Foucault, Michel. *The History of Sexuality*. Vol. 1: *An Introduction*. 1978 (U.S.). Trans. Robert Hurley. New York: Vintage, 1990.

Fox, Alice. *Virginia Woolf and the Literature of the English Renaissance*. Oxford: Clarendon, 1990.

Freud, Sigmund. *The Interpretation of Dreams*. Trans. A.A. Brill. New York: Modern Library, 1978.

– *The Standard Edition of the Complete Psychological Works of Sigmund Freud*. 24 vols. Trans. and ed. James Strachey. London: Hogarth, 1964.

Gallagher, Catherine. *Nobody's Story: The Vanishing Acts of Women Writers in the Marketplace, 1670–1820*. Oxford: Clarendon, 1994.

Garber, Marjorie. *Vested Interests: Cross-Dressing and Cultural Anxiety*. New York: Routledge, 1992.

Garrity, Jane. *Step-Daughters of England: British Women Modernists and the National Imaginary*. Manchester: Manchester UP, 2003.

Gerzina, Gretchen Holbrook. 'Bushmen and Blackface: Bloomsbury and Race.' 14th Annual International Conference on Virginia Woolf. Senate House, London. 25 June 2004.

– *Carrington: A Life*. New York: Norton, 1989.

Gilbert, Sandra. 'Costumes of the Mind: Transvestitism as Metaphor in Modern Literature.' *Critical Inquiry* 7 (1980): 391–417.

– 'Orlando.' *Virginia Woolf: Introductions to the Major Works.* Ed. Julia Briggs. London: Virago, 1994. 187–217.

Gilbert, Sandra, and Susan Gubar. *The Madwoman in the Attic: The Woman Writer and the Nineteenth-Century Literary Imagination.* New Haven: Yale UP, 1984.

Gillespie, Diane. 'The Biographer and the Self in *Roger Fry.*' *Virginia Woolf: Texts and Contexts.* Ed. Beth Daugherty and Eileen Barrett. New York: Pace UP, 1996.

– 'The Texture of the Text: Editing *Roger Fry: A Biography.*' *Editing Virginia Woolf: Interpreting the Modernist Text.* Ed. James Haule. Basingstoke, Eng.: Palgrave, 2002.

Gilmore, Leigh. 'Obscenity, Modernity, Identity: Legalizing *The Well of Loneliness* and *Nightwood.*' *Journal of the History of Sexuality* 4.4 (1994) 603–24.

Glendinning, Victoria. *Vita: A Biography of Vita Sackville-West.* New York: Knopf, 1983.

Goreau, Angeline. *Reconstructing Aphra: A Social Biography of Aphra Behn.* New York: Dial, 1980.

Gosse. Edmund. 'Aphra Behn.' *Dictionary of National Biography Founded in 1882 by George Smith; Edited by Sir Leslie Stephen and Sir Sidney Lee; From the Earliest Times to 1900.* London: Oxford UP, 1967–8. 2:130.

Graham, John. 'The "Caricature Value" of Parody and Fantasy in *Orlando.*' *Virginia Woolf: A Collection of Critical Essays.* Ed. Claire Sprague. Englewood Cliffs, NJ: Prentice, 1971.

Green, David. '*Orlando* and the Sackvilles: Addendum.' *PMLA* 71.1 (1956): 268–9.

Grosskurth, Phyllis. *Havelock Ellis: A Biography.* New York: Knopf, 1980.

Grosz, Elizabeth, and Elspeth Probyn, eds. *Sexy Bodies: The Strange Carnalities of Feminism.* New York: Routledge, 1995.

Gubar, Susan. 'Blessings in Disguise: Cross-Dressing as Re-Dressing for Female Modernists.' *Massachusetts Review.* 22.4 (1981): 477–508.

Guiguet, Jean. *Virginia Woolf and Her Works.* Trans. Jean Stewart. New York: Harcourt, 1966.

Hacking, Ian. *Rewriting the Soul: Multiple Personality and the Sciences of Memory.* Princeton: Princeton UP, 1995.

Hafley, James. *The Glass Roof: Virginia Woolf as Novelist.* New York: Russell, 1963.

Hall, Radclyffe. *The Well of Loneliness.* New York: Doubleday, 1928.

Heilbrun, Carolyn. *Toward a Recognition of Androgyny.* New York: Knopf, 1973.

Hirsch, Marianne. *Mother/Daughter Plot: Narrative, Psychoanalysis, Feminism.* Bloomington: Indiana UP, 1989.

Hirsh, Elizabeth. 'Writing as Spatial Historiography: Woolf's *Roger Fry* and the National Identity.' *Mapping the Self: Space, Identity, Discourse in British Auto/Biography*. Ed. Frédéric Regard. Saint-Etienne, Fr.: U de Saint-Etienne, 2003.

Hoberman, Ruth. *Modernizing Lives: Experiments in English Biography, 1918–1939*. Carbondale: Southern Illinois UP, 1987.

Hollis, Patricia. *Ladies Elect: Women in English Government, 1865–1914*. Oxford: Oxford UP, 1987.

Homans, Margaret, ed. *Virginia Woolf: A Collection of Critical Essays*. Englewood Cliffs, NJ: Prentice, 1993.

Hovey, Jaime. '"Kissing a Negress in the Dark": Englishness as a Masquerade in Woolf's *Orlando*.' *PMLA* 112.3 (May 1997): 393–404.

Hughes, Derek. *The Theatre of Aphra Behn*. New York: Palgrave, 2001.

Hutch, Richard A. 'Strategic Irony and Lytton Strachey's Contribution to Biography.' *Biography* 11.1 (1988): 1–15.

Hunter, Heidi. *Rereading Aphra Behn: History, Theory, and Criticism*. Charlottesville: U of Virginia P, 1993.

Irigaray, Luce. *Speculum of the Other Woman*. Trans. Gillian Gill. Ithica: Cornell UP, 1983. Trans. of *Spéculum de l'autre femme*. Paris: Minuit, 1974.

– *This Sex Which Is Not One*. Trans. Catherine Porter with Carolyn Burke. Ithaca: Cornell UP, 1985. Trans. of *Ce sexe qui n'en est pas un*. Paris: Minuit, 1977.

Johnson, Erica. 'Giving Up the Ghost: National and Literary Haunting in *Orlando*.' *Modern Fiction Studies* 50.1 (2004): 110–28.

Johnston, Georgia. 'Virginia Woolf Revising Roger Fry into the Frames of "A Sketch of the Past."' *Biography: An Interdisciplinary Quarterly* 20.3 (1997): 284–301.

Jones, Danell. 'The Chase of the Wild Goose: The Ladies of Llangollen and *Orlando*.' *Virginia Woolf: Themes and Variations: Selected Papers from the Second Annual Conference on Virginia Woolf*. Ed. Vara Neverow-Turk and Mark Hussey. New York: Pace UP, 1993. 181–9.

Juhasz, Suzanne. *A Desire for Women: Relational Psychoanalysis, Writing, and Relationships between Women*. New Brunswick: Rutgers UP, 2003.

Jung, C.G. 'Versucheiner Darstellung der psychoanalytischen Theorie.' *Jahrbuch für psychoanalytishe Forschungen* 5 (1913): 229.

Kaivola, Karen. 'Revisiting Woolf's Representations of Androgyny: Gender, Race, Sexuality, and Nation.' *Tulsa Studies in Women's Literature* 18.2 (1999): 235–61.

– 'Virginia Woolf, Vita Sackville-West, and the Question of Sexual Identity.' *Woolf Studies Annual* 4 (1998): 17–40.

Kamuf, Peggy. 'Penelope at Work: Interruptions in *A Room of One's Own*.' *Novel* 16.1 (1982): 5–18.

Kapnist, Elisabeth, and Elisabeth Roudinesco. *Jacques Lacan: Psychoanalysis Reinvented*. France: ARTE France: INA, 2001.

Kellerman, Frederick. 'A New Key to Virginia Woolf's *Orlando*.' *English Studies* 59 (1978): 138–50.   2101.22

Knopp, Sherron E. '"If I Saw You Would You Kiss Me?": Sapphism and the Subversiveness of Virginia Woolf's *Orlando*.' *PMLA* 103 (1988): 24–34.

Kristeva, Julia. *Tales of Love*. Trans. Leon S. Roudie. New York: Columbia UP, 1987.

Lacan, Jacques. *Écrits: A Selection*. Trans. Alan Sheridan. New York: Norton, 1977.

– *On Feminine Sexuality: The Limits of Love and Knowledge: Book XX: Encore, 1972–1973*. Ed. Jacques-Alain Miller. Trans. Bruce Fink. New York: Norton, 1998.

– *Le Séminaire livre XX : Encore*. Ed. Jacques-Alain Miller. Paris: Seuil, 1975.

– *The Seminar of Jacques Lacan: Book VII: The Ethics of Psychoanalysis, 1959–1960*. Ed. Jacques-Alan Miller. Trans. Dennis Porter. New York: Norton, 1992.

– 'The Subversion of the Subject.' *Écrits: A Selection*. Trans. Alan Sheridan. New York: Norton, 1977. 292–325.

LaCapra, Dominick. *Writing History, Writing Trauma*. Baltimore: Johns Hopkins UP, 2000.

Laqueur, Thomas. *Making Sex: Body and Gender From the Greeks to Freud*. Cambridge: Harvard UP, 1990.

Laurence, Patricia Ondek. *Lily Briscoe's Chinese Eyes: Bloomsbury, Modernism and China*. Columbia: U of South Carolina P, 2003.

Lawrence, Karen R. 'Orlando's Voyage Out.' *Modern Fiction Studies* 38.1 (1992): 253–77.

Leader, Darian, and Judy Groves. *Introducing Lacan*. New York: Totem, 1996.

Leaska, Mitchell, ed. and intro. *Pointz Hall: The Earlier and Later Typescripts of 'Between the Acts.'* New York: University Pub., 1983.

Lee, Hermione. *Virginia Woolf*. London: Chatto, 1996.

Levinson, Brett. 'Sex without Sex, Queering the Market, the Collapse of the Political, the Death of Difference, and AIDS: Hailing Judith Butler.' *Diacritics* 29.3 (1999): 81–101.

Lilienfeld, Jane. '"The Gift of a China Inkpot": Violet Dickinson, Virginia Woolf, Elizabeth Gaskell, Charlotte Brontë, and the Love of Women Writing.' *Virginia Woolf: Lesbian Readings*. Ed. Eileen Barrett and Patricia Cramer. New York: New York UP, 1997. 37–56.

Little, Judy. '(En)gendering Laughter: Woolf's *Orlando* as Contraband in the Age of Joyce.' *Women's Studies: An Interdisciplinary Journal* 15 (1988): 179–91.

Love, Jean O. '*Orlando* and Its Genesis: Venturing and Experimenting in Art,

Love, and Sex.' *Virginia Woolf: Revaluation and Continuity*. Ed. Ralph Freed-
man. Berkeley: U of California P, 1980. 189–218.

MacCannell, Juliet Flower. *The Regime of the Brother: After the Patriarchy*. New
York: Routledge, 1991.

Marcus, Jane. *Hearts of Darkness: White Women Write Race*. New Brunswick:
Rutgers UP, 2003.

– *Virginia Woolf and the Languages of Patriarchy*. Bloomington: Indiana UP, 1987.

Marshik, Celia. 'Publication and Public "Women": Prostitution and Censorship in Three Novels by Virginia Woolf.' *Modern Fiction Studies* 45.4 (1999):
853–86.

McNaron, Toni A.H. '"The Albanians, or Was It the Armenians?" Virginia
Woolf's Lesbianism as Gloss on Her Modernism.' *Virginia Woolf: Themes and
Variations: Selected Papers from the Second Annual Conference on Virginia Woolf*.
Ed. Vara Neverow-Turk and Mark Hussey. New York: Pace UP, 1993. 134–41.

– 'A Lesbian Reading of Virginia Woolf.' *Virginia Woolf: Lesbian Readings*. Ed.
Eileen Barrett and Patricia Cramer. New York: New York UP, 1997. 10–20.

Meese, Elizabeth. *(Sem)erotics: Theorizing Lesbian: Writing*. New York: New
York UP, 1992.

Millett, Kate. *Sexual Politics*. London: Virago, 1977.

Minow-Pinkney, Makiko. *Virginia Woolf and the Problem of the Subject*. New
Brunswick: Rutgers UP, 1987.

Mitchell, Juliet. *Psychoanalysis and Feminism*. New York: Pantheon, 1974.

Mitchell, Juliet, and Jacqueline Rose, eds. *Feminine Sexuality: Jacques Lacan and
the école freudienne*. Trans. Jacqueline Rose. New York: Norton, 1982.

Moi, Toril. *Sexual/Textual Politics: Feminist Literary Theory*. London: Routledge,
1985.

Moore, Lisa. *Dangerous Intimacies: Toward a Sapphic History of the British Novel*.
Durham: Duke UP, 1997.

Moore, Madeline. '*Orlando*: An Edition of the Manuscript.' *Twentieth Century
Literature* 25.3–4 (1979): 303–55.

– *The Short Season between Two Silences: The Mystical and the Political in the
Novels of Virginia Woolf*. Boston: Allen, 1984.

Muller, John P., and William J. Richardson, eds. *The Purloined Poe: Lacan,
Derrida and Psychoanalytic Reading*. Baltimore: Johns Hopkins UP, 1988.

Nadel, Ira Bruce. *Biography: Fiction, Fact and Form*. New York: St Martin's,
1984.

Nargourney, Peter. 'The Basic Assumptions of Literary Biography.' *Biography:
An Interdisciplinary Quarterly* 1.2 (1978): 86–104.

Naremore, James. *The World Without a Self: Virginia Woolf and the Novel*. New
Haven: Yale UP, 1973.

RAITT *had written a book on*
VW + VS-W /45 a

Newman, Herta. 'Regarding *The Hours*: A Transposition in Fiction and Film.' *Virginia Woolf Miscellany* 64 (Fall–Winter 2003): 8–9.

Newton, Esther. 'The Mythic Mannish Lesbian: Radclyffe Hall and the New Woman.' *Signs: Journal of Women in Culture and Society* 9.4 (1984): 557–75.

Nicolson, Nigel. *Portrait of a Marriage*. New York: Atheneum, 1973.

OED Online. 2004. *Oxford English Dictionary*. 17 August 2004 <http://dictionary.oed.com/entrance.dtl>.

Parkes, Adam. *Modernism and the Theater of Censorship*. New York: Oxford UP, 1996.

Pope, Alexander. 'The First Epistle of the Second Book of Horace.' *The Works of Alexander Pope*. 10 vols. New York: Gordian P, 1967. 3: 349–73.

Raitt, Suzanne. 'Sex, Love and the Homosexual Body in Early Sexology.' *Sexology in Culture*. Ed. Lucy Bland and Laura Doan. Chicago: U of Chicago P, 1998. 150–64.

– *Vita and Virginia: The Work and Friendship of V. Sackville-West and Virginia Woolf*. Oxford: Clarendon P. 1993.

Riviere, Joan. 'Womanliness as Masquerade.' *Formations of Fantasy*. Ed. Victor Burgin, James Donald, and Cora Kaplan. New York: Routledge, 1989. 35–44.

Rolley, Katrina. 'Cutting A Dash: The Dress of Radclyffe Hall and Una Troubridge.' *Feminist Review* 35 (Summer 1990): 54–66.

Roof, Judith. *Come As You Are: Sexuality and Narrative*. New York: Columbia UP, 1996.

– *A Lure of Knowledge: Lesbian Sexuality and Theory*. New York: Columbia UP, 1991.

– 'The Match in the Crocus: Representations of Lesbian Sexuality.' *Discontented Discourses: Feminism/Textual Intervention/Psychoanalysis*. Ed. Marleen Barr and Richard Feldstein. Urbana: U of Illinois P, 1989.

Rosario, Vernon A., ed. *Science and Homosexualities*. New York: Routledge, 1997.

Rose, Gillian. 'As If the Mirrors Had Bled: Masculine Dwelling, Masculinist Theory and Feminist Masquerade.' *Body Space*. Ed. Nancy Duncan. New York: Routledge, 1996. 56–74.

Rose, Phyllis. *Woman of Letters: A Life of Virginia Woolf*. New York: Oxford UP, 1978.

Rosenbaum, S. P., ed. *The Bloomsbury Group: A Collection of Memoirs, Commentary and Criticism*. Toronto: U of Toronto P, 1975.

Rosenman, Ellen Bayuk. 'Sexual Identities and *A Room of One's Own*: "Secret Economies" in Virginia Woolf's Feminist Discourse.' *Signs: Journal of Women in Culture and Society* 14 (1989): 634–50.

Rosenthal, Michael. *Virginia Woolf*. New York: Columbia UP, 1979.

Sackville-West, Vita. *All Passion Spent*. 1931. Garden City, NY: Doubleday, 1984.
– *Andrew Marvell*. London: Faber, 1929.
– *Aphra Behn: The Incomparable Astrea*. London: Howe, 1927.
– *Challenge*. Introduction by Nigel Nicolson. London: Collins, 1974.
– *The Dragon in Shallow Waters*. London: Collins, 1921.
– *Grey Wethers: A Romantic Novel*. New York: Doran, 1923.
– *The Heir: A Love Story*. London: Heinemann, 1922.
– *Heritage*. New York: Doran, 1919.
– *Knole and the Sackvilles*. 1922. London: Lindsay Drummond, 1949.
– *The Letters of Vita Sackville-West to Virginia Woolf*. Ed. Louise DeSalvo and
  Mitchell Leaska. New York: Morrow, 1985.
– *Passenger to Teheran*. London: Hogarth, 1926.
– *Saint Joan of Arc*. 1936. New York: Grove, 2001.
– *Seducers in Ecuador & The Heir*. 1924, 1927. Intro. Lisa St Aubin de Teran.
  London: Virago, 1987.
– *Twelve Days: An Account of a Journey across the Bakhitari Mountains in South-
  Western Persia*. New York: Doubleday, 1928.
Sackville-West, Vita, and Harold Nicolson. *Vita and Harold: The Letters of Vita
  Sackville-West and Harold Nicolson*. Ed. Nigel Nicolson. New York: Putnam's,
  1992.
Schlack, Beverly Ann. *Continuing Presences: Virginia Woolf's Use of Literary
  Allusion*. University Park: Pennsylvania State UP, 1979.
Schneiderman, Stuart. *Jacques Lacan: The Death of an Intellectual Hero*. Cam-
  bridge, MA: Harvard UP, 1983.
Schwartz, Beth C. 'Thinking Back through Our Mothers: Virginia Woolf Reads
  Shakespeare.' *ELH* 58.3 (1991): 721–46.
Scott, Bonnie Kime. *Refiguring Modernism*. 2 vols. Bloomington: Indian UP
  1995.
Scott, Geoffrey. *The Portrait of Zélide*. London: Constable, 1925.
Sedgwick, Eve Kosofsky. *Between Men: English Literature and Male Homosocial
  Desire*. New York: Columbia UP, 1985.
– *The Epistemology of the Closet*. Berkeley: U of California P, 1990.
Shanley, Mary Lyndon. *Feminism, Marriage, and the Law in Victorian England*.
  Princeton: Princeton UP, 1993.
Shakespeare, William. *Cymbeline. The Riverside Shakespeare*. Ed. Herschel Baker,
  et. al. New York: Houghton, 1997. 1565–611.
Shaw, George Bernard. *Saint Joan: A Chronicle Play in Six Scenes and an Epi-
  logue*. New York: Brentano's, 1924.
Showalter, Elaine. *A Literature of Their Own: British Women Novelists from Bronte
  to Lessing*. Princeton: Princeton UP, 1977.

Silver, Brenda. *Virginia Woolf Icon*. Chicago: U of Chicago P, 1999.

Smith, Sidonie, *Subjectivity, Identity and the Body: Women's Autobiographical Practices in the Twentieth Century*. Bloomington: Indiana UP, 1993.

Smith-Rosenberg, Carroll. 'Discourses of Sexuality and Subjectivity: The New Woman, 1870–1936.' *Hidden from History: Reclaiming the Gay and Lesbian Past*. Ed. Martin Bauml Duberman, Martha Vicinus, and George Chauncey, Jr. New York: NAL, 1989. 264–80.

– *Disorderly Conduct: Visions of Gender in Victorian America*. New York: Knopf, 1985.

Spalding, Frances. *Vanessa Bell*. New Haven: Ticknor, 1983.

Sproles, Karyn Z. 'Cross-Dressing for (Imaginary) Battle: Vita Sackville-West's Biography of Joan of Arc.' *Biography* 19.2 (1996): 158–76.

Squier, Susan. 'Tradition and Revision in Woolf's *Orlando*: Defoe and "The Jessamy Brides."' *Virginia Woolf*. Ed. Rachel Bowlby. London: Longman, 1992.

Stein, Gertrude. *The Autobiography of Alice B. Toklas*. New York: Harcourt, 1933.

Stephen, Adrian. *The 'Dreadnought' Hoax*. 1936. Intro. Quentin Bell. London: Chatto, 1983.

Stephen, Leslie. 'Charlotte Bronte.' *Dictionary of National Biography Founded in 1882 by George Smith; Edited by Sir Leslie Stephen and Sir Sidney Lee; From the Earliest Times to 1900*. London: Oxford UP, 1967. 3:68.

– *Hours in a Library*. 3 vols. London: Smith, 1892.

Stevens, Michael. *V. Sackville-West: A Critical Biography*. London: Joseph, 1973.

Stevens, Wallace. 'Anecdote of the Jar.' *Harmonium*. New York: Knopf, 1953. 129.

Stimpson, Catharine R. 'Zero Degree Deviancy: The Lesbian Novel in English.' *Critical Inquiry* 8.2 (1981): 363–80.

Strachey, Lytton. *Eminent Victorians*. 1918. New York: Harcourt, 1969.

Summers, Montague. 'Memoir of Mrs. Behn.' *The Works of Aphra Behn*. Vol. 1. New York: Blom, 1915. xv–lxiii.

Symons, A.J. *Quest for Corvo: An Experiment in Biography*. 1935. New York: New York Review of Books, 2001.

Teran, Lisa St Aubin de. Introduction. *Seducers in Ecuador & The Heir*. By Vita Sackville-West. London: Virago, 1987. v–x.

Todd, Janet. *The Secret Life of Aphra Behn*. New Brunswick: Rutgers UP, 1997.

Torok, Maria. 'Mourning *or* Melancholia: Introjection *versus* Incorporation.' *The Shell and the Kernel*. Nicolas Abraham and Maria Torok. Ed. and trans. Nicholas Rand. Vol. 1. Chicago: U of Chicago P, 1994. 125–38.

Traub, Valerie. 'The Ambiguities of "Lesbian" Viewing Pleasure: The (Dis)articulations of *Black Widow*.' *Body Guards: The Cultural Politics of*

Gender Ambiguity. Ed. Julia Epstein and Kristina Straub. New York: Routledge, 1991. 305–28.

– *Desire and Anxiety: Circulations of Sexuality in Shakespearean Drama*. New York: Routledge, 1992.

– 'The (In)significance of "Lesbian" Desire in Early Modern England.' *Erotic Politics: Desire in the Renaissance*. Ed. Susan Zimmerman. New York: Routledge, 1992. 150–69.

– 'The Psychomorphology of the Clitoris.' *Generation and Degeneration: Tropes of Reproduction in Literature and History from Antiquity through Early Modern Europe*. Ed. Valerie Finucci and Kevin Brownlee. Durham: Duke UP, 2001. 153–86.

– *The Renaissance of Lesbianism in Early Modern England*. Cambridge: Cambridge UP, 2002.

Trautmann, Joanne. *The Jessamy Brides: The Friendship of Virginia Woolf and V. Sackville-West*. Pennsylvania State University Studies No. 36. University Park: Pennsylvania State UP, 1973.

– '*Orlando* and Vita Sackville-West.' *Virginia Woolf: a Collection of Criticism*. Ed. Thomas S.W. Lewis. New York: McGraw, 1975. 83–93.

Trefusis, Violet. *Don't Look Round*. London: Hutchinson, 1952.

Trombley, Stephen. *All That Summer She Was Mad: Virginia Woolf: Female Victim of Male Medicine*. New York: Continuum, 1982.

Vicinus, Martha. 'Distance and Desire: English Boarding School Friendships, 1870–1920.' *Hidden From History: Reclaiming the Gay and Lesbian Past*. Ed. Martin Bauml Duberman, Martha Vicinus, and George Chauncey, Jr. New York: NAL, 1989. 212–29.

Warhol, Robyn, and Diane Herndl, eds. *Feminisms: An Anthology of Literary Theory and Criticism*. New Brunswick: Rutgers UP, 1997.

Washington Post. Thurs., Jan. 3, 2002. C-3.

Watchman, Gay. *Lesbian Empire*. New Brunswick: Rutgers UP, 2001.

Watson, Sara Ruth. *V. Sackville-West*. New York: Twayne, 1972.

Weeks, Jeffrey. *Coming Out: Homosexual Politics in Britain from the Nineteenth Century to the Present*. London: Quartet, 1977.

– 'Inverts, Perverts, and Mary-Annes: Male Prostitution and the Regulation of Homosexuality in England in the Nineteenth and Early Twentieth Centuries.' *Hidden From History: Reclaiming the Gay and Lesbian Past*. Ed. Martin Bauml Duberman, Martha Vicinus, and George Chauncey, Jr. New York: NAL, 1989. 195–211.

Whitlock, Gillian. '"Everything Is Out of Place": Radclyffe Hall and the Lesbian Literary Tradition.' *Feminist Studies* 13.3 (1987): 555–82.

Wiegman, Robyn. 'Introduction: Mapping the Lesbian Postmodern.' *The Lesbian Post Modern*. Ed. Laura Doan. New York: Columbia UP, 1994. 1–22.

Wilson, J.J. 'Why Is *Orlando* Difficult?' *New Feminist Essays on Virginia Woolf*. Ed. Jane Marcus. Lincoln: U Nebraska P, 1981. 170–84.   ᴇ /ᴧᴧᴜᴊ

Winnicott, D.W. *Playing and Reality*. New York: Basic, 1971.

Woodcock, George. *The Incomparable Aphra*. London: Boardman, 1948.

Woolf, Leonard. 'Review of Freud's *Psychopathology of Everyday Life*.' *A Bloomsbury Group Reader*. Ed. S.P. Rosenbaum. Cambridge, MA: Blackwell, 1993. 189–91.

Woolf, Virginia. 'The Art of Biography.' *Collected Essays*. Vol. 4. New York: Harcourt, 1950. 221–8

– *The Diary of Virginia Woolf*. 5 vols. Ed. Anne Olivier Bell. New York: Harcourt, 1977–84.

– 'Lapin and Lapinova.' *The Complete Shorter Fiction of Virginia Woolf*. Ed. Susan Dick. San Diego: Harcourt, 1985. 255–62.

– *The Letters of Virginia Woolf*. Ed. Nigel Nicolson and Joanne Trautmann. 6 vols. New York: Harcourt, 1975–80.

– 'Modern Fiction.' *Collected Essays*. Vol. 2. New York: Harcourt, 1950. 41–50.

– 'Mr. Bennett and Mrs. Brown.' *Collected Essays*. Vol. 1. New York: Harcourt, 1950. 103–10.

– *Mrs. Dalloway*. 1925. New York: Harcourt, 1981.

– 'The New Biography.' *Collected Essays*. Vol. 4. New York: Harcourt, 1950. 229–35.

– 'Old Bloomsbury.' *A Bloomsbury Group Reader*. Ed. S.P. Rosenbaum. Cambridge, MA: Blackwell, 1993. 355–72.

– *Orlando: A Biography*. 1928. New York: Harcourt, 1956.

– *A Room of One's Own*. 1929. New York: Harcourt, 1957.

– 'A Sketch of the Past.' *Moments of Being: Unpublished Autobiographical Writings*. New York: Harcourt, 1976. 64–159.

– *To the Lighthouse*. 1927. New York: Harcourt, 1955.

– '22 Hyde Park Gate.' *Moments of Being: Unpublished Autobiographical Writings*. New York: Harcourt, 1976. 140–55.

Young-Bruehl, Elizabeth. *Subject to Biography: Psychoanalysis, Feminism, and Writing Women's Lives*. Cambridge: Harvard UP, 1998.

Zimmerman, Bonnie. 'Is "Chloe Liked Olivia" a Lesbian Plot?' *Women's Studies International Forum* 6.2 (1983): 169–75.

– 'What Has Never Been: An Overview of Lesbian Criticism.' *Feminism Studies* 7.3 (1981): 451–75.

Žižek, Slavoj. *The Sublime Object of Ideology*. London: Verso, 1989.

Index

236   Index

Goreau, Angeline, 113, 211n5, 211–12n6

Gosse, Edmund, 114

Graham, John, 95–6, 206n9, 207–8n15, 208–9n16

Grant, Duncan, 57, 58, 184n6, 204–5n3

Green, David, 210n22

Grosskurth, Phyllis, 192n20

Grosvenor, Rosamund, 24–5, 27–8, 37, 42, 47, 191n14

Groves, Judy, 134

Gubar, Susan, 163–4

Guiguet, Jean, 207n14

Hacking, Ian, 39, 195n37, 199–200n4

Hafley, James, 208–9n16

Hall, Radclyffe, 7, 30, 31–6, 46, 75, 114, 121, 129–30, 186–7n19, 192n17, 193nn25, 26, 196–7n46, 202n6, 214n17

Hankins, Leslie, 185n15

Heir, The. See under Sackville-West, Vita

Hirsch, Marianne, 111

Hirsh, Elizabeth, 185–6n17

Hirschfield, Magnus, 22, 29

History of Sexuality, The (Foucault), 9, 42, 183–4n3, 192n22, 192–3n24

Hoberman, Ruth, 204–5n3

Hogarth Press, 19, 62, 142, 145, 151, 190–1n8, 216n9

Hollis, Patricia, 195–6n41

Hours, The (Cunningham), 165

Hovey, Jaime, 203n12, 205n4

Hughes, Derek, 212n7

Hussey, Mark, 218n4

Hutch, Richard A., 207n12

hysteria, 21–2, 30, 39, 40, 163, 190n7

invert, sexual, 29, 30, 36, 37, 41–2, 189n3

Irigaray, Luce, 16, 82, 187n24, 197n47

Jane Eyre (Brontë), 203n13

Johnston, Georgia, 185–6n17

Jones, Danell, 201n4

Juhasz, Suzanne, 198–9n1

Jung, C.G., 188n26

Kaivola, Karen, 185n15

Kamuf, Peggy, 111

Kapnist, Elisabeth, 16

Kavanagh, Julia, 120

Kellerman, Frederick, 210n22

Keynes, J.M. (Maynard), 104, 204–5n3

Klein, Melanie, 198–9n1

Knole, 22, 23, 32, 40, 43–50, 51, 54, 62, 64, 70–3, 89, 110, 139, 196n42, 198n50, 201nn1, 2, 203n11, 210n22, 217n16

Knole and the Sackvilles. See under Sackville-West, Vita

Knopp, Sherron E., 12, 145, 185n13, 207n13

Krafft-Ebing, Richard, 22, 30, 186–7n19

Kristeva, Julia, 16, 187n24, 203n10

Labouchère Amendment. See Criminal Law Amendment Act

Lacan, Jacques, 14–17, 48–50, 82, 93, 97, 133–4, 146–51, 161–5, 188n26, 195n40, 197n48, 197–8n49, 198–9n1, 207n11, 209n18, 214n1, 216nn11, 13, 217nn17, 1, 2; desire, 14–17, 67–9, 87, 207n11, 216n11; feminine, feminine position, feminine sexuality, 15, 43, 48–50,

82, 148–51, 159–60, 161–3, 195n40,
197–8n49, 214n1, 216n11, 217nn1,
2; *jouissance*, 48–50, 51, 134,
148–51, 158, 197–8n49, 198n50;
Law, Law of the Father, 15, 34, 43,
47–50, 70, 73, 78, 84, 87–9, 90–108,
120, 133, 149–51, 161–5, 187n23,
195n40, 197n48, 198n50, 209n18,
216n11 (*see also* superego); mirror
stage, 188n26; not-all, 133, 149,
195n40, 216n11; subject, subjectivity, 15–16, 207n11 (*see also under*
Woolf, Virginia: *Orlando*); Woman,
82, 133, 161–5, 187n24, 216n11;
works: *Écrits*, 188n26, 207n11,
217n17; *Feminine Sexuality* (ed.
Mitchell and Rose), 187n24, 217n1;
On Feminine Sexuality, 146–51,
216n11; *Le Séminaire livre XX :
Encore*, 197n49, 216n11, 217nn1, 2;
'The Subversion of the Subject,'
16, 93, 207n11
LaCapra, Dominick, 198n50
Laplanche, Jean, 214n1
Laurence, Patricia Ondek, 184–5n9
Law. *See under* Lacan
Leader, Darian, 134
Lee, Hermione, 5, 9, 52, 53, 153,
201nn4, 14, 206n9, 214n18,
216–17n 14
Lee, Sir Sidney, 101–2
Lehmann, John, 216n9
lesbian, 6–14, 25–6, 127–30, 133,
198–9n1; development and usage,
19, 25, 186–7n19; mannish, 29, 30,
31–8, 41–2, 47, 67. *See also* desire;
erotic practice; queer; sapphism;
sexuality
Letters of Virginia Woolf, The (Woolf),
3, 5, 14, 18, 51, 53, 54, 60, 61, 62, 65,

66, 70, 71, 72, 91, 109, 112, 131–3,
135–44, 147–57, 164, 165, 184nn5,
15, 188n27, 200nn6, 3, 211n4,
214n18, 215n6, 217nn16, 19
*Letters of Vita Sackville-West to Vir-
ginia Woolf, The* (Sackville-West), 3,
4, 8, 53, 62, 64, 65, 66, 67, 70, 71, 72,
121, 109, 131–2, 136–44, 147–57,
164, 188n27, 211n4, 215n4, 216n10,
217n15
Levi-Strauss, Claude, 187n23
Lilienfeld, Jane, 8, 185n15
Little, Judy, 207n13
Lombroso, Cesare, 22, 29
*Longman Anthology of British Litera-
ture, The*, 211n5
Lopokova, Lydia, 104
Love, Jean, 136, 145, 215n5

MacCannell, Juliet Flower, 216n12
MacCarthy, Desmond 141, 204–5n3,
211n3
MacCarthy, Molly 60, 204–5n3
Mansfield Park (Austen), 76
Marcus, Jane, 7, 12, 75, 111, 126,
185nn9, 10, 13, 187n21, 193n26,
198–9n1, 213n13, 214nn16, 17
Marmorstein, Jack, 195n35, 197–8n49
Marshik, Celia, 212n8
Maynard, Constance, 26
McNaron, Toni A.H., 6, 191n15,
204n16
Meese, Elizabeth, 7, 12, 128, 207n13,
213n15, 214n3
Memoir Club, 4, 55, 204–5n3
Millett, Kate, 163–4
Minow-Pinkney, Makiko, 82, 188–
9n25, 203nn10, 14, 206n9, 213n15
Mitchell, Juliet, 16, 187n24, 214n2
Moi, Toril, 16, 111

Room of One's Own, 7, 10, 14, 41, 74, 75, 82, 109–12, 121–30, 166, 202n7, 210–11nn1, 3, 213nn13, 15, 213–14n16, 214n17; 'A Sketch of the Past,' 54, 55, 58, 59, 134, 143; *Three Guineas*, 16, 82, 158; *To the Lighthouse*, 6, 8, 10, 52–4, 72, 90–2, 103, 122, 132, 137–8, 140, 143, 146, 151, 156, 157, 198–9n1, 200n7; '22

Hyde Park Gate,' 55–6; *The Voyage Out*, 75, 91; *The Waves*, 16
Wordsworth, William 13, 85
Wuthering Heights (Brontë), 203n13

Young-Bruehl, Elizabeth, 205n6

Zimmerman, Bonnie, 10
Žižek, Slavoj, 187n22

restaurants in

Sienna *upsetting*

French

La Taverna — *Blu* — BD
It's in a *back st*
basement

RAJPUT

Peking Garden

Summer Lodge *b*
Evershot
10 mi
NW

Little Barwick
House
18 mi *Yeovil*
SW

43   KNOLE
the largest house
in England